POLITICS
AS
USUAL

Contemporary American Politics

The **Contemporary American Politics** series is intended to assist students and faculty in the field of American politics by bridging the gap between advanced but oft-times impenetrable research on the one hand, and oversimplified presentations on the other. The volumes in this series represent the most exciting work in political science—cutting-edge research that focuses on major unresolved questions, contradicts conventional wisdom, or initiates new areas of investigation. Ideal as supplemental texts for undergraduate courses, these volumes will examine the institutions, processes, and policy questions that make up the American political landscape.

Books in This Series

DO CAMPAIGNS MATTER?
Thomas M. Holbrook

GENDER DYNAMICS IN CONGRESSIONAL ELECTIONS
Richard Logan Fox

THE CONGRESSIONAL BLACK CAUCUS: Racial Politics in the REU.S. Congress
Robert Singh

POLITICAL TOLERANCE: Balancing Community and Diversity
Robert Weissberg

UP THE POLITICAL LADDER: Career Paths in U.S. Politics
Wayne L. Francis & Lawrence W. Kenny

POLITICS AS USUAL: The Cyberspace "Revolution"
Michael Margolis & David Resnick

POLITICS AS USUAL

The Cyberspace "Revolution"

Michael Margolis

David Resnick

CONTEMPORARY
AMERICAN
POLITICS

Sage Publications, Inc.
International Educational and Professional Publisher
Thousand Oaks ▪ London ▪ New Delhi

For information:

Sage Publications, Inc.
2455 Teller Road
Thousand Oaks, California 91320
E-mail: order@sagepub.com

Sage Publications Ltd.
6 Bonhill Street
London EC2A 4PU
United Kingdom

Sage Publications India Pvt. Ltd.
M-32 Market
Greater Kailash I
New Delhi 110 048 India

Printed in the United States of America

Library of Congress Cataloging-in-Publication Data

Margolis, Michael.
  Politics as usual: The cyberspace "revolution" / by Michael Margolis and David Resnick.
      p. cm.—(Contemporary American politics; v. 6)
  Includes bibliographical references and index.
    ISBN 0-7619-1330-0 (cloth: acid-free paper)
    ISBN 0-7619-1331-9 (pbk.: acid-free paper)
    1. Internet (Computer network)—Political aspects. 2. Internet (Computer network)--Political aspects—United States. 3. Cyberspace—Political aspects. 4. Cyberspace--Political aspects—United States. I. Resnick, David. II. Title. III. Series.
  HM851 .M37 2000
  303.48'33--dc21   99-050650

00   01   02   03   10   9   8   7   6   5   4   3   2   1

Acquiring Editor:	Peter Labella
Production Editor:	Diana E. Axelsen
Editorial Assistant:	Cindy Bear
Typesetter:	Marion Warren
Cover Designer:	Candice Harman

Contents

Preface

When we began our study of cyberspace in the early 1990s, we hoped that the Internet's communication capabilities, its information sources, virtual communities, newsgroups, and mailing lists would inspire unprecedented levels of active intelligent participation by citizens in politics. We took seriously the claim that cyberspace would initiate a revolutionary change in the way we conduct our democratic politics. Alas, these expectations proved far too optimistic. Over the course of a few short years, the Internet became a mass medium dominated by the World Wide Web, and the Web itself rapidly evolved from a medium for research and information exchange into one dominated by commercial interests.

Far from revolutionizing the conduct of politics and civic affairs in the real world, we found that the Internet tends to reflect and reinforce the patterns of behavior of that world. Politics on the Internet is politics as usual conducted mostly by familiar parties, candidates, interest groups, and news media. Government itself is no longer simply a silent partner, but is coming to play an increasingly important role in shaping the new medium. Moreover, as in the real world, most people who use the Internet have less interest in participating in political and civic affairs online than they have in following sports, seeking entertainment, pursuing hobbies, shopping, or gathering information about a variety of other subjects. While the Internet may still have the potential to greatly enrich our public life, thus far that potential has not been realized.

Acknowledgments

We want to thank the Sage Series editor, Dick Niemi, who shepherded this project from inception to completion. His critical comments and suggestions helped us to develop the original proposal, improve the book's organization, discover new material, and clarify our prose. He also provided comments from an anonymous reader on the first complete draft of manuscript, and he coordinated our efforts with those of the editors at Sage.

Peter Labella came up with the title that encapsulated our thesis, and Diana Axelsen handled the final stages of preparation for publication with aplomb.

In winter quarter of 1999, students in the University of Cincinnati's Undergraduate Honors Program who were enrolled in Margolis's seminar on Politics and the Internet provided additional feedback on the first complete draft. We also received research assistance from Larry Gache, Melicent Homan, Chin Chang Tu, Lillian Vasi, Robert Wheeler, and other graduate students in the Department of Political Science.

Our colleagues at the Center for the Study of Democratic Citizenship, George Bishop, Bonnie Fisher and Joel Wolfe, provided helpful suggestions and resources. Our wives, Elaine Camerota and Kathy Resnick, read our drafts with the critical eyes of English teachers and editors. Our special thanks go to Kathy for editing the final draft and preparing the index.

Despite all the contributions of our colleagues, students, relatives and friends, we alone must bear the blame for any mistakes that readers may discover. Then again we happily claim the credit for all the comments and suggestions that we have incorporated into our work. That, dear readers, is also politics as usual.

* * * * *

For Elaine and Kathy

The Normalization of Cyberspace

Cyberspace is no longer a strange realm. It has become intertwined with everyday life. Millions of us now feel so at home online in cyberspace that it is hard to imagine how we got along without it. We use email to keep in touch with family, friends, and colleagues. We use the World Wide Web (WWW) to check out the weather, to read the news, to find out sports scores, to order books, and to do a thousand things as the spirit moves us. Our lives have been enriched by the Internet. We are told that a revolution is occurring, that we are now in a new era. Yet, how much has all this computer power and global reach changed our lives?

Not long ago, the Internet was heralded as a technology for creating new forms of community, empowering citizens, and challenging existing power structures, as seen in a statement by Rheingold (1993), one of the leading popularizers of the idea:

> The political significance of CMC [computer-mediated communication] lies in its capacity to challenge the existing political hierarchy's monopoly on powerful communications media, and perhaps thus revitalize citizen-based democracy. . . . The vision of a citizen-designed, citizen-controlled worldwide communications network is a version of technological utopianism that could be called the vision of "the electronic agora." (p. 14)

There was also a darker contrary vision, an Orwellian dystopia of computers, electronic databases, and new media, a panopticon in which governments employ powerful new information technologies to oppress, manipulate, and dominate ordinary citizens.

Although cyberspace has become wildly popular and undergone major technological transformations in recent years, it has not had nearly the effects on society that either its proponents or its detractors predicted. Perhaps it is too early to fully assess its effects, but, so far, both the utopians and dystopians had it wrong. Cyberspace is neither a mass breeding ground for liberated virtual communitarians nor a launching pad for electronic storm troopers bent on stamping out free expression and dissent.

We have titled our book *Politics as Usual: The Cyberspace "Revolution"* because we are convinced that the cyber-revolution, like most revolutions, is not turning out quite as expected. Revolutions have a way of dashing utopian hopes, as revolutionaries have to grapple with the mundane problems of running a society. We have tried to step back from the hyperbole about cyberspace and reflect on what actually has happened in the past few years. What we see affords little comfort to utopians. It has become a mass medium inundated by millions and millions of people who are concerned with pursuing their own agendas, not some idealized vision. Whatever the future revolutionary implications of cyberspace, we are convinced that it will be molded by the everyday struggle for wealth and power. This book places these crucial aspects of ordinary life at the center of the analysis of the Internet and its future.

What has occurred is the normalization of cyberspace. Cyberspace has not become the locus of a new politics that spills out of the computer screen and revitalizes citizenship and democracy. If anything, ordinary politics and commercial activity, in all their complexity and vitality, have invaded and captured cyberspace. Virtual reality has grown to resemble the real world.

Chapter 1 presents a framework for understanding the transformation of cyberspace. We call it the *normalization thesis* to emphasize the fact that cyberspace is taking on the characteristics of ordinary life. We offer a theoretical perspective illuminating the social structural changes that have occurred in cyberspace as it has developed from a simple text-based communication medium with limited access into a multimedia phenomenon with a mass audience. As political scientists, we are concerned with analyzing and understanding the types of politics and political possibilities generated by the Internet. We discuss the new types of communities that exist in cyberspace with their own politics, but we emphasize that the Internet is being used by citizens of the real world to pursue their own agendas. We then turn to the political implications of this transformation and discuss three types of politics spawned by this new mass medium. We conclude by suggesting that the evidence shows that cyberspace increasingly reflects the political forces that dominate politics and social life in the real world.

The Great Transformation and Beyond

Once the Net was like a Lockean state of nature. All individuals were free and equal. Each was a producer and a consumer, although some were more likely to consume than to produce. The dominant ethos was altruism, and there was a spirit of mutual aid. Although some people were more skilled, there was no rigid division of labor. The land of cyberspace seemed to stretch from virtual horizon to horizon, but it was sparsely settled. There was hardly any real politics—certainly no concerted effort to manipulate the opinions and actions of a mass public. Communities formed around common interests, and differences of opinion served to spur thought and discussion. People were more innocent. They led simple lives online, and life was fun, if not particularly profitable.

What happened? Locke attributes the transformation of the original state of nature to the invention of money, a medium of exchange that made it rational for men and women to work hard and to use the surplus created by their labor. When it became profitable for people to invest more and more of their time in productive activities, the division of labor intensified, and the ways in which men and women interacted and organized themselves were radically transformed. With the invention of money came the need for laws and the creation of civil society and politics (Locke, 1689/1988). We suggest that something similar happened on the Internet. There is no question that the Net today looks much more like a pluralistic civil society than an individualistic state of nature. It has its own economy, complete with overly optimistic business forecasts; it has developed a complicated division of labor, with its attendant inequalities; and it has heard the call for laws and regulation and the protection of private property. The Net has lost its political innocence.

Once activity on the Net came to be seen as a form of productive labor, the potential value of time spent online greatly increased. Then, new institutions, organizations, practices, and politics appeared. The primitive exchange economy of altruistic producers and consumers was pushed to the periphery. The center became dominated by a relatively sophisticated political economy that, in traditional fashion, can be divided into three sectors: the public, the nonprofit, and the for-profit. Now, the amateurs and hobbyists have been crowded out by professionals and by a mass audience of consumers, entertainment and information seekers, and curious tourists. Some of the early stalwart settlers online dropped off in disgust. Those who remained online did not need their own Frederick Jackson Turner to tell them the frontier was fading fast.

When various professionals began to see time spent on the Internet as work rather than recreation, things changed forever. Now, professionals are paid to construct Web pages, provide content for Web sites, or log onto the Web in the course of their paid work. Political, economic, social, and recreational life on the Net for the mass public is increasingly designed and guided by Web professionals.

The fluid and unstructured politics of newsgroups and listservs was once the only significant politics that existed on the Net. Cyberspace sheltered an individualistic, free-flowing, inchoate politics of discussion and polemic, of conversation and passion. It was relatively egalitarian and participatory and often was bounded by the discussion group itself. Newsgroups are, by nature, interactive, because they are conversations transplanted to a new medium. Conversation is not a finished product but an ongoing process. Any bit of dialogue in the middle of a conversation is open at both ends; it responds to what has gone before and looks forward to a response. Whether it is conducted on the Net in real time or asynchronously, it still feels alive and spontaneous. Those who lurk, logging onto newsgroups without actually posting anything, are like those who stand around and listen to a conversation at a party, able to add to the conversation if they wish or move on to another conversation. Engaging in conversation requires no special training. Creating and maintaining a successful, sophisticated Web site that attracts a significant number of hits requires, at least up to now, both dedication and technical skills. A lot of advertising, both offline and online, also helps to increase the number of people who visit the site.

If human conversation is the real-world paradigm of a newsgroup, a presentation is the paradigm of a Web site. By "presentation," we mean such things as a published book, a dramatic or musical performance, a TV program or advertisement, and the like. A presentation is based on a script, can be repeated without losing its essential qualities, and, most importantly, is intended for an audience. Although there are brilliant conversationalists, conversations are essentially egalitarian. Presentations may use some of the same skills we use in conversation, but they also call on a host of other aptitudes and abilities. Unlike conversations, presentations value talents and demand expertise. They are fundamentally inegalitarian.

Presentations encourage experiments in new media to convey meaning in more sophisticated and elaborate ways. They develop expertise in speech, the visual arts, dance, or music. An audience ordinarily is not expected to participate in the presentation. They are there to be entertained, informed, inspired, awed, manipulated, energized, and the like. The real class division in cyberspace is between the Webmasters and the surfers. Undoubtedly, all producers of presentations are consumers of other presentations, but, assuredly, relatively few consumers are producers.

The Web is structured by formal presentations that are the product of thought and deliberation and that are open to all comers, but that limit freedom and expression. Movement within a site appears to be totally free, but there are only various degrees of structured freedom. Web sites are intended to sell, entertain, or present coherent political positions and inform, influence, and persuade those who log onto them. Although the majority of political sites probably are still created by individual volunteers, the most important, most visited sites are now sponsored, designed, and paid for by organizations and professionals.

The Web site is typical of the new Net, just as the newsgroup or listserv is typical of the old Net. Current popular press stories on politics and the Net almost always refer to the Web. Although there may be a few passing references to newsgroups, those citizens who are interested in politics are guided to the flashy Web sites. The Web presents itself as the first and most exciting place for those new to cyberspace. It creates a very different type of political experience, unlike the amorphous dialogue of newsgroups and listservs. Web sites are designed to be graphic, attractive, and informative. Politics on the Web is structured in a double sense, presenting a structured experience and reflecting the organized structure of pluralistic political life in the real world. It is truly a creature of modern democratic politics.

On the day of the 1996 U.S. presidential election, there was a tremendous increase in Net traffic. Traffic jams at the various Web sites promising election data led some to claim that the Net was not yet ready for prime time

(Angwin, 1996). Although this phenomenon was a sign of the great number of people who see the Web as a ready source of information, such use is not significantly different from using newspapers, radio, and television.

Many of those who are organized to influence electoral outcomes and bring the pressure of public opinion to bear on public policy now feel that they must have their own Web sites. Although an organized group occasionally may respond to a posting on a newsgroup, these groups are not seen as the main vehicles for influencing a mass public. The public that is ripe for persuasion and manipulation, if it exists at all on the Net, is a free-floating agglomeration of Web surfers and searchers. The WWW has transformed cyberspace, creating new opportunities for the politically skilled and sophisticated. But for all the hype about a qualitatively new virtual world, cyberspace nevertheless is coming to resemble our old familiar world of everyday economics and politics (van de Donk & Tops, 1995).[1]

The initial expansion of the Net from its early beginnings as a project of the Department of Defense occurred when those online started using it for communication; email became the "killer app," and the functionality of the Net increased along with its popularity. The creation of the Web, with its graphical interface and its hypertext site-based focus, opened up cyberspace to the masses. No longer was the Net a text-based system centered around dialogic communication and postings, an anarchic mélange of newsgroups, listservs, and gopher sites. It had become a multimedia phenomenon of linked Web sites, in which search engines, advertisements, commerce, and entertainment existed alongside the traditional text-based Net of old.

The invention and rapid spread of the WWW has changed the Net dramatically for the overwhelming majority of users. Web browsers, with their graphical user interfaces and point-and-click technology, have led to a dramatic increase in the Internet population. Despite all the hype about interactivity, Web browsers and home pages are also largely responsible for transforming the Net into a relatively passive medium, significantly more passive than it is claimed to be by those who celebrate the Web as a spectacular breakthrough in interactivity. Web boosters seemed to believe that the Net could miraculously transform couch potatoes into actively engaged seekers of knowledge and new experiences, but surfing and using hypertext are still very much like clicking a TV remote—albeit a remote freed from the tyranny of the fixed broadcast schedule and able to choose from an enormously expanded list of channels. The ability to respond actively to Web sites by posting email is only one step above being able to write fan letters to TV programs. Chat rooms and other opportunities to interact with like-minded individuals do exist, but they are not central features of the most popular politically relevant Web sites. To be sure, the Web can involve more participation on the part of the person online than can other media, but it is not the kind of active participation that is required of someone engaged in conversation.

Web pages are Net-based presentations that are more suitable to a mass audience than are text-based conversations. It takes less effort to be an anonymous member of an audience, to go from presentation to presentation as the spirit moves you, than to engage in conversation actively, whether on the Internet or in the real world. Unlike being a member of an audience, participating in a conversation often requires discipline and effort. It is truly utopian to believe that the Internet could transform politics radically in advanced industrial society by making politics more like a conversation among equals than a series of elaborate presentations that attempt to elicit the support and approval of relatively passive consumers.

Political life on the Internet has moved away from fluid cyber-communities, in which civic life centers around free discussion and debate. It has entered an era of organized civil society and structured group pluralism with a relatively passive citizenry. A randomly selected online citizen is certainly more able and, for now, probably more willing to air personal and political opinions than his or her counterpart offline, but this is not sufficient reason to conclude that cyberspace will transform the nature of citizenship in advanced industrial countries in the next century. As virtual reality comes to mirror the real world, cyberspace simply becomes another arena in the ongoing struggle for wealth, power, and political influence.

The Web today has a strong and growing commercial sector. Revenue for electronic commerce in 1997 was estimated to be $26 billion and is expected to reach the $1 trillion mark by 2005 (Organization for Economic Cooperation and Development, 1998). Although the federal government had always subsidized and owned significant parts of the Internet, until recently, it remained virtually invisible to the average user. With the advent of the Web, a formal public sector emerged. Now, American governments at all levels increasingly use the Web to disseminate and gather information, deliver services, improve government operations, and pursue the public interest as they see it, both nationally and internationally. As the Web increasingly becomes a venue for commerce, governments become increasingly interested in extending their regulatory supervision and taxing authority.

In the early days of the Internet, people posted data for altruistic reasons, and no one thought much about its costs or reliability. Although now there are many more people able to provide information, the sheer quantity of information has led to problems with quality and selectivity. Good information is often costly to the provider and increasingly to the consumer who values accuracy and whose time is not a free good. How can providers be adequately compensated and true costs be reduced for the consumer? To try to solve the latter problem, commercial services that provide search engines and media conglomerates that run elaborate Web news sites have appeared on the Net. How providers will be compensated is still to be worked out. People are reluctant to pay for information that was once free, so advertisements have proliferated.

What we call "news" on the Internet has moved beyond the simple sharing of information among people online. Amateur news gatherers and presenters have been all but supplanted by the pros, with their superior resources and technical expertise. Although going online is hardly profitable now, big media corporations hope to turn a profit in the future. Alternative news sources are still flourishing, but they seem destined to remain minor niche players or, if successful, to be bought out by the majors.

Three Types of Internet Politics

Internet politics comprises three political phenomena: politics within the Net (intra-Net politics), politics that affects the Net, and political uses of the Net. *Politics within the Net* encompasses the political life of cyber-communities and other identifiable online groups that regulate their own affairs and settle disputes among themselves. *Politics that affects the Net* refers to the host of public policy issues and actions taken by governments that arise from the fact that the Internet is both a new form of mass communication and a vehicle for commerce. *Political uses of the Net* include the activities of ordinary citizens, political activists, organized interests, political parties, and governments to achieve political goals having little or nothing to do with the Internet per se.

Intra-Net Politics

Intra-Net politics, or politics within the Net, has as its object the operation of the Net or some portion of it. It concerns matters that can be settled without reference to political or legal entities outside the Net community itself, and it includes such things as establishing technical standards and behavioral norms, settling disputes internal to newsgroups and listservs, and creating and structuring new virtual communities. This type of Net politics conceives of cyberspace as a virtual state of nature. The communities that exist there are thought to be perfectly able to run their own affairs. Each community believes that its members should exercise authority over their own domain and that there is no need for outsiders to regulate their behavior or even assist them in enforcing their own rules. Certainly, it is believed, terrestrial governments should not attempt to extend their jurisdiction into cyberspace. Intra-Net politics is based on a mixture of consensus, participation, and in the technical area, deference to civic-minded technical elites. The overall ethos is laissez-faire and libertarian. Rule enforcement is through moral suasion, shunning, and in extreme cases, excommunication (outlawing Web sites, blocking postings, and so on).

Politics within the Net in the old days inspired utopian speculation. It was personal, egalitarian, and voluntary, in contrast to the corrupt politics of elites and organized interests of money and power in the real world. This type of political life continues on the Web, but it has not turned out to be a model for politics in the real world, nor has it affected the consciousness of many of the millions of new users who have signed on in the past few years. If anything, the newcomers have introduced a number of attitudes and assumptions about politics that have upset the older generation of Internet users.

The millions of people who have entered cyberspace in the past few years, often known as *netizens,* have not been attracted by the possibility of creating their own meaningful self-governing virtual communities. Cyberspace for them is simply an extension of their everyday lives and concerns. They buy computers and sign up with Internet service providers in the expectation that they will receive something of value for their time and money. For them, being online means primarily email and the WWW. Email is a faster, cheaper, and better way to communicate than surface mail. They expect the Web to provide diversion, amusement, information, educational benefits, and commercial opportunities. But they also expect it to be a safe and secure place. Both new netizens and commercial interests require a modicum of law and order and show relatively little sympathy for the idea of totally unregulated freedom. Their lack of interest in intra-Net politics has caused it to decline in importance.

As the Internet has become a mass medium, the more controversial consequences of an unregulated environment have attracted the attention of organized groups, both online and offline. Free speech is one thing, but pornography is another. A totally unregulated business environment may seem attractive to both producers and consumers, but not if it brings crime and fraud in its wake. The most important type of politics that involves cyberspace now is taking place in real space, and it is hardly the stuff of utopia. Those who are committed to having the Net remain as free and unregulated as it is now must engage in organized political advocacy. Cyberspace has become a focus for contending social and political forces that wish to tame it. When it comes to governance, the age of laissez faire and self-regulation belongs to the past of the Net; the future belongs to government.

Politics That Affects the Net

Politics that affects the Net consists of actions and policies taken by political entities, usually, but not always, nation-states. This type of Net politics is seen as an unwarranted, if not an illegitimate, intrusion by those who believe that the only legitimate Net politics is intra-Net politics. Because the Net has become an important and popular phenomenon offline, it has come under the scrutiny of governments that assert jurisdiction over what happens online. Governments certainly do not accept any claim of extraterritoriality for cyberspace, and they cannot and will not acknowledge that cyberspace is a free territory inhabited by free people acting beyond the writ of governments.

Those who log onto the Internet are citizens over whom states have ordinary legal authority. However, it is not completely obvious how we are to extend to cyberspace legal concepts such as property, libel, copyright, fair use, community standards, and free speech. The unsettled state of the law has not stopped lawyers who see cyberspace as a growth area from staking their own claims in the new territory. In September 1995, UCLA created the Online Institute for Cyberspace Law and Policy, which is dedicated to furthering the development of cyberspace law as a separate discipline. The Institute provides an extensive online bibliography on cyberspace law. In major U.S. cities in 1996, there were at least 53 law firms that claimed expertise in the digital domain, and more than a score of U.S. law schools offered courses on aspects of law and the Internet (Macavinta, 1996).

Since then, there has been a virtual explosion of interest and scholarship on the legal aspects of the Internet spurred by the growth of electronic commerce and the transformation of the Internet into a mass communication medium. Elite law schools are competing to be at the forefront of the new field of

Internet law, both to bolster their claims to be at the center of innovative legal studies and to attract students to a new and lucrative field. In 1997, Harvard Law School established the Berkman Center for Internet and Society with a $5.4 million donation from the estate of an alumnus. Harvard's rival Yale Law tried to get into the game by offering visiting professorships to two experts in the field, James Boyle of American University and Robert Mergess, codirector of the Berkeley Center for Law and Technology at the University of California. According to Pam Samuelson, one of the founders of Berkeley's center, "The competition has definitely heated up" (Harmon, 1998).

In 1999, John Marshall Law School posted on its Web site a list of 48 courses on Internet law at 39 law schools, each with a hotlink so you could check them out (John Marshall Cyberspace Law Web site, 1999). There is even a free online course, "Cyberspace Law for Non-Lawyers," that covers copyright law, trademarks, libel, free speech issues, contract law, content regulation, and dispute resolution in cyberspace. The course lists two law professors on its faculty, Lawrence Lessig of Harvard Law School and David Post, a Visiting Associate Professor at Georgetown University Law Center, who are prominent in the field of cyberspace law (Cyberspace Law for Non-Lawyers, 1999).

In the United States, most legal issues probably will be decided not by new legislation but by the old-fashioned case-by-case method of common-law adjudication. Although there is debate about how various legal concepts and principles are to be applied in cyberspace, lawyers and judges undoubtedly will find satisfactory solutions—that is, solutions satisfactory to lawyers and courts (Huber, 1996). If this method of extending and adapting the law proves unsatisfactory in particular policy areas, politicians and regulators will step into the breach.

The impact of politics on the Net will only increase. The Communications Decency Act (1996), though struck down by the U.S. Supreme Court in *Reno v. American Civil Liberties Union* (1997), still demonstrates the sensitivity of politicians to public pressure and their attempt to respond to it (Greenhouse, 1997). Though no doubt a great triumph for free speech, it is only one victory in an ongoing war against attempts by governments to interfere with the free flow of information in cyberspace. Furthermore, with the rise of commerce on the Net, politicians have become increasingly interested in the tax consequences. As the Net becomes more a part of ordinary life, it provides governments with excuses and opportunities to extend both their general regulatory and taxing authority (see Chapter 6, this volume).

The process of normalization means that activities in cyberspace become more varied and involve greater participation by the general public. The days of relatively benign neglect are behind us, as the Internet has come under the intense scrutiny of political authorities. Politicians express shock at some Internet activities and are moved to take actions to remedy what they take to be the abuse of freedom. The impact of actions contemplated or taken by states that infringe on user freedom has become a hot issue among dedicated netizens. At the forefront of this struggle to protect privacy and free expression on the Net is the Electronic Frontier Foundation. Its Web site (http://www.eff.org) once boasted that it was one of the four most-linked-to sites on the entire WWW. Freedom of expression in cyberspace is also seen by many as a human rights issue. The renowned human rights organization Human Rights Watch has included an analysis of threats to freedom of expression on the Internet as a special issue initiative in its comprehensive annual world reports on human rights abuses (Human Rights Watch, 1998, 1999).

Fears have centered around efforts by governments to censor visual and textual material on the Net that runs afoul of moral and cultural values. In addition to protecting children from pornography, a concern of all governments, authoritarian governments want to protect their citizens from dangerous social and political ideas. Singapore has a system of regulation that bans access to pornography not only for children but also for adults. It closes off access to Web sites and newsgroups that provide information on homosexuality, defame any race or religion, or contain what the government judges to be politically dangerous and subversive materials. China has blocked access to many Web sites, including those that discuss China's human rights record. German prosecutors have used threats of legal action to pressure online services to restrict access to Web sites providing neo-Nazi propaganda and information useful to terrorists. The French government sued an English-language Web site in France affiliated with an American university because it offered services in English but not in French (Chaddock, 1997; Guissani, 1997a; King, 1997; Swardson, 1996).[2] In September 1996, the Association of Southeast Asian Nations agreed that the Internet should be regulated to protect "our cherished values, traditions and cultures" from the onslaught of Western values (Boyle, 1996a).

The call to regulate has caused a furor among those devoted to privacy and freedom in cyberspace. Many believe that attempts to control information on the Internet are likely to fail: The Net's ability to provide uncensored instantaneous information has proven invaluable in international trade, and the attempt to regulate it might prove more costly than it is worth. Attempts to block information also might prove useless because of the sheer size of cyberspace and the ability of sophisticated users to circumvent limits on freedom of speech. Many Internet users put their faith in sophisticated encryption techniques to preserve privacy and block governments from snooping. Strong encryption would make it virtually impossible for the government to "wiretap" or "eavesdrop"—interestingly, both words refer to earlier technologies, but you get the point.

Policing cyberspace clearly transcends national borders. The U.S. government, as well as the Organization for Economic Cooperation and Development, is exploring ways to establish guidelines for encryption. There have been calls for the United Nations to get involved in regulating cyberspace to catch pornographers, neo-Nazis, and terrorists. In fact, many in the legal community believe that a new area of international law will emerge as the Internet becomes subject to international treaties (Boyle, 1996b).[3]

The impact of the Net on society in general generates a host of political controversies. Issues of distributive justice are raised by the creation of this new and powerful good. Should everyone have a right to share in it? Should we subsidize its distribution? Many people fear that the new computer communication technology will further widen the gap between the rich and the poor. They worry that lack of either financial resources or technical skill will effectively deny the Internet to significant segments of the population. There are policy proposals that range from former House Speaker Newt Gingrich's offhand comment that we might consider giving every poor person a laptop to more serious proposals. In the 1997 State of the Union address, President Clinton repeated his call for connecting every classroom and library to the Internet by the year 2000. He linked the Internet to education goals: "Every 8-year-old must be able to read; every 12-year-old must be able to log on to the Internet; every 18-year-old must be able to go to college, and every adult American must be able to keep on learning" (Clinton, 1997). The U.S. government has taken steps to realize the vision of universal Internet access by adopting a policy of subsidizing public school and library Internet connections through the so-called e-rate (see Chapter 6, this volume).

It is hard to predict the outcome of the national and international struggle between the civil libertarians and the regulators. We will see the politics of distributive justice internationally as well as the clash of cultural values and issues of free speech and privacy. As the Internet becomes enmeshed in the fabric of everyday life, demand will grow for universal access within nations and equitable access across nations. The pressure to spread the benefits of the *Rechtsstaat* to cyberspace, if not ultimately the welfare state, will increase. The regulation of cyberspace is part of the process of normalization—of transforming a marginal frontier into a populous settled territory of advanced industrial society. For some people, this transformation marks the loss of freedom, but settling the frontier means establishing law and order; it means building fences, rounding up outlaws, and making cyberspace a nice place to raise a family and conduct a business. It also means lawyers, tax collectors, and government officials, but that is the price of "progress."

Political Uses of the Net

Political uses of the Net refers to employing the Net to influence political activities offline. Political parties and candidates design Web sites to affect the political behavior of those who visit the sites. Political sites urge visitors to take actions, such as emailing Congress to get citizens involved in real-world politics. Special interests, pressure groups, and nonpartisan public interest groups have found the Net a cheap and fast way to communicate with their members and inform and plead their causes to the general Web population. There is an extensive political life on the Net, but it is mostly an extension of political life off the Net.

The types of political activities conducted on the Internet—such as campaigning, lobbying, policy advocacy, and organizing—existed before the Net and would exist without it. The Net, and especially the Web, certainly will have an influence on offline political life, although the nature of this influence is unclear. Speculation about the impact of the Net often takes a metaphor—cyberspace—and reifies it, as if cyberspace actually exists in a parallel universe. Our mundane existence is presumably transformed when we enter this free space. Long ago, Marx observed the false freedom that results from positing us as free, all-powerful, sovereign citizens in our public capacity, while actually living out limited and alienated lives in civil society (Marx, 1843/1978). Is the abstract freedom of cyberspace really liberating, or is it deeply illusory? The more we experience life online, the more it looks like life offline.

The new pluralistic politics of the Web will not necessarily entail a politics of elite domination. There are countervailing tendencies. It has been suggested that voting via the Net would be a great boon to democratic life. The problem of the depressingly low turnout of the American electorate could be solved. If voters could log on at home, the voting process would be immune from the vagaries of weather, take hardly any time at all, be a boon to the sick and disabled, and so on. A survey of the American electorate conducted after the 1996 national election suggested that turnout could be increased by Internet voting. It found that 51% favored voting via the Internet as long as there were proper safeguards in place; 28% were strongly in favor, but 42% were opposed (Proxicom, 1996).

Voting via the Net could increase not only the amount but also the quality of participation. Before voting, a citizen could visit both partisan and nonpartisan Web sites for information about the issues and candidates. In the 1996 American national election, a surprising number of people used the Net to follow the campaign and gather political information. A survey on American Internet use, according to Andrew Kohut of the Pew Research Center in Washington, D.C., found that 12% of the voting-age population said that they followed the campaign through their computers, and a great many more sought news about local elections. Observers have noted that although national newspapers and television do a fair job covering presidential and congressional races, local papers and local television carry much less political news than they did a decade ago. Web sites dedicated to local politics may be filling this gap in coverage (Randolph, 1996).[4]

The 1996 American national election was the first for which there was significant campaigning on the Web (Margolis, 1996; Margolis, Resnick, & Tu, 1997). Nonpartisan public interest groups constructed sites to educate voters about candidates and issues. Major media corporations set up political news sites that attracted great attention and loyal followers. These sites provided a wealth of information about candidates, policies, and positions for citizens who were genuinely interested in becoming well-informed voters, and they detailed election news for political junkies who follow campaigns the way others follow sports (Armstrong, 1996; Saunders, 1996).[5]

There were official and unofficial candidate and party sites, including the Democratic and Republican parties and several minor parties. Although the minor parties had a jump in using the Internet before the growth of the Web, particularly through Usenet newsgroups and listserv email lists, during the campaign major party sites greatly outnumbered those of the minor parties. The Web accelerated the growth of Internet use, bringing millions of new users online. It put a premium on sophisticated Web sites that are easy to access, visually attractive, and fun to use. Constructing, maintaining, and updating such sites requires much more time and money than running a newsgroup or a mailing list (Miley, 1996; Ubois, 1996). Newsgroups and mailing lists can count on active subscribers to create content and continually update it. Those responsible for Web sites have to rely on their own resources to keep the sites fresh and appealing for both first-timers and repeat visitors.

If we ask which political parties and candidates are likely to provide sophisticated Web sites, the answer is clear: those who command the resources to hire the talent to produce them. Our study of campaigning on the Internet during the 1996 American national election confirmed this hypothesis. A comparison of the Web sites of the Democratic and Republican parties and their candidates with those of minor parties and candidates showed that the major parties dominated. They not only had more sites, but the sites were more technically sophisticated and attractive and contained more information, graphics, and links to other sites. They also were updated more often. Although most minor parties and candidates relied heavily on amateur talent (the leading exception was Ross Perot), the major parties hired professionals (Margolis et al., 1997).

Campaigning on the Internet is still in its infancy. Party and candidate Web sites undoubtedly will grow in sophistication as more hot java is available for creating them, but it is not yet clear that the returns are there to justify the monies invested. If sales are the bottom line for businesses on the Web, so votes are for politicians. Campaigners have hoped that the Web would not only win votes but also help perform other functions important to campaigning, such as fund-raising and mobilizing volunteers.

To evaluate the effectiveness of the Web as a means for campaigning, at least from the point of view of those who put parties and candidates online, contact persons and Webmasters at the national, state, and local levels were reached by email or telephone after the campaign. No one claimed that his or her Web site affected the election outcome, changed public opinion, raised substantial sums of money, or turned out numerous activists (Margolis, 1996). A Web journalist who covered the campaign online reached the same conclusion: "What effect did the Web have on the conduct of the presidential campaign? Answer: non, nada, zip, zilch" (Heilemann, 1996). The fact that American politicians had so little to show for their efforts on the Web in the 1996 election does not mean that they will abandon cyberspace. No doubt, they will simply try harder next time.

The last presidential campaign did show that conventional American political parties and candidates feel they must have a presence on the Web. The Web encourages what we have called "presentations," and these are suited to mass audiences and traditional top-down electoral politics. Entering such a site is like entering a little campaign headquarters, with literature tables, candidates' pictures, and solicitations for funds and volunteers. The more sophisticated sites have graphics that move around, but they are certainly not up to the standards of broadcast television. Yet the Internet does have a distinct advantage over the broadcast media because it enables a citizen to stop the show and concentrate on an interesting aspect of the presentation and, if desired, to download and preserve it for future consideration or mark the site for a return visit. In this sense, the Web is like traditional print media. No doubt Web sites will get glitzier in the future, but up until now campaigns in cyberspace have been dependent on tried and true real-world campaign techniques. Campaigning on the Web might capture the attention of those who are unreachable by traditional campaign techniques, but for now, a Web site seems merely to demonstrate that a candidate is aware of current trends and is committed to the latest technology.

On the other hand, the Internet might facilitate the particular style of democratic politics favored by activists, a style that, unlike that of traditional political parties, does not concentrate on voting and elections. One of the great advantages of the Web for political activists is that it enables them to access up-to-the-minute information on a huge variety of topics that are relevant to developing their own policy positions and political strategies. Policy-relevant research developed by one group and put up on the Web also can be of great value to other groups that share their general political orientation.

Yet, in his book *Net Activism: How Citizens Use the Internet*, Edward Schwartz has argued that the political activist should not think only in terms of the Web, because the older text-based area of the Internet still will have a crucial role to play in the politics of the future. He observed, "The public discussion of the Internet now revolves almost entirely around the World Wide Web. . . . That's fine, but what activists—in fact, most people—want from the Internet is email" (Schwartz, 1996, p. 179). The Internet can be used to build up discussion lists of activists who can develop political strategies and policy positions and to connect with those who, though devoted to different issues and policies, share similar general political orientations. Listservs and email can help organize political activity, and activists not affiliated with major political parties are always chronically short of resources. Online organizing is one way of substituting time and effort for money; online solicitation of funds also can substitute donors' money for the scarce time and effort of activists.

If the Internet were to provide a significant boost to nonparty political activism, the traditional American political parties, already in decline, might be further weakened. A form of hyper-pluralism might emerge in issue areas in which popular participation is facilitated by old progressive participatory reforms. Many states have adopted the initiative, which permits citizens to put an issue on the ballot by petition for public approval or rejection, thus bypassing the standard legislative procedure. In those states the Web could be a focus for continuous campaigns. The Net reduces transaction costs. The high cost of petition drives serves as a barrier to many interest groups that would like to circumvent the ordinary process of representative democracy and go directly to the voters. If it were legal to sign petitions on the Net, the actual dollar costs of putting new initiatives on the ballot would decrease significantly. If this practice became commonplace, representative institutions would be significantly undermined.

It is far more likely that political activists will use the Net to locate and disseminate information, to contact and organize political sympathizers, and to lobby government officials and political representatives. For all the commitment of activists to radical change, their presence on the Net is part of the process of political normalization. Along with the political parties and interest groups, they represent a familiar element of democratic pluralism.

Organized interest groups are another type of player in democratic politics. They also advocate familiar types of political participation. They urge visitors to learn more about the group and its policy concerns, to contact public officials, to contribute to the cause, to support candidates sympathetic to the group, to vote, and the like (Margolis, 1996). They offer Web presentations of their positions, some more glitzy than others, but it is hard to see how their presence in cyberspace will add anything to ordinary interest-group politics. Traditional political parties and interest groups probably will not increase their power and influence by going online. They construct Web sites now because it is expected of them and perhaps because they need to prevent being outflanked by newer groups. For most, it is simply part of the struggle to remain competitive in all areas of mass appeal. As part of their constituency moves into cyberspace, traditional organized groups migrate with them.

Traditionally, mass media serve a mass public, whereas specialized media serve select audiences. The Web is a hybrid, both a specialized medium and a mass medium. There is room for groups and causes that appeal to narrow constituencies. A presence on the Web could greatly increase the exposure of a narrow interest group to its own potential constituency and to the public at large. They probably have more to gain by going online than do mainstream, well-established groups that are skilled in using traditional mass media. Because of the hypertext linkages, which permeate the Web, even a very specialized interest can be categorized in more general terms and become linked to more popular sites. In any case, no matter how obscure or outré the cause, if it has a home page, it can most likely be located by employing a search engine (although this is often not as simple as it is made out to be).

Although groups sponsoring such Web sites may not approach the number of hits in a year that the National Democratic Party site receives in a day, any exposure is important to them. Obscure groups and causes typically lack the money and membership to do offline what they can do online. Because it is relatively inexpensive for them to operate online, they can spread their message, recruit new members, raise funds, lobby politicians, mount petition drives, and the like. Many of these familiar political strategies and activities would have been impossible even to attempt without the Web. Currently, the effects of such political activity are hardly visible in the real world as measured by electoral success or influence on the public policy agenda; nevertheless, such activity does have some potential. Any significant political movement in the near future arising in the industrial world probably not only will have a strong presence on the Internet, but that presence will be one factor among many explaining its rise to prominence. Yet communication technology is no magic bullet. For the most part, marginal movements will remain marginal.

Just as activists, interest groups, and parties use the Net for their purposes, governments are discovering that the Net is a way to achieve their own political objectives. Just as activists wish to know what the government is doing, so the government wants to know what activists are doing. An assessment of the strategic impact of the Internet written by Charles Swett (1995), an assistant for Strategic Assessment for the U.S. Department of Defense (DOD), claimed, "The Internet is a potentially lucrative source of intelligence useful to the DOD. This intelligence can include . . . information about the plans and operations of politically active groups." It can even be used for counterintelligence. Swett cited as an example a message posted to a left-wing newsgroup that repeated for their benefit an Associated Press article about an army training exercise directed at the St. Moritz Hotel in Miami Beach,

Florida. He added a cautionary note that if it became known that the DOD was monitoring the Internet for intelligence or counterintelligence purposes, then people would start leaving false messages, and "our analysis function would need to account for this" (Swett, 1995).[6]

The world of spies and counterspies, intelligence and counterintelligence already has invaded the Internet, and more lies ahead. Swett (1995) suggested that as more foreign officials, military officers, businesspeople, and journalists get email addresses, the Internet could be used as a medium for psychological operations campaigns. The Net could rapidly convey the official government perspective on a host of issues to a wide and influential audience. It also could be used in unconventional warfare to communicate with sympathetic groups abroad who might undertake missions that otherwise would be performed by U.S. special forces (Swett, 1995).

Since Swett's assessment was written, there has been a marked increase in concern about the implications of unconventional warfare in cyberspace, and the threats that are foreseen are more frightening than using the Internet for clandestine communication. The Internet has now been designated a vital part of the national infrastructure and considered prone to terrorist attacks. Protecting the Internet from enemies at home and abroad is now a task that the U.S. government considers part of the national defense (see Chapter 8, this volume). And if it is part of the national defense, no doubt it is also part of the national offense.

Swett (1995) also envisioned the use of the Internet as a tool of statecraft. Citing the use of dueling Web sites by Ecuador and Peru to lambaste each other in a dispute over the Ecuadorean border, he saw a future in which nation-states use the Internet for their diplomatic and propaganda efforts. To date, most official foreign government Web sites have been limited to routine public affairs information, heavy on statistics and descriptions of businesses, culture, industries, and population. It is commonplace on the Web to see policy advocacy by political dissenters and activists of every persuasion. In 1995 Swett predicted that when countries become embroiled in disputes in the future, Web sites will be created to advocate government policies and positions. It was reported in 1997 that Sri Lanka did exactly that. It launched a national Web site to counter the Tamil Tigers, who have been fighting a long civil war to establish a homeland for Tamils in Sri Lanka. The Tamil Tigers already had set up their own Web site giving their side of the dispute. Sri Lankan officials said their Web site will "help in countering anti-Sri Lanka propaganda by enabling Internet surfers world wide to have access through a single window to authentic news and information on Sri Lanka" ("Sri Lanka Takes War Against Rebels to Cyberspace," 1997).

Little did Swett know at that time that in a few years not only would governments use Web sites for policy advocacy, they would be engaging in attempts to sabotage Web sites that they found offensive. In January 1999, the Indonesian government was blamed for organized attacks on computers in Ireland that disrupted an East Timor virtual country domain ".tp." Top-level domains are usually reserved for sovereign nations, and because East Timor was occupied and claimed by Indonesia, the creation of the site was a virtual declaration of independence in cyberspace. When the East Timor domain was first established, a spokesperson for the Indonesian embassy said that although Indonesia fully respected the freedom of cyberspace, it was

> concerned that this freedom has been misused by Connect-Ireland [the Irish Internet service provider] to spread a campaign against Indonesia. . . . The handover of the domain to the government of East Timor is beyond imagination since the government of East Timor will not exist. ("Virtual Country 'Nuked' in Cyberwar," 1999)

With the normalization of cyberspace, the political uses of the Net are becoming more varied and intense. The Internet is no longer simply a space for online political discussion. It has now become a mass medium for influencing public opinion and public policy, and a great number of new actors have entered cyberspace to pursue their political agendas. It is home to political parties and political activists, to lobbyists seeking to influence government, and to politicians seeking to influence voters. Although most political uses of the Net are limited to advocacy, we also are witnessing the emerging use of Internet as a form of direct action directed at political opponents (see Chapter 8, this volume). The political uses of the Net will certainly continue to flourish.

Looking Forward

The Internet will make it more difficult for repressive regimes to withhold vital information from their citizens and to censor ideas that those governments find morally and politically subversive. Because the Internet is becoming a crucial component of world commerce, there will be increasing pressure for Internet access. Unless a nation decides to cut itself off totally from the international economy, it will have to live with the consequences of a new and potentially destabilizing technological window on the outside world. Internet access brings with it more than just commercial information and contacts. It facilitates a whole range of interactions with foreigners and expatriates. It thus continues the trend to open up closed societies that was begun by such new media as satellite TV, cell phones, and faxes.

The Internet will continue to harbor a great variety of opinion and controversy. Many hope that it can serve as a school for a truly democratic politics because it is not limited to official establishment sources. The Web is a wonderful vehicle for citizens who are already interested in politics. If they choose, ordinary citizens can acquire a plethora of data and gain access to the public face of the democratic political process. It has functioned well as a tool for citizen awareness campaigns, although so far these have mostly concerned politics that affect the Net. It can mobilize activists and facilitate political organizing, campaigning, and lobbying.

Although some still hope cyberspace can bring radical political change, that hope must be tempered by the facts. Both official government information and independent information have their limits. No matter how copious and detailed, government-provided materials will not make modern governments transparent to their citizens, and the unofficial sources of information on the Internet are only as reliable as the providers themselves. Things are not always what they seem: Manipulation, deception, and misinformation occur in cyberspace. Even if we do manage to select what we need and sort the good from the bad, good information by itself does not make good citizens. Information is no substitute for education and motivation.

Cyberspace has undergone a great transformation. Although those working on the cutting edge might still see it as a wide-open frontier, it has taken on the characteristics of a settled territory. The utopian vision of a worldwide agora that would revitalize democracy has to confront the harsh reality of lawsuits and regulations, commerce and entertainment, political parties, organized interest groups, political activists, and, most important, masses of bored and indifferent citizens. Although revitalization is still possible, it is much more difficult than the optimists once imagined.

In the chapters that follow, we examine the extent to which politics in cyberspace reflects the politics of the real world. Chapter 2 presents a brief history of the Internet, noting its origins, expansion, and recent changes. We focus in particular on how the Net evolved from a community of scientific peers supported largely by government to a privately funded commercial medium used by a mass audience.

The next three chapters concern aspects of mass politics. Chapter 3 examines the growing presence of political parties, candidates, and interest groups on the Net. We focus on the functions served by their Web pages, newsgroups, and listservs, and we attempt to assess their impact on politics and elections. In Chapter 4, we move into the spotlight bureaucrats and elected officials. We examine the extent to which U.S. governmental agencies and elected officials have used cyberspace to provide information about public policies, political issues, and other matters of public concern. In addition, we consider the content of the information, how it is organized, and the opportunities it provides for increasing political participation for ordinary citizens. We speculate on the ramifications of moving governmental information onto the Internet regarding the making of public policy and the conduct of democratic politics. In keeping with our general model, we consider mainly politics that affects the Net and political uses of the Net. These considerations anticipate problems of regulation and privacy, which are discussed in Chapters 6 and 7.

Chapter 5 traces the manner and extent to which established and alternative news media have migrated to the Net. We ask how media in this new form affect the formation and expression of public opinion. We examine the evolution of early patterns from newsgroups, bulletin boards, mailing lists, and the like—on which users provided alternative sources of information—into the WWW, where mainstream news media have developed a formidable presence. The movement from text-based communication to multimedia Web sites changed the nature of netizens from active participants in an ongoing civic life to more passive audiences who use the Web for information, entertainment, or business.

In Chapters 6 through 8, the focus shifts from mass politics to the politics of conducting public and private business over the Internet. Chapter 6 looks at doing business in cyberspace. We examine the dual role of government in supporting and at the same time regulating the Internet; we also analyze the problem of taxation. Using gambling as a case study, Chapter 7 takes a closer look at regulation of business on the Internet. We assess the extent to which commercial regulation of the Internet and the politics surrounding this regulation mirror the politics of commercial regulation in the real world. We also consider claims that there are special problems unique to regulating cyberspace. Chapter 8 deals with crime in cyberspace. We distinguish between network crime and computer crime. *Network crime* consists of a variety of criminal activities that employ the Internet but do not entail corrupting or breaking into computers. *Computer crime* has computers as its objects. The section on computer crime deals with methods that have been used to break into computers and computer networks. It concludes with a discussion of the Presidential Commission's Report on Critical Infrastructure and the response of the government to the threat of hackers and cyber-terrorists.

In discussing the impact of developments in each of the chapters, we return to our concepts of intra-Net politics, politics that affects the Net, and political uses of the Net. In Chapter 9, we evaluate the extent to which the evidence supports our thesis that in cyberspace normalization proceeds apace, and we discuss the implications of this judgment for the conduct of democratic politics in the twenty-first century.

Notes

1. "Orwell or Athens" in van de Donk and Tops's title refers to the fact that the new technologies have evoked both negative and positive images. For optimistic assessments of the use of the Internet for enhancing democratic citizenship, see Mann (1995), Rheingold (1993), and Schwartz (1996).

2. Although the lawsuit was thrown out of court on procedural grounds, at almost the same time a Quebec computer store owner got in similar trouble with Quebec's *Office de la Langue Francaise* for having an English-only Web site (King, 1997).

3. For an analysis of the problems of trying to adapt concepts grounded on territorial sovereignty to cyberspace—a territory without traditional geographical boundaries—see Johnson and Post (1997).

4. For the entire survey and detailed results, see the Web site of the Pew Research Center for the People and the Press (http://www.people-press.org/tec96que.htm).

5. For those interested in following campaigns around the world, not just in the United States, Klipsan Press provides *Election Notes,* an excellent wide-ranging daily summary of electoral news (http://www.klipsan.com/elecnews.htm).

6. The views expressed in the document by Swett (1995) are those of the author and do not necessarily represent the policies or positions of the DOD.

Democracy in Cyberspace

A Brief History

Hardly anyone uses computers to compute anymore. Instead we use them to communicate.

Steven McDonald, 1997, p. A68

If democracy entails equal opportunity to participate in politics, then the Internet creates that opportunity. Computer-mediated communication (CMC) technology provides individual citizens, interest groups, and public officials with the information necessary to decide questions of politics and public policy, and it provides them with the communication tools necessary to organize themselves for collective action. An "electronic" agora actually seems possible, in which the ordinary citizen's voice can be amplified cheaply and broadcast as widely as the voice of the richest plutocrat.

This chapter presents a brief history of the origin and development of computer networks and how they became the Internet. It provides readers with a basic understanding of the structure of the Net and of its fundamental protocols; it then focuses on the theoretical and practical relations between the Internet and democratic politics (Hafner & Lyon, 1996). The three typologies described in Chapter 1 underpin the discussion: politics within the Net, politics that affects the Net, and political uses of the Net.

The thesis of the discussion is that as the population of cyberspace has expanded, the politics of cyberspace has evolved from a self-regulating system dominated by internal concerns to a system in which politics that affects the Net and political uses of the Net predominate. Furthermore, although communication over the Internet still has the potential to democratize political discourse, in fact, it increasingly resembles the one-to-many pattern of broadcast media.

The Rise of ARPANET

In the 1960s, when the authors of this book began using computers, we relied on large "mainframes" to do our work. We used these computers mostly for data processing and for statistical data analysis. We even did our own programming, writing out specific instructions in various computer languages that directed the mainframe to complete its assigned task. Most mainframes at the time processed each job (a discrete set of instructions to complete a task) serially.[1] By the end of the decade, however, two significant developments occurred that benefited researchers in the social sciences: (a) refinement and adoption of time-sharing, which allowed users to make more efficient use of a mainframe's computing capacity (Kemeny, 1972, Chapter 3); and (b) distribution of integrated packages of programs written in languages that allowed users to process and analyze data without having to write special programs for their own computers (Margolis, 1970).

Time-sharing meant that a computer would select jobs in a manner that apportioned the central processing unit (CPU) and peripheral sources as needed instead of devoting all its resources to running jobs serially. For instance, while it was doing one job that required CPU time, it might be using peripherals to read in data for other jobs, or it could apportion the CPU among several small jobs at once. A time-shared computer could be thought of as a quickly moving servant of slowly moving masters.[2] A multitude of users could connect terminals—teletype-like machines or cathode ray tubes with keyboards attached—to a properly programmed computer all at the same time, yet each of them would seem to have the computer's full attention. Feedback about and output from jobs could be received right at the terminal. This circumstance democratized computing in the sense that users logging in from decentralized computer stations could exert greater control over their jobs than they could before.

Among the vigorous advocates of time-sharing was J. C. R. Licklider, a visionary social psychologist and computer scientist, who in 1962 became Director of the Command and Control Research Division of the Advanced Research Projects Agency (ARPA) of the U.S. Department of Defense.[3] Before joining ARPA, Licklider had written of the possibilities of citizens using a network of "home computer consoles" to keep themselves "informed about, and interested in, and involved in, the process of government. . . . The key is the self-motivating exhilaration that accompanies truly effective interaction with information through a good console and a good network to a good [central] computer" (Hafner & Lyon, 1996, p. 34; see also Margolis, 1979, pp. 158-170). Building on his academic and private sector connections, Licklider distributed research contracts aimed at improving user-computer interface among the country's foremost computer centers, including Stanford, the Massachusetts Institute of Technology (MIT), UCLA, and UC-Berkeley. Shortly before his tenure, he had begun a legendary series of memos addressed to the "Intergalactic Computer Network." The memos noted that realizing the potential power of computer networks required dispersed computer centers to "agree upon some language or, at least, upon some conventions for asking such questions as 'What language do you speak?' " (Hafner & Lyon 1996, p. 38; see also Discovery Channel Online, http://eagle.online.discovery.com/online.html). During his 2 years as director, Licklider shifted his division's emphasis from playing out war-game scenarios to developing time-sharing systems and computer graphics and to improving computer languages. The division's new name, Information Processing Technology Office (IPTO), reflected this change of emphasis.

In the social sciences, the impetus behind the availability of integrated packages for data processing and analysis had been the growth of archives of computerized information. The Inter-University Consortium for Political and Social Research (ICPSR, originally ICPR), centered at the Institute for Social Research at the University of Michigan, is among the most prominent of these. Founded in 1962 as a partnership of the University of Michigan and 21 U.S. universities, it has expanded to become the "world's largest archive of computer-based research and instructional data for the social sciences" (ICPSR, 1994), with a membership of more than 300 North American colleges and universities plus several hundred affiliates worldwide.

From its inception, the ICPSR strove not only to acquire and preserve social science data but also to provide effective distribution and use of the data. This included developing standards for coding and storing digitized information on media suitable for distribution to member universities and also providing consultation and training in data processing and analysis for social scientists. As common standards emerged, data could be moved from ICPSR's computers, first by punched cards and later by magnetic tape and disk, to members' computers, where researchers could use standard data processing and statistical packages to organize and analyze the data. Distributing these data and the associated packages of computer programs democratized empirical research in the social sciences. Access to major sets of social science data, particularly on public opinion and electoral behavior, no longer belonged almost exclusively to researchers at the few centers that had the resources to collect them. Now faculty and students at member universities could replicate or otherwise test the original researchers' findings. They also could analyze hitherto unused combinations of variables within the same sets of data to develop and test their own theories.

Moving data in machine-readable form was a great advance, but it still involved shipping information on a storage medium from one computer center to another. Documentation in either machine-readable or printed form also had to be included. Once users had received the data, documentation, and programs, they still had to write special instructions for their own computers to read the information and activate the programs. In principle, researchers would have an easier time if they shared a common protocol that allowed them to use their own computer facilities to access both the information and the programs directly from computers at remote locations.

Social scientists comprised only a small fraction of computer users, but the problems they encountered in transferring data and programs between machines were typical of those being encountered by the larger scientific research community. Robert Taylor, who became the third director of IPTO in 1966, found himself frustrated not only by the difficulties of running three separate terminals to connect to three separate mainframe computers from his office, but also by the increasing cost of funding some 17 separate mainframes at research centers across the country, most of which required unique protocols for access and many of which contained redundant programs and data. Both he and his boss, Charles Herzfeld, Director of ARPA, were familiar with Licklider's ideas. Taylor convinced Herzfeld to fund a project for IPTO to create a network of 4 to 12 computers. With Herzfeld's help, Taylor hired Lawrence Roberts from MIT's Lincoln Laboratory, a major government contractor, to manage the project (Discovery Channel Online; Hafner & Lyon, 1996).

By 1967, Roberts was able to present the first design paper of what came to be called ARPANET. It capitalized on Leonard Kleinrock's theoretical work on packet switching. This system broke messages down into separate portions or packets and sent them between networked computers via any route available, in contrast to relaying the full messages via a direct circuit between two computers.

As it happened, researchers headed by Kleinrock at MIT, Paul Baran at RAND Corporation, and Donald Davies at National Physical Laboratory in Middlesex, England, had proceeded independently with parallel work on network packet switching. Only the RAND project dealt with building a network that would be resistant to nuclear attack. The ARPANET was conceived for reasons of budgetary and scientific efficiency, not as an effort to secure communications in the event of nuclear war (Hafner & Lyon, 1996, chap. 2; Leiner et al., 1998; Zakon, n.d.).

Development of the network proceeded. Throughout 1968 Roberts worked with representatives of ARPA-funded centers to refine the specifications of the network. These individuals, mostly graduate students, later became the core of the Network Working Group (NWG). The key to linking computers would be Interface Message Processors (IMPs) that would exchange packets with distant computers and then relay the information to local "host" computers. A "request for proposals" to develop these processors was issued in December 1968. The contract was won by Bolt, Beranek, and Newman (BBN) of Boston, whose research team worked under the direction of Frank Heart and Robert Kahn. Meanwhile, a research team headed by Howard Frank of Network Analysis Corporation worked with Roberts on costing out the network, and another team worked under Kleinrock, who was now with the Network Measuring Center at UCLA, on monitoring and managing network traffic. The three teams' efforts were coordinated through meetings with Roberts and the NWG (Hafner & Lyon, 1996, chaps. 3-4; Hauben, n.d.; Leiner et al., 1998).[4]

The first IMP was installed at UCLA and connected to its first host computer in September 1969. Connections were expanded quickly by adding IMPs to hosts at the Stanford Research Institute (SRI), UC-Santa Barbara, and the University of Utah. The Stanford node supported an early hypertext system, whereas the latter two nodes specialized in applications that involved graphics. By the end of the year, a simple four-node network was in operation. UCLA, SRI, and UC-Santa Barbara connected with one another, but all of Utah's connections were routed through SRI. Thus, the network lacked the redundancies necessary to make the connections impervious to breakdowns at key nodes, as envisioned by Baran. Indeed, even as it matured, ARPANET never achieved the levels of redundancy that the RAND studies had contemplated. Significantly, however, ARPANET represented an effort to combine research on specific defense projects with research on the more general problem of developing communication among computers to harness and combine their capacities across great distance (Hafner & Lyon, 1996, pp. 72, 78, 113, 151-152; Leiner et al., 1998).[5]

As ARPANET expanded—by 1971 there were 15 nodes with 23 host computers that stretched from coast to coast—the need for common protocols to link local networks of computers to other hosts or other local networks grew more acute. Steve Crocker, one of Kleinrock's graduate students at UCLA, headed the NWG task force on this matter. Rather than having the NWG develop and then implement standards on its own, Crocker employed a strategy of releasing "requests for comments" that encouraged the participation of researchers at all the major centers that handled Defense Department contracts. The process was remarkably open: "Documentation of the NWG's effort is through notes such as this. Notes may be produced at any site by anybody and included in this series." The purpose of these notes, or comments, was to air any and all ideas that might be used to develop the network in a timely fashion. No requirements for polished ideas were imposed. "The minimum length for a NWG note is one sentence." Indeed, the NWG aimed "to promote the exchange and discussion of considerably less than authoritative ideas" (Hauben, n.d.; see also Hafner & Lyon, 1996, p. 144; Zakon, n.d.).

This openness was all the more remarkable when we consider that during the late 1960s and early 1970s, the FBI and CIA were busy infiltrating and otherwise disrupting various civil rights and anti-Vietnam War organizations in which students participated. At the same time, the National Security Agency was tapping international telephone calls; the Post Office was opening international mail; and the Justice Department's Law Enforcement Intelligence Unit was funding "red squads" of local police, whose members spied on, acted as *agents provocateurs* for, or sometimes did worse to the civil rights and antiwar organizations they deemed dangerous. Nor did President Nixon hesitate to use the Internal Revenue Service to audit and otherwise harass those who opposed his policies on these matters (Greenberg & Page, 1995, pp. 362-363, 498, 504).

In short, despite the federal funds that drove it, ARPANET was mostly self-regulating in its early years. Neither the press nor Congress paid close attention to the emerging computer network from 1969 through 1974. To the extent that they did look at computer networks, both tended to focus on three types of problems: (a) issues of privacy as computerized data from state and local governments were consolidated by federal agencies, (b) the USSR's effort to develop its own computer network augmented by American and British technologies, and (c) the dangers of abuses by agencies of government that collected and consolidated computerized data on protesters and political opponents. IPTO and ARPANET were not in the public limelight.[6] The ARPANET community was a rather small group of research students, scientists, engineers, and technicians. Regulation of the emerging computer network, however, was comparable to what we have called politics within the Net. Present and anticipated ARPANET users made the decisions democratically.

Expanding and Linking Computer Networks

In December 1970, the NWG introduced Network Control Protocol (NCP) as ARPANET's host-to-host protocol. Implementation of NCP facilitated the network's growth to more than 40 machines by summer 1972. During the same period, other computer networks were being developed independently. Computer scientists had devised programs for sending electronic messages within a time-sharing system, but now there was a need for a cheap means for researchers to communicate directly with one another over a network. Beyond that, researchers needed to address the problem of how users from different networks could communicate with one another.

In March 1972, Ray Tomlinson at BBN wrote the first successful email program within ARPANET. Lawrence Roberts refined Tomlinson's software so that users could selectively read, file, forward, and respond to messages. Email was piggybacked onto the file-transfer protocols (FTPs) then being implemented, and it was available in time for the first public demonstration of ARPANET at the inaugural meeting of the International Conference on Computer Communications in October 1972. The highly successful demonstration, put together under Robert Kahn's direction, involved more than 40 different types of terminals, coordinated through a Terminal IMP that allowed users to access any of 29 ARPANET nodes. The amazing thing that Kahn discovered from the conference, however, was that practically all the users began to use the network to send electronic mail rather than to access scientific resources on distant computers. Communication had taken precedence over computation (Hafner & Lyon, 1996, pp. 86, 191-192; Leiner et al., 1998).

Having demonstrated that packet-switching technology allowed communication among users of different types and makes of computers across the ARPANET, Kahn and Roberts were ready to devote more resources to interconnecting computers on different networks. Representatives from several networking projects in the United States and abroad already had established the International Network Working Group (INWG) to take on this problem. Vinton Cerf, who had worked on NCP at UCLA, was designated the leader of the group.

Kahn already had four features in mind when he formally asked Cerf to join him to design an Internet protocol:

1. Open architecture: Each network could be separately designed, and none would require internal changes to connect to the Internet.
2. Each packet sent on a "best effort" basis: If the source did not receive confirmation that a packet had reached its final destination, the source would retransmit it.
3. Networks interconnected through simple "black boxes" (later called "gateways" or "routers"); to ease recoveries from breakdowns, these gateways would retain none of the information that they used for routing data.
4. There would be no global control of operations. (Leiner et al., 1998)

Features 1 and 4 were remarkably democratic, foreshadowing some utopian aspects of intra-Net politics.

The Kahn-Cerf collaboration was highly productive. The two prepared the first version of what eventually became Transmission Control Protocol/ Internet Protocol (TCP/IP) for a special meeting of the INWG held in conjunction with a communications conference at the University of Sussex. IP would encapsulate each information packet, telling where the packet came from and where it was bound, much like an ordinary postal envelope. The gateways or routers would read only this information, ignoring what the packet contained. In contrast, TCP would handle information within each sending and receiving computer. It would tag each message or data transmission and break it into packets, identify the order of each packet within each message, place each packet in an electronic envelope, send and acknowledge receipt of it, and resend any packet that was not acknowledged by the receiving computer. Once all the packets had reached their destination, TCP would reassemble the message (Hafner & Lyon, 1996, pp. 226-227; Leiner et al., 1998).[7]

During 1975, researchers working with Cerf at Stanford refined the Cerf-Kahn concepts into a set of concrete specifications. ARPA then let contracts to centers at Stanford (Cerf), BBN (Tomlinson), and University College London (Peter Kirstein) to implement the protocols independently. These efforts were so successful that the next year all three implementations could operate with one another. With these versions in hand, full-blown experimentation with interconnecting networks took off, and by mid-1977 ARPANET was linked to Packet Radio and to SATNET. Cerf and Kahn led a demonstration of this internet, sending messages 94,000 miles across all three networks without losing a single bit of information (Leiner et al., 1998).[8]

From that point network development accelerated. While computer scientists associated with defense projects were experimenting with ARPANET, other network communities blossomed. Some were governmental, such as the U.S. Department of Energy's MFENet for Magnetic Fusion Energy, and its HEPNet for High Energy Physics, or the NASA space physicists' network called SPAN. Some were marketed commercially, such as BBN's TELENET, a private packet-switching network service (not to be confused with remote logins called "telnet"). Others linked academic units. These included Lawrence Landweber's THEORYNET, which linked more than 100 University of Wisconsin researchers via TELENET and a local email program, and MEDLINE, a Johns Hopkins University project that linked researchers to the National Library of Medicine database.

Because ARPANET was limited to defense contractors—only 15 of its 61 sites were universities in 1979—Landweber, head of computer science at the University of Wisconsin, put together a conference on the feasibility of developing an academic network for computer science (CSNET).[9] Representatives from the National Science Foundation (NSF) and ARPA attended, as well as representatives of several universities and other ARPANET members. In summer 1980, Landweber's group successfully proposed a three-tiered (low to high capabilities) network that would run more cheaply, though more slowly and with fewer redundancies, than ARPANET. All three tiers would connect to one another via gateways. NSF agreed to underwrite the network for 5 years, gradually turning management and financing over to the member universities and nondefense private computer research firms.

AT&T's Bell Labs developed Unix-to-Unix CoPy (UUCP) in 1976 and began to distribute it with its UNIX operating system in 1977. Among other things, UUCP facilitated using dial-up connections for email, which as mentioned previously, was the network service most in demand. This led to nonresearch as well as research-oriented networks. By 1979, three graduate students, Tom Truscott and Jim Ellis at Duke and Steve Bellovin at the University of North Carolina (UNC), established the first Usenet newsgroups using UUCP protocols, with Duke and UNC as the hosts. The same year, Richard Bartle and Roy Trubshaw created the first Multi-User Dungeon at the University of Essex (Gilster, 1994; Hafner & Lyon, 1996; Leiner et al., 1998; Zakon, n.d.).[10] In 1981, BITNET, the first general-purpose academic network, had become operational. Designed by Ira Fuchs of the City University of New York and Greydon Freeman of Yale, BITNET used an IBM-based "store and forward" protocol to connect mainframe computers at separate universities via dedicated telephone lines. By 1984 more than 100 universities were included (Gilster, 1994). Although all of these networks supported email internally, they or their successors would need to use some form of TCP/IP to connect to the Internet via gateways.

While Cerf and Kahn were working on Internet protocols, researchers at Xerox's Palo Alto Research Center (PARC) were developing one of the first personal computers (PCs), called Alto. An immediate concern was how to link these computers to more powerful hosts. Robert Metcalfe, a researcher at PARC, learned of the University of Hawaii's ALOHAnet radio packet technology through his friend, Steve Crocker. After consulting with Norman Abramson, the principal designer of ALOHAnet, Metcalfe and his team put together a hardwired local area network (LAN) at PARC. Thanks to the hardwired connections and an improved internal design, the new network operated 1,000 times faster than did ALOHAnet. Initially called Aloha Alto Network, it was renamed "Ethernet" in 1973 (Hafner & Lyon, 1996).

Development of Ethernet technologies, combined with the adaptation of TCP for the Xerox Alto and the IBM-PC, eventually changed the entire nature of the Internet. Instead of a few national-scale networks like ARPANET, each with a relatively large number of hosts (Class A), or regional scale networks that still have many hosts per network (Class B), most networks that form the Internet—such as those at universities or large businesses—are LANs. These usually consist of many PCs and workstations connected by means of an Ethernet to a relatively small number of host computers (Class C) (Leiner et al., 1998).

Having so many separate computer workstations presents a problem of addressing. Every computer that receives a message over the Internet needs an IP address. The IP address currently consists of four numbers separated by periods; for example, 129.137.72.182 has been the IP address of the Macintosh 6100/66 in Michael Margolis's departmental office. The address proceeds from general to particular: 129 indicates University of Cincinnati; 182 indicates the 182nd computer on the campus network to which the Political Science Department's computers are linked. Needless to say, this address is difficult to memorize. Although a directory of all the addresses of one network might be kept on a central computer, millions of users of Internet email on thousands of independently managed networks render impractical maintaining a central directory of IP addresses. A simpler hierarchical system of addressing is needed.

Even though some rival systems for Internet addressing were proposed, TCP/IP replaced NCP as the official ARPANET standard on January 1, 1983. At the same time, a team led by Jonathan Postel at the Information Sciences Institute (ISI) of the University of Southern California developed Simple Mail Transfer Protocol (SMTP) as the new standard for addressing. Although SMTP included both mnemonics that simplified the addressing of email and protocols that improved communication between sending and receiving computers, the traffic across the Internet had burgeoned so rapidly that the existing means to locate addresses or mailboxes on some 2,000 separate hosts became slow and cumbersome (Hafner & Lyon, 1996; Postel, 1982).

The Domain Name System (DNS) solved the problem and is the hierarchical addressing system used today. Invented by Paul Mockapetris at ISI and developed primarily by Mockapetris, Postel, and Craig Partridge of BBN, DNS effectively translates the four-part IP address into a mnemonic that proceeds from particular to general. For example, Michael Margolis's original email address at the University of Cincinnati was Margolis@ucbeh.san.uc.edu. This indicated a mailbox for user "Margolis" on the UC VAX computer in Beecher Hall on the Student Access Network at the University of Cincinnati, an educational institution. There were six primary domains for the United States: (a) *edu* for educational institutions; (b) *com* for commercial sites; (c) *gov* for U.S. civilian governmental sites; (d) *mil* for U.S. military sites; (e) *net* for network administrative organizations; and (f) *org* for organizations that do not fit into the previously stated categories, usually nonprofits. The first four top-level domains originally applied only to U.S. organizations. Other countries sometimes used these, especially "com," but many developed their own top-level domain names, such as "de" for Germany or "kr" for (South) Korea. Each domain is divided into zones, where computers called "nameservers" translate each mnemonic into appropriate IP addresses. Any given mnemonic address automatically passes through one or more of these nameservers until the correct IP address is located. Once located, the IP address is returned to the sending computer, and the message (in packets) is sent out (Gilster, 1994; Leiner et al., 1998; Mockapetris, 1983). The information held by each nameserver can be updated within its appropriate zone without referral to a centralized file.[11]

The implementation of TCP/IP and DNS in 1983 marks the birth of the Internet as we recognize it today. With these two features in place, networks could be linked seamlessly, and information—email in particular—could be directed between network hosts without difficulty. As networks like CSNET, BITNET, and Usenet were now free to link up with ARPANET, the Defense Department thought it prudent to carve off the 68 ARPANET nodes that primarily dealt with military research and information into a new network called MILNET. The remaining 45 nodes became the Internet's first backbone.

With the technology in place, academics from disciplines outside the computer and engineering sciences added their demand for greater access. In 1983, the European Academic and Research Network was established, and in 1984 Britain opened its Joint Academic Network. The success of CSNET already had convinced NSF that facilitating low-cost direct communication among professional academics produced enormous research benefits and that those without access to network communications would become increasingly disadvantaged. It was not until 1985, however, when the United States needed to provide access to five newly established regional supercomputers, that both the academic and economic benefits provided NSF with the impetus to fund a high-speed backbone. The Foundation agreed to build a backbone called NSFNET and to provide access to any regional academic network. Academic institutions were required to use TCP/IP for linkages and to provide access for all qualified users, regardless of discipline. In January 1986, DNS was made mandatory for connections to NSFNET. With this infrastructure in place, Internet growth took off. In 1984, there were 1,000 hosts; by 1987, there were 10,000; and in 1989 the number of hosts reached 100,000 (Hafner & Lyon, 1996; Leiner et al., 1998; Zakon, n.d.). The Internet was poised for the next great expansion: the advent of the World Wide Web.

From ARPANET to the Internet

Before we turn to the WWW, however, let us pause to consider how the transition from ARPANET to the Internet was accomplished. How were decisions made? Who made them? Separate networks essentially had been self-governing. To what extent did the participation of outside entities, both public and private, begin to affect governance of the Internet?

In 1979, Vinton Cerf, who had moved to ARPA to manage the Internet Program, established two invitational groups: (a) the Internet Configuration Control Board (ICCB), chaired by David Clark of MIT, as an informal committee to advise Cerf's department regarding Internet development; and (b) the International Cooperation Board (ICB), chaired by Peter Kirstein of University College London, to coordinate European activities. In addition, Cerf put together a more inclusive body, the Internet Research Group (IRG), to facilitate overall exchange of information. Although membership in the first two bodies was invitational, there was little concern that they would be unrepresentative. The Internet leadership and its research community were composed largely of groups of experts in Internet technology, and most of them knew one another's work (Froomkin, 1995, I-A; Leiner et al., 1998; Zakon, n.d.). In any case, even with the essentially open membership of the IRG, governance of the Net remained largely in control of those who used it most heavily, and the sources we have reviewed cite no serious complaints about how decisions were made.

The intrusion of politics that affects the Net began in earnest with the increased number of users following the implementation of TCP/IP. When Barry Leiner succeeded to Cerf's position at ARPA in 1983, he and David Clark collaborated on creating a new structure of governance to accommodate the rapidly growing Internet research community. In place of the ICCB, they created a series of task forces overseen by a new body called the Internet Activities Board (IAB). The IAB was composed of the heads of these task forces. Each task force focused on developing standards for particular technological aspects of the Net: routers, protocols, means for assigning domain names, and so forth. Not surprisingly, those named to lead the task forces were all former members of the ICCB, and Clark was appointed as the IAB's first chairman.

The Internet Engineering Task Force (IETF) turned out to be the most important of the task forces. As access to the Internet spread, there was growth in the numbers of engineers and computer scientists who (like most social scientists) used the Net for applied rather than research purposes. These users began to attend IETF meetings and to demand that the task force pay more attention to their concerns. Moreover, as NSF poured money into the Internet backbone, it wanted to encourage the development of appropriate connections to regional academic networks and an Acceptable Use Policy (AUP) for use of the backbone.

As a result, AUP established a general principle:

> NSFNET backbone services are provided to support open research and education in and among U.S. research and instructional institutions. . . . Use for other purposes [e.g., extensive personal or commercial business] is not acceptable.

In fact, there were so many exceptions that AUP permitted just about anything short of blatant for-profit operations (Gilster, 1994).[12]

The upshot of the policy was to encourage the creation of private long-distance networks to link local and regional commercial networks. In 1988, NSF even initiated a series of conferences at the Kennedy School of Government at Harvard on commercialization and privatization of the Net and sponsored continuing discussions on a "com-priv" mailing list. Commercial networks from Performance Systems International (PSINET), UUNET Technologies (ALTERNET), Advanced Network Services, Inc., IBM and MCI (ANSCO+RE), and others soon emerged. All these brought new constituencies and new concerns into the governance of the Internet. The pioneers were still influential in determining standards and policies, but now they had to take into account the interests and desires of a rapidly growing population of users, who could be described better as consumers of Internet services than as Internet developers, researchers, or technicians.

Expansion continued. In 1985, the influential virtual community Whole Earth Lectronic Link (WELL) was formed. In 1986, Cleveland Freenet, the first of several networks to offer the general public free access to numerous Internet services, came online. The same year, Usenet implemented Net News Transfer Protocol (NNTP) to accommodate TCP/IP connections that permitted greater access and outreach. In 1987, FIDONET, the network system of bulletin boards for IBM compatibles, connected to Usenet. By 1988, NSFNET had established direct links to Canada and seven European countries, and shortly thereafter *Reseaux IP Europeans* was formed to establish standards for network services in Europe. The first major disruption of the Internet also occurred in 1988, when a graduate student loosed a "worm" that disrupted services on nearly 6,000 (about 10%) of the existing hosts. The Computer Emergency Response Team, headquartered at Carnegie-Mellon University (CMU), was quickly established to handle and, more importantly, prevent future disruptions. Meanwhile, proprietary networks, such as CompuServe, America Online, and Prodigy, also expanded and began to offer selected Internet services, especially email (Froomkin, 1995, I-B; Zakon, n.d.).

Parallel developments in governance occurred among various networks that connected to the NSFNET backbone. Throughout the 1980s, Usenet newsgroups, for example, expanded in numbers and areas of interest. The expansion that followed the implementation of NNTP led to the "great renaming" during 1986 and 1987, when Usenet groups were classified into the now familiar categories, such as *biz* (business), *comp* (computers), *news* (news about Usenet), *rec* (recreation), *sci* (science), *talk* (politics and related topics), and so forth. This structure, in turn, was governed by a backbone group that included many of the experts who had been responsible for establishing and upgrading the network (Gaffin, 1996; Hardy, 1993; Zakon, n.d.). The group set ground rules to which the various newsgroups were supposed to conform. There was general acceptance of the classification scheme, but when the group balked at allowing proposed "rec.drugs" and "rec.sex" newsgroups to have access to the backbone, several dissidents decided to set up alternate routes to carry them. The "alt" classification using these routes for controversial issues was thereby established, and Brian Reid of CMU simply sent the "backbone cabal" a fait accompli:

> To end the suspense, I have just created alt.sex. That meant that the alt network now carried alt.sex and alt.drugs. It was therefore artistically necessary to create alt.rock-n-roll, which I have done also. I have no idea what sort of traffic it will carry.[13]

This somewhat whimsical and disorderly governance by technocracy remained dominant until the mid-1990s, when commercial interests and established governments began in earnest to impose greater control over the structure and operations of the Internet. The popularity of the WWW and the desire of American business and political leaders to implement "free market" policies provided much of the impetus for this intrusion.

The World Wide Web and the
Popularization of Cyberspace

Despite its accelerating pace of growth, by 1990 the Internet remained a relatively esoteric medium. NSFNET had displaced ARPANET as the backbone of the Internet and was connected to countries as remote as Argentina, India, and Japan. ARPANET was decommissioned on June 1, 1990. But even in 1992, as the number of host computers on six continents (all but Antarctica) exceeded 1 million, most of the users were still computer-savvy individuals involved in research or educational activities. Although treasure troves of software and data were added almost daily as networks linked with one another, the contents available on new hosts remained essentially unknown. Anonymous FTP, which allowed access to publicly held files on remote computers, was useful only to the extent that users knew where to find the information they sought. To use FTP efficiently also required learning how data were stored on the remote computers being accessed and mastering a sizable set of commands.

Until Peter Deutsch, Alan Emtage, and William Wheelan of McGill University introduced "Archie" in 1990, users had no easy means to acquire the addresses or contents of the computers that held the information they wished to access. Archie allowed users to inquire about the existence of a filename in the public FTP areas of any computer on the Net. Archie was followed by Gopher in 1991. Gopher, invented by Mark McCahill and his team of programmers at the University of Minnesota, provided system administrators with the ability to place the contents of information on menus. Gopher was the first widespread system that allowed users to access data by pointing at menu titles or topics instead of learning to issue special commands. Gopher capabilities soon were enhanced when Fred Barrie and Steven Foster of the University of Nevada added "Veronica," a tool that enabled users to search Gopher menus by topic. By 1993, Veronica could peruse more than 1 million entries on Gopher menus around the world (Discovery Channel Online; Gilster, 1994, 1997; Zakon, n.d.).

Real popularization of the Internet finally took place when the WWW was coupled with the invention of Mosaic, the first widespread graphical browser. When the European Laboratory for Particle Physics (*Conseil Européen por la Recherche Nucléaire,* or CERN) connected CERNET to the Internet in 1989, one of its physicists, Tim Berners-Lee, seized the opportunity to propose implementation of a hypertext-based system that he had ruminated on for nearly a decade. The idea was to exchange information by embedding links within documents. The links, which users could activate as desired, would contain the computer addresses needed to access the desired information. Berners-Lee dubbed the system the "World Wide Web" and circulated his proposal in March 1989. The WWW was placed in operation on a NeXT server at CERN the following year. It was not an immediate success. The typical Internet users were accustomed to employing hierarchical and linear search paradigms like those of Archie or of related Wide Area Information Servers (WAIS), not following nonlinear hyperlinks (Discovery Channel Online; Gilster, 1997; Kazmierczak, n.d., sections 5-6).

While his research partner Robert Cailliau focused on connecting the WWW to physics networks, Berners-Lee worked on spreading the technology across the Internet. Berners-Lee shared a notion that was functionally similar to the Apple Macintosh vision of friendly graphical user interfaces (GUIs), in contrast to the powerful but less friendly UNIX-based interfaces that still dominated Net protocols and MS-DOS protocols still used on most PCs. In his view, "When you turn on your computer, what you should see is information.... You should be able to create it, to absorb it ... [and] exchange it freely in the informational space" (Gilster, 1997, p. 45). Based on existing Internet protocols and document languages, he refined HyperText Transfer Protocol (HTTP) and introduced HyperText Markup Language (HTML). To access the WWW, all someone needed was a "client" or "browser" that would ask the Web servers to locate and transfer information of interest. By November 1992, there were 26 WWW servers, including the National Center for Supercomputing Applications (NCSA) at the University of Illinois.

Marc Andreesen, then an undergraduate student in engineering and part-time programmer at NCSA, became intrigued with the idea of improving the WWW by adding a user-friendly GUI to the hypertext. He convinced Eric Bina, a full-time senior engineer, to apply his skills to the task, and together they spearheaded the development of a new browser for the WWW, which they called Mosaic. NCSA released the first version of NCSA Mosaic for X, designed for UNIX machines, in February 1993, and versions for PC/Windows and Macintosh in September. All versions could be downloaded free from NCSA's WWW server. The GUI allowed users not only to navigate the Web via hypertext but to gather information by pointing and clicking on graphics, symbols, hot buttons, or the like. Mosaic X proved popular, and, following the release of Windows and Macintosh versions, an explosion began: The number of WWW servers jumped to approximately 630 in January

1994. News of Mosaic spread not only among Internet users but through featured articles in *The New York Times,* the *Economist,* and the *Guardian.* The Internet had entered the mainstream of popular Western culture (December & Randall, 1994; Kazmierczak, n.d., section 7; Reid, 1997).[14]

Before Mosaic, WWW transactions accounted for a negligible percentage of packets sent over the NSFNET backbone. By April 1995, when NSFNET turned the backbone over to private hands and reverted to a research network, WWW packet transactions equaled those of FTP, accounting for 24% of the traffic. Between January 1994 and July 1995, the number of Web servers grew from 600 to 23,500. By July 1996, this number exceeded 200,000.

The nature of the servers changed greatly also. Not only did they support more powerful graphics, often accompanied by sound, but they overwhelmingly represented commercial rather than educational or other types of domains. Only 2 of the 130 WWW servers had "com" as their domain in June 1993. In contrast, by July 1996, more than two thirds of the estimated 230,000 WWW servers were commercial.[15] Commercial development also was boosted when Marc Andreesen joined with James Clark (principal of Silicon Graphics Inc.) in March 1994 to found what became Netscape Communications Corporation. The corporation redesigned, rebuilt, and extended the functionality of the original Mosaic. Their primary product, Netscape Navigator 1.0, released in December 1994, soon became the dominant Web browser. Netscape gave users the ability to transact business: It could support not only sound and graphics but also interactive forms for ordering services or merchandise, and it provided encryption to help protect payment transfers and privacy (Kazmierczak, n.d., section 7; Reid, 1997).

Web sites and Web pages within those sites each carry a unique Web identifier called a Universal Resource Locator (URL). Even though a browser like Netscape can take users to any particular site and follow the links found there, users must direct the browser, either by citing the URL or by activating a link displayed on their current Web page. As the WWW grew, the need for functional equivalents of search engines like Archie and Veronica became apparent. During 1994, several important search engines were launched, all of which eventually became commercial. Among these were WebCrawler, a text-oriented engine by Brian Pinkerton of the University of Washington; Lycos, a strategic search engine that employs probability models, by Michael Mauldin, John Leavitt, and Eric Nyberg of CMU; and, most popular of all, Yahoo!, a hierarchically arranged search engine with categories based on users' search patterns, by David Filo and Jerry Yang of Stanford. Finally, the advent of user-friendly Web browsers and search engines brought about a rapid change in the services offered by proprietary networks, such as America Online. Whereas prior to 1995 these networks attracted customers by advertising access to their own easy-to-use features—graphics, markets, information services, games, chat rooms, special interest groups, and the like—now they advertise their prowess as Internet service providers (ISPs), with their proprietary features as bonuses. Indeed, no general-purpose proprietary network could survive today if it did not offer its customers easy and economical access to the WWW (December & Randall, 1994; Kazmierczak, n.d., section 7; Reid, 1997).[16]

The upshot of these developments was a transformation of the Internet from a research-oriented vehicle dominated by technocrats to a commercially oriented one dominated by businesses that supply products and services ranging from information to entertainment and from software to merchandise. This is not to say that the old interests have disappeared. Far from it. Researchers, candidates, parties, governmental bodies, educational institutions, cause groups, public interest groups, nonprofit organizations, and others all have increased their presence on the Net. However, the proportion of Internet traffic they drive has shrunk relative to the activities of commercial enterprises.

Even as this transformation took place, the organizations that governed technical aspects of the Internet continued to evolve. In response to the needs of the growing commercial sector, the IAB leaders spearheaded the formation of the Internet Society (ISOC) in 1991. The Society was organized under the auspices of Robert Kahn's nonprofit Corporation for National Research Initiatives (CNRI), and Vinton Cerf, who had by then joined CNRI, served as the Society's first president. In 1992, the IAB reorganized, renaming itself the Internet Architecture Board, subordinating itself to the Internet Society. By 1998, the Society included 7,000 individual members who paid nominal annual dues. But, more importantly, its 150 or so organizational members, who paid from $1,000 to $50,000 in annual dues, included major providers of network access, telecommunications and computer products, research and information services, systems management, shipping, education, and media services, as well as governmental agencies (Leiner et al., 1998).[17]

In 1994, the World Wide Web Consortium (W3C) was formed to coordinate the activities and to develop standards for major organizations (mostly commercial) doing business on the Web. W3C was initiated by CERN, MIT, and the French National Institute for Research in Computing and Automation, and Tim Berners-Lee served as its first president. Membership was open only to organizations. Full memberships required $50,000 (U.S.) as annual dues. Affiliate memberships at $5,000 annual dues were available to governmental agencies, nonprofit organizations, and small for-profit businesses. The membership was a formidable list of major firms that offered a huge range of products and services, including not merely telecommunications and the like but manufacturing, publishing, banking—just about any line of business worldwide, except perhaps direct retail merchandising of small consumer products (Leiner et al., 1998).[18]

As the Internet expanded, the U.S. government stepped back from direct ownership and control of the high-speed backbone. After turning over the backbone to commercial carriers in 1995, the government also delegated many of its regulatory functions to privately run (mostly nonprofit) organizations. Assignment of TCP/IP addresses, their correlation with unique domain names, and related technical matters were handled by the Internet Assigned Numbers Authority (IANA), headquartered at ISI and headed by Jonathan Postel until his untimely death in 1998. Chartered by the ISOC and the FNC, IANA enforced protocols developed by IETF. Registration of the actual top-level domain names for com, net, org, gov, and edu, however, was contracted to Network Services Inc. (NSI), and AT&T was assigned the associated Directory and Database Services. NSF then joined with NSI and AT&T to form InterNIC, a nonprofit network administrative organization that provides information and support services (such as Netscout) to research and educational institutions to support their own Internet users. Finally, the U.S. government helped to charter the Coordinating Committee for Intercontinental Research Networking (CCIRN), an international organization devoted to promoting development and coordination of standards for commercial and research networks throughout the world.[19]

Figure 2.1 summarizes the growth and evolution of the Internet and its governing mechanisms as described throughout this chapter. The pattern indicates (a) the growth in complexity of the governing bodies that attempt to set technical standards for the Internet, and (b) the tremendous growth in the number of users and networks. Although many of the individual participants in these governing bodies have been active and influential in the development of the Internet from the inception of ARPANET in the late 1960s, the newer participants represent stakeholders not merely from governmental, educational, and research institutions but also from commercial organizations interested in using the Internet to conduct business for profit. These new inter-

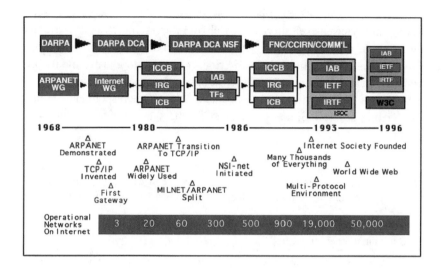

Figure 2.1. Internet Governance and Development
SOURCE: Internet Society (http: www.ISOC.org/internet/history/timeline.gif).

ests represent a familiar type of pluralism among the elite. The organizational participants reflect what is often called the "establishment": large corporate, educational, and governmental interests.

Because most of the participants are drawn from the top leadership of European and North American institutions, those who determine the technical standards and protocols are predominantly white and male. That the Asian Pacific Networking Group has substantial representation in CCIRN may mitigate the Euro-American influence, but it also exacerbates the male dominance. In addition to the sparsity of women and non-whites among the governing bodies, there is very little individual or organizational representation of the laboring classes, let alone the poor. The class structure of the interests that determine and enforce the technical standards of the Internet resembles that of the most influential interests represented in the governmental institutions of the real world.

As recently as 1994, the old rules of intra-Net politics still held. When the law firm of Canter and Siegel sought business with a mass emailing, it was considered not only a "spam" (an indiscriminant slathering of junk mail, particularly across Usenet) but also a general violation of "netiquette" (rules of Internet etiquette, which forbade commercial advertisements in most of cyberspace, as did AUP). Many who subscribed to listservs or Usenet newsgroups viewed even survey research over the Internet as an unwarranted intrusion or, worse yet, a spam. Indeed, in summer 1994, our first effort to survey the political activities of subscribers caused a stir and eventually precipitated a cancel order that removed the survey from a random sample of 80 newsgroups (Fisher, Margolis, & Resnick, 1996b). One respondent's lament for the days before ordinary folks invaded cyberspace was particularly poignant:

> Ah, the Internet. . . . I remember when the name didn't even exist. Back then it wasn't politics. . . . It was people exchanging some ideas and programs and such over the net, talking to friends in Israel, or playing an interactive war game, etc.
>
> POLITICS! of the network. . . . Yee gads.
>
> Get your society off our net!!!
>
> The Internet has been awfully nice over the years, and now it is being ruined by people who feel it has to be somehow defined, measured, analyzed, have laws made on it, charges assessed against every byte, and on and on and on. . . . WILL YOU PLEASE STOP??? Leave the net as it is. (Fisher et al., 1996b, p. 399)

As the Internet has become crowded with traffic of the hoi polloi pursuing goods, services, and information of all varieties, the research community has established the University Corporation for Advanced Internet Development (UCAID) and moved toward establishing a limited-access high-speed information highway called Internet2 (I2). Plans call for this new network to link some 120 member universities, a dozen corporate partners, and an additional 30 or more organizations designated as "Corporate Sponsors and Members" or "[nonprofit] Affiliate Members." I2's avowed mission and goals include the following:

> The development, deployment, operation, and technology transfer of advanced, network services to further U.S. leadership in research and higher education . . . [and to] catalyze partnerships with governmental and private sector organizations, [and to] encourage transfer of technology from Internet2 to the rest of the Internet.

Initially, I2 will use the NSF very-high-speed Backbone Network Service (vBNS), but eventually it will develop and use other high-speed networks, with speeds estimated at 100 to 1,000 times faster than those currently available.[20]

The developmental model here is different from that of the Internet. Instead of governmental agencies coordinating the overall effort, an independent, ostensibly nonprofit, public-private corporation has taken charge. Instead of the network being used for public purposes, the expectation is that "After the universities develop and debug these new lanes over the next two to five years, commercial interests will probably take over, imposing charges on those using Internet 2's premium services" (Meredith, 1998, p. C3).[21] The corporate partners are network, hardware, software, and service providers and developers who expect to profit from their efforts sometime in the near future. They include 3Com Corporation, ANS, IBM, Cabletron Systems, Cisco Systems, and Nortel. In short, I2 also looks like business as usual.

Political Consequences of Popularization

The history recounted in this chapter is replete with the names of white male engineers and scientists, many of whom made their mark on the Internet at an early age. Indeed, until well into the 1990s, the Internet and most of cyberspace were the bailiwick of young white males with relatively high incomes and educational levels. The first systematic user surveys conducted in 1994, for instance, estimated that as few as 1 in 10 users was female.[22] The median age of respondents hovered at about 30, the median annual household income for American respondents was at least $10,000 above the median for white households, and more than two thirds reported having completed a bachelor's degree program. Half the respondents were affiliated with educational domains; only 30% used commercial ISPs. Approximately one in five users was a student. Another 50% classified themselves as university faculty, researchers, or technical specialists. More than 90% identified themselves as white, and fewer than 2% said they were unemployed. They were highly proficient in using Internet technology, and they were unusually active politically. Obviously, these users were hardly typical of the general population (Fisher, Margolis, & Resnick, 1996a; Fisher et al., 1996b; Georgia Tech [GVU], 1999).[23]

Barely 5 years later, the characteristics of the respondents had radically changed. Quite simply, users had come to resemble the general middle-class population. By virtually every demographic and socioeconomic measure—gender, educational attainment, race, income, and occupation—the user population had become more representative of the general population. Among Americans, for instance, more than half the novice users were women, and more than 10% who classified themselves by race were non-white. Technical and educational occupations had dropped to about 30%, and more than 75% of users reported that they accessed the Net from home daily.

The rapid rise of commercialism, however, illustrated the most significant normalization. Whereas commercial uses of the Internet were just beginning in 1994, by fall 1997, more than two thirds of the GVU respondents from both Europe and the United States reported having ordered products or services via the WWW. Moreover, the longer the respondents' experience on the Web, the more likely they were to have used it to make purchases. That the new users were less likely than the old hands to have accessed the Web for work-related purposes as opposed to recreational and other purposes should reinforce this trend.

Not only is commercial traffic expanding on the WWW, but its nature may soon change. Advertising, particularly in the form of banners and click-through boxes, is commonplace. So, too, are the ubiquitous "cookies," persistent session identifiers that allow Webmasters to keep track of the selections that each particular user makes and to automatically adjust the advertising or the links accordingly in subsequent sessions. Magazines like *Slate,* journals like the *Chronicle of Higher Education,* and newspapers like *The New York Times* are seeking or in some cases have implemented ways to charge readers for access to their Web pages or to limit such access to those who subscribe to the publications offline. Although GVU survey respondents have declared their unwillingness to pay such charges—more than 80% indicated that they already pay enough just for access to the Internet or that they can find the same information from free sources—consolidation of high-quality sources and attempts to impose fees for access to them undoubtedly will increase. The GVU surveys themselves are now driven not merely by academic interest but also by the interests of a council of corporate sponsors, whose membership includes Sun Microsystems, NCR, Andersen Consulting, CyberDialog, and Yahoo.[24]

In sum, the interactions we find in cyberspace increasingly resemble those of the pluralistic market space of the real world. The same enterprises that dominate business and (as we shall see) politics in the real world appear to be emerging to dominate the business and politics of cyberspace. Moreover, the Internet users themselves act primarily as consumers or audience members, not as producers, discussants, technical wizards, or political participants.

Vestiges of the traditional politics within the Net remain, especially where individual network communities have formed around a Usenet newsgroup, a listserv mailing list, or a membership group like the WELL. The technical community also holds sway regarding guidance of the task forces and organizations that determine the international standards and protocols. But even these communities have been affected by politics that affects the Net. Private organizations, including both ordinary and network service businesses, have claimed representation on the councils that determine how the Internet is run, as have governmental organizations. Governments may shrink from attempting to run the Internet, but they remain concerned with how business is conducted over the Net, particularly with the manner and extent to which such business should be regulated or taxed. Meanwhile, established organizations and businesses have built up their own private networks, "intranets," or intra-organizational CMC. Although they can link to the Internet via email or WWW browsers, they maintain "firewalls" to prevent outsiders from accessing information. Finally, established parties, interest groups, and others are trying to use their presence on the Net to influence politics offline. The political activities of parties and interest groups on the Net is the focus of the next chapter.

Notes

1. Users would estimate the central processing unit (CPU) time required to complete the job. Short jobs were given priority during ordinary working hours when computer traffic was heavy; jobs requiring longer CPU time were usually run overnight.

2. The analogy is based on Kemeny (1972, pp. 23-28); see also Hafner and Lyon (1996, pp. 36-37).

3. ARPA was renamed Defense Advanced Research Projects Agency (DARPA) in 1971; its name reverted to ARPA from 1993 to 1996, and it was renamed DARPA in 1996 (Leiner et al., 1998, n. 4).

4. Network Analysis Corporation was bought out by Contel in the early 1980s, which in turn was absorbed by GTE in 1991 (Maryland Business School Web site).

5. Vinton Cerf, Steve Crocker, and Jon Postel were students of Leonard Kleinrock at UCLA. (Hauben, n.d., "History of ARPANET," http://www.dei.isep.ipp.pt/docs/arpa—5.html). Douglas Englehart was in charge of the "Augmentation of Human Intellect" project at SRI (Englehart, 1962), which included use of oNLineSystem (NLS) that contained hypertext. See http://www.histech.rwth-aachen.de/www/quellen/engelbart/ahi62index.html. The University of Utah project, led by Robert Taylor and Ivan Sutherland, involved using networks for transmission of three-dimensional representations. Taylor left IPTO to join Sutherland at Utah in October 1969. Sutherland had been Licklider's successor and Taylor's predecessor as Director of IPTO (Kazmierczak, n.d.). The UCSB team was led by Glen Culler and Burton Fried. The graphics and network developments stemmed from the need to communicate with and service the Defense Department's first spy satellites (Bryan, 1995).

6. Lexis-Nexis Universe lists no stories on ARPANET or IPTO among the 71 stories on computer networks carried by major newspapers from 1969 through 1974. *The New York Times* (January 21, 1972) ran one small story about the Nixon administration proposing an electronic mail system that would provide routine "overnight mail delivery between stations and 1-hour priority delivery." Otherwise, our search turned up only one other story devoted to email during the period: a book review of Thomas E. Mails's *The People Called Apache* in *The New York Times* (December 1, 1974).

7. The original paper was by Vinton Cerf and Robert Kahn, titled "HOST and PROCESS Level Protocols for Internet Communication," *Notes of the INWG, 39* (September 13, 1973), subsequently published as "A Protocol for Packet-Network Communication," *IEEE Transactions on Communication Technology, 5* (May 1974), pp. 627-641.

8. University College London and the Royal Radar Establishment in Norway had become the first international nodes on ARPANET in 1973 (Zakon, n.d.). SATNET was a transatlantic packet-switching network that linked computers by bouncing radio signals off satellites. Packet Radio sends similar signals among computers terrestrially (Hafner & Lyon, 1996, pp. 221-222, 236-237).

9. Part of the difficulty lay with the Defense Communication Agency's policy of restricting ARPANET access to defense contractors (Hafner & Lyon, 1996, 235-237).

10. UUCP was used to establish European UNIX Network (EUNET) and Japan UNIX Network (JUNET) in 1981 and 1982, respectively. Network services included email and Usenet (Zakon, n.d.).

11. To prevent interruptions, Internet standards require that the nameservers be redundant (see Mockapetris, 1987, pp. 17-18).

12. The Federal Networking Council included representatives from NSF, (D)ARPA, the Department of Energy, the Department of Education, the Environmental Protection Agency, NASA, NSA, USAID, and other agencies. See http://www.fnc.gov /FNC_org_chart.html.

13. Quoted in Hardy (1993): "The 'breaking of the backbone cabal.' " Hardy added that because "there is no 'official' written history, most of what is known about the past is in the minds and postings of these 'old ones.' " To this day, some Usenet servers still refuse to carry certain "alt" newsgroups.

14. For December 1993, a Lexis-Nexis UNIVerse search uncovered 133 stories in major periodicals that referred to cyberspace, the Internet, Mosaic, or the WWW.

15. Statistics on Web and Internet usage are notoriously unreliable (NUA Internet Surveys). Figures reported in the text are based on Reid (1997, pp. xxii-xxiv, 16-17, 38) and on Gray (n.d.).

16. In December 1995, Microsoft, chagrined by Netscape's spectacular growth, felt pressure from investors to greatly expand its presence on the Net. It quickly bulked up Internet Explorer, allowed users to download it freely, and soon began to integrate the browser with Windows 95, a process that led Netscape and eventually the U.S. government to accuse the company of acting illegally in restraint of trade. In fall 1998, as the antitrust case came to trial, America Online purchased Netscape.

17. ISOC's orientation suggests an unabashed emphasis on commercial markets:

> The success of many organizations depends on Internet related decisions being made every day by policy makers, standards organizations, and legislators around the world. Those decisions have a direct impact on how well organizations can plan for the future, serve their customers, and compete in the digital age. See http://www.isoc.org.

18. See also http://www.w3.org.

19. http://www.internic.net/; http://www.netsol.com; http://scout.cs.wisc.edu/scout/indextxt.ht ml; http://www.fnc.gov; http://www.fnc.gov/CCIRN_charter.html. Critics like Robert McChesney

(1997) argue that privatization of the Internet backbone, which originally was developed by investing taxpayers' dollars, is hardly more than another example of corporate welfare.

20. http://www.internet2.edu/index.html. As of January 1998, regular university members must commit to developing I2 applications and local aggregation points known as "GigaPoPs (Points of Presence that can send and receive gigabits of information per second)" that provide broadband connectivity. Dues are $25,000 annually, plus an estimated $500,000 commitment per campus for research, development, and deployment of I2 hardware and software. Corporate partners pay $10,000 in dues annually and are expected to contribute $1 million or more in goods and services over the expected (but not officially specified) 5-year "life of the Internet2 project." Corporate sponsors pay $10,000 annually, plus contribute $100,000 in goods and services over the lifetime of the project. Corporate members and nonprofit affiliates pay $10,000 in annual dues. Douglas E. Van Houweling, former Vice Provost for Academic Outreach and Information Technology at the University of Michigan, is UCAID's President and CEO. The Board of Trustees is composed of officers of member universities. For further details, see http://www.internet2.edu/html/membership_faq.html#1 and http://www.internet2.edu/html/who_is_ucaid.html.

21. The maintenance of common communication standards is a major developmental concern regarding new I2 applications. The big concern in this matter, however, is likely to center on the big money associated with business-to-business transactions via CMC, not educational research, not retail sales, and certainly not participatory politics.

22. For links to additional sources on Internet surveys, see http://www.gvu.gatech.edu/user_surveys/others/.

23. No claim is made that the data are truly representative of the user population. On the difficulties of obtaining reliable samples for survey research in cyberspace, see Fisher, Margolis, Resnick, and Bishop (1995), Fisher et al. (1996a), and Georgia Tech (GVU) (1999).

24. The corporate interest is evident:

> To increase the value of the GVU WWW Survey, we have decided to expand our focus on commercial uses of the Web. Web advertising, electronic commerce, intra-Net Web usage, and business-to-business transactions are important application areas, in that they provide the motivation for financing Web technology development.

See http://www.gvu.gatech.edu/user_surveys/council_members.html.

3

Parties and Interest Groups

Organizing, Lobbying, and Electioneering in Cyberspace

The Internet provides a new medium for political interactions. As discussed in Chapter 1, optimists have hoped that communication via the Net will create a demand for more choices in politics. After all, computer-mediated communication (CMC) greatly reduces the organizational costs of building coalitions. The politically engaged can use email, bulletin boards, Usenet groups, listserv mailing lists, gopher sites, and the WWW to form new political groups. Democratic participation in politics, whether an adversarial contest among competing interests, a unitary process for building consensus, or some combination of the two, could spread from cyberspace to the real world. The United States could see a flowering of new parties and interest groups that could break the dominance of the major parties and established interests (Bonchek, 1995; Hauben & Hauben, 1997; Mann, 1995; McGookin, 1995; Phillips, 1995; Rheingold, 1993; Schwartz, 1996).

This chapter suggests that the flowers are not blossoming in the way the optimists expected, at least in ordinary American electoral and interest group politics. The Republican and Democratic parties at all levels—county, state, and federal—and many of their candidates and officeholders now have a large, growing, and increasingly dominant presence on the Internet. Moreover, familiar commercial and political interests are establishing prominent Web sites that mirror the metrotowns of the "real" America. The sprawl of these new "cybertowns" threatens to pave over the delicate growths that have sprung up along the information superhighway. Far from remaking American politics, the development of cyberspace, and particularly of the WWW, seems more likely to reinforce the status quo.

As late as 1994, the preponderant number of American political party Web sites belonged to minor parties (Mann, 1995, part I). By midsummer 1996, however, as the Republican Party gathered for its national convention, major party Web sites formed 59.2% of 477 direct links to the party home pages listed on Yahoo. Even when the number of links to party sites had grown to more than 600 in July 1998, the Democratic and Republican sites still comprised just less than 60%.[1] When Yahoo purged its first-level U.S. party listing down to 525 in September 1998, this proportion jumped to 70%, where it remained nearly constant (377 of 548) through 1999, as shown in Figure 3.1.[2]

The banner at the top of Figure 3.1 displays a hotlink to Find law (http://findlaw.com) a popular legal research and service site, which claims to be "the leading Web portal focused on law and government." Other banners have included LinkExchange (http://www.linkexchange.com), a commercial Web site developer that offers members free reciprocal exchanges of advertising. Claiming more than 1 million members, LinkExchange describes itself as the Web's largest advertising network. Members must agree to accept full unmodified HTML code for banner ads and to place these ads on at least one of their Web pages. Although sponsors pay for widespread distribution of their advertisements among members' sites, all members are entitled to have their Web sites registered with major search engines and to have their banner ads distributed to a modest number of relevant sites for free. This free service can be useful to minor parties. We discovered that the Web sites of several Libertarian state party organizations belonged to LinkExchange or one of its rival companies. The general aim is to match the relevance of the advertisement to the interest of the user.

The figure also illustrates a more general trend discussed in Chapter 2: the commercialization and combination of popular sites on the Web. When we visited Yahoo's home page in January 1996, it contained no advertisements. Three years later, it offered not just advertisements but hotlinks for a whole list of "in-house" or partnered goods and services. These included Today's News (Reuters), *Yahoo! Internet Life Magazine* (Ziff-Davis), Visa (Yahoo's own card), travel, yellow and white pages, classified ads, email accounts,

YAHOO! Personalize   Help - Check Email

Home > Government > U.S. Government > Politics >
Parties

Search [FindLaw Legal Guide   ◆]   FindLaw **CLICK HERE!**
       [Miranda   ] [Search]   LawCrawler

[   ] [Search] [all of Yahoo! ◆]

- America's Party - a new party for Americans wanting responsive government.
- **American Conservative Party** (2)
- American Reform Party - free-standing, national group that in 1997 formally split from Ross Perot and his Dallas-based Reform Party.
- **Communist Party U.S.A.** (5)
- **Constitution Party** (8)
- Constitutionalist Party - new political party dedicated to the advancement of human liberty and adherence to the U.S. Constitution.
- **Democratic Party** (164)
- **Green Party** (21)
- **Labor Party** (2)
- **Libertarian Party** (63)
- National Patriot Party - affiliates in 26 states, including several with ballot status. Its focus is on democratic political restructuring and fiscal reform.
- **Natural Law Party** (2)
- New Party
- New Union Party - socialist organization with theoretical foundations in the writings of Marx, Engels, and Daniel DeLeon.
- Pansexual Peace Party - Platform and propaganda of this radical grass-roots party.
- Puritan Party - aims to revive the nation as a theocracy.
- **Reform Party** (47) NEW!
- **Republican Party** (213)
- Socialist Labor Party of America
- **Socialist Party USA** (7)
- **Southern Party** (3)
- United States Independent American Party - united by a common Religious Right ideology.
- Workers Party USA
- Workers World Party - working-class party that fights against capitalism.
- Web Directory: The Political Lighthouse - comprehensive linked index to most of the major political parties in America today, complete with humorous commentary.

Inside Yahoo!

News: 2000 Presidential Race

News: Campaign Finance Reform

News: Democratic Party

News: Hillary Rodham Clinton

News: Reform Party

News: Republican Party

Get a **FREE CD-ROM** from **Yahoo! Internet Life**. Click Here.

Figure 3.1. Yahoo List of Political Parties, October 1999

stock quotations, chat rooms, personal and classified advertising, senior adult and children's Yahoos, the company's own regional and international sites, and even its own accessories and wearing apparel. These services had become so popular that two out of three visitors actually used them as end points as opposed to conducting a Yahoo search for external Web pages (Flynn, 1998).[3]

Banners change rapidly, in some cases each time a user accesses the page. In March 1998, the lead banner of Yahoo's "Government: Politics" page advertised *The Hill*, a nonpartisan political newsweekly with a circulation of 22,000 that focuses on Congress. *The Hill*'s target population included the 535 voting members of Congress, 40,000 congressional aides and staff, cabinet members, top-level appointees and civil servants, the news media, trade associations, public interest groups, and lobbyists (http://www.casey.com/index.html). At the same time, Yahoo users who chose "literature" under "Arts and Humanities" instead of "Politics" under "Government," were greeted with a banner and a hot button for Amazon.com, the Web's largest online bookseller at that time. Appropriate to the season, the banner touted books on gardening.

Although the connections made between the users' interests and the advertisers' aims are by no means perfect, the Web provides the potential to deliver well-targeted messages to potential customers. When the Electronic Privacy Information Center (EPIC) surveyed 100 of the most popular Web sites in December 1997, it found that 55 used online registration to collect personal information, often at the user's option. In addition, 30 passed persistent cookies to their users, usually without notification (Helling, 1998). The upshot is that Web sites not only can display relevant advertisements or recommended links to categories of users, but also can tailor their displays to the specific user or at least the Internet protocol address of the user's computer.[4]

Ninety-two of the sites that EPIC surveyed were in the "com" domain. None was "gov," and none was an overtly political organization. This pattern of commercial dominance, however, is not surprising. We have seen that in cyberspace, as in the real world, most people's interest in government and politics pales in comparison to their interest in business, commerce, sports, entertainment, and matters of family or personal concern.[5] Notwithstanding the acclaimed importance of public policy decisions, communication about government and politics comprises only a small proportion of the traffic on the Internet. By and large, the business of the Internet, and especially of the WWW, is business.[6] With advertising revenue on the Web projected to be as high as $5 billion by the year 2000, this is serious business, far more important to most people than the political activities of parties, candidates, or interest groups in cyberspace. This is a perspective to keep in mind during the discussion of political activities on the Internet in the next three sections of this chapter.

Will the Internet provide the means for electoral politics to assume a more democratic character as CMC reduces the organizational costs of political participation? The evidence suggests that the nature and popularity of the Web are more likely to foster an electoral politics that replicates the real world, albeit in a slick electronic form. Notwithstanding the novelty and explosive growth of electioneering in cyberspace, the Internet in general, and the WWW in particular, it seems more likely to reinforce the existing structure of American politics than to change it (Birdsall et al., 1996; Fisher et al., 1996b; Graber, 1996; Hiskes, 1996; Margolis et al., 1997; Raney, 1999).

In support of this thesis, the next three sections describe and characterize the electoral activities of selected parties, candidates, and interest groups as they appeared on the WWW primarily from January 1996 through spring 1998.[7] The final section summarizes these observations, presents conclusions, and speculates about the likely effects that political uses of the Net will have on electoral outcomes.

Political Parties on the Internet

Figure 3.1 suggests that sources of information about politics available to citizens of cyberspace tend to replicate those familiar to denizens of the real world. Electronic affiliates of mainstream media, whose sites are supported in part by corporate advertising, have become commonplace. Users do not have to go to a publication as specialized as *The Hill*. They can find Web sites for nearly every familiar mainstream newspaper or periodical, from *The New York Times* to *Time* magazine. These professionally designed sites aim to inform, amaze, and entertain their visitors. Updated regularly, they want visitors habitually to return.

As if to embody this trend, the Republican National Committee's (RNC) home page (http://www.rnc.org/) used "Main Street" as its principal metaphor from the primary season of 1996 through summer 1998. From January through June 1996, visitors encountered a stylized image of the Main Street of some hometown USA (no tall buildings, shopping malls, or slums), complete with representations that included a cafe, gift shop, post office, travel agency, newsstand, school, party headquarters, and a satellite TV receiver, all of which formed hypertext links to other Republican sites. The obvious purpose of these links was to lead the visitor further into Republican territory: Republican candidate pages, issue positions, state and local party organizations, affiliates, conservative ideological groups, and the like. However, the party also provided a link to the Democratic National Committee's (DNC) home page ("Find out what our competitors are saying about us") and to numerous nonpartisan information sites.

The flexibility of Web pages permits rapid change of organizational or personal images, an attractive feature for parties and candidates during a campaign. The primary electorate "tends to have more dyed-in-the-wool party supporters than would be true in a general election" (Polsby & Wildavsky, 1996, p. 139). Whereas the image of small-town America invoked old-fashioned family values that appealed to Republican primary voters and convention delegates, it did not reflect where most registered voters live or work. To win the presidency and Congress, the party needed to broaden its appeal. Once Bob Dole had clinched the nomination, the Republicans transformed the image of Main Street from a small town of the heartland to the more inclusive metropolitan environment. By October 1999 the RNC home page had evolved through several forms and emerged as the active news site shown in Figure 3.2.[8]

Established in October 1995, the RNC Web site is updated almost daily. Since 1996, it has been professionally maintained. By spring 1998, the Republicans had made available "I-chat," "QuickTime," "Adobe Acrobat," "RealAudio," and "RealVideo" technology, together with improved links to state party organizations. The content of the updates tends to follow the news in the mass media. When politics dominates the front pages and television newscasts, use increases from the usual daily average of 3,000 hits. Webmaster Jon Knisley claimed that on election day of November 1996, the site received more than 3.5 million hits.[9] Visitors can sign up to join Republican groups, to receive Republican publications and email, and to participate in various party activities. In March 1999, the party began sending visitors persistent cookies.

As indicated previously, Democratic and Republican party sites have outnumbered all other American political party Web sites since 1996. The numbers, however, tell only part of the story. The minor parties once had the jump on major parties in using the Internet, particularly through Usenet

Figure 3.2. Republican National Committee Web Site, October 1999

newsgroups and listserv mailing lists that could attract the politically attentive and maintain the interest of their own supporters. The advent of the
WWW, however, brought millions of new and unsophisticated Net users and
put a greater premium on easy-to-use sites that contain multimedia and interactive components as well as attractive graphics. Developing and then maintaining and updating such Web sites requires a greater investment of time and
money than does running a newsgroup or mailing list (Miley, 1996; Ubois,
1996). Although newsgroups and mailing lists can rely on active subscribers
to post items of interest, for Web sites, "the real work is in creating a place
[unsophisticated] users will want to visit over and over" (Ubois, 1996, p. 28).

State-of-the-art Web sites attempt to grab users' attention with everything
from dynamic graphics, sound, and music to graffiti walls, questionnaires,
quizzes, and even conferences (Miley, 1996). The variety, quality, and ease of
use of the better Web sites overshadow much of what commercial online services like America Online and CompuServe had offered in-house. The attrac-
tion of such Web sites forced these services to transform themselves from essentially in-house providers to ISPs with full access to the Internet (Ziegler,
1996).

If new users are likely to focus on attractive Web sites, which political parties, candidates, and interests are in the best position to provide them? The
question is rhetorical. The short answer is those with sufficient resources to
hire the talent to produce the pages: mostly the Republicans and the Democrats. Moreover, as state laws mandate that the major parties have their organizational representatives in every county down to nearly every voting precinct, the Democrats and the Republicans have ready-made organizations to
develop local sites linked to their national sites. Superior resources and organization already on the ground have helped the major parties achieve rapid
growth in the number and quality of their Web sites.

As examples, consider Figures 3.3, 3.4, and 3.5, the DNC, Libertarian, and
Communist party home pages.[10] Compared to the Libertarian and the Communist home pages, the DNC home page, professionally developed by Trav-
ellers Crossroad, a full-service Internet marketer, is arguably the most
user-friendly and dynamic. There are daily press notices, and the "Progress
vs. Partisanship" feature is updated daily. The site has its own search capabilities driven by "Excite!" Like the RNC, the DNC altered its home page
shortly after the 1996 primary season. It changed from an impersonal patriotic design that suggested the American flag to formats that featured the increasingly popular Bill Clinton. As the Lewinsky scandal mounted, however,

the party changed to a design in which Clinton's visage alternated with those of other past and present party luminaries. In fall 1999 the design changed to the one in Figure 3.3, which placed heavier emphasis on campaign 2000.

In comparison, the Libertarians present a sophisticated home page but one that is devoid of party personalities. Various party links repeat the thematic image of Miss Liberty, but the party relies on statements of principle more than on prominent party leaders or candidates to attract supporters. As you follow the links, it becomes clear that, notwithstanding the Libertarian Party's status as "the third largest political party in the United States" and having "the first WWW site established by any political party" (http://www.lp.org/lp-site.html), many of the links are maintained by volunteers. Nevertheless, the Libertarians' organization on the Net improved considerably between 1996 and 1998. By spring 1998, nearly all the state affiliates had Web sites of their own, and the College Libertarians of the University of Illinois at Urbana-Champaign no longer turned up as one of the party's most elaborate sites. Despite its prowess in Web site construction, however, the party lacks the funds to have its sites advertised as broadly or placed as prominently at the top of the parties' lists of search engines or general "nonpartisan" political sources.[11] Nor do its candidates or leaders have the personal notoriety or celebrity to match that of their Democratic and Republican counterparts.

The contrasts between the two major parties and the Libertarians with other minor parties are somewhat starker. Many of the minor party sites are maintained by volunteers who tend to be slow to update their pages. The Communist Party USA (see Figure 3.5), which redesigned its site in fall 1998, still typifies the unremarkable graphics, interactive features, and paucity of substantial numbers of links to party branches or to candidates below the national level.[12] Minor party sites are also less noticed on the Net: They typically have many fewer "backpointers," that is, hotlinks from other sites that connect to their Web site (Margolis, Resnick, & Wolfe, 1999). Even minor parties that seek general support, such as the Greens, Socialists, Reform, or Natural Law, nonetheless describe themselves as outside the mainstream. The Web gives them more exposure relative to the Democrats and the Republicans than they receive in the mass media, but it certainly does not level the playing field. As in the real world, they remain—and sometimes even look like—marginal political operations.

The Democratic and Republican party sites do not display uniformly high quality. The number and quality of sites vary significantly among the states,

(Text continued on page 65)

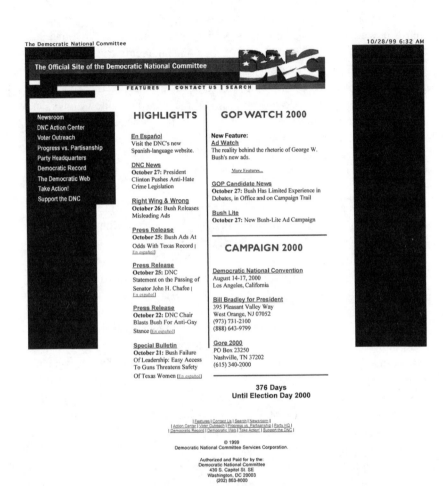

Figure 3.3. Democratic National Committee Web Site, October 1999

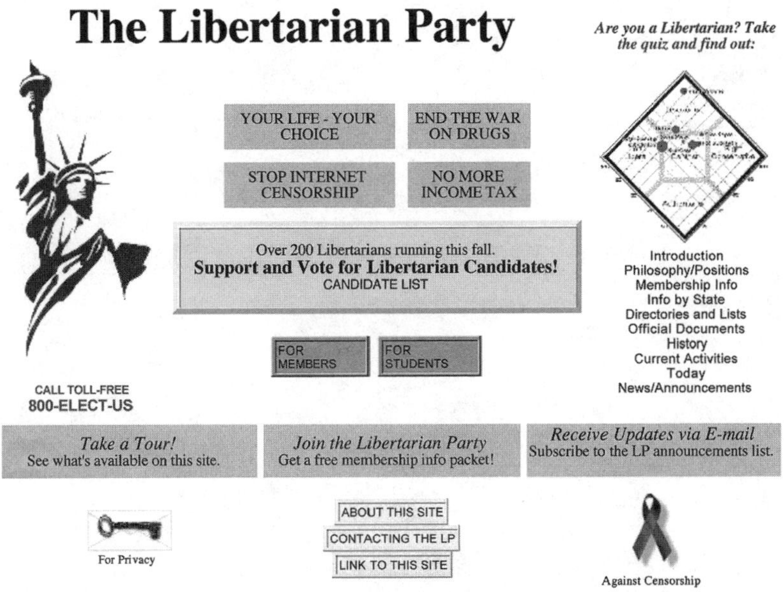

The Libertarian Party

Are you a Libertarian? Take the quiz and find out:

YOUR LIFE - YOUR CHOICE

END THE WAR ON DRUGS

STOP INTERNET CENSORSHIP

NO MORE INCOME TAX

Over 200 Libertarians running this fall.
Support and Vote for Libertarian Candidates!
CANDIDATE LIST

Introduction
Philosophy/Positions
Membership Info
Info by State
Directories and Lists
Official Documents
History
Current Activities
Today
News/Announcements

FOR MEMBERS

FOR STUDENTS

CALL TOLL-FREE
800-ELECT-US

Take a Tour!
See what's available on this site.

Join the Libertarian Party
Get a free membership info packet!

Receive Updates via E-mail
Subscribe to the LP announcements list.

For Privacy

ABOUT THIS SITE

CONTACTING THE LP

LINK TO THIS SITE

Against Censorship

Figure 3.4. Libertarian Party Web Site, October 1999

COMMUNIST PARTY

U.S.A.

Welcome to the Communist Party U.S.A.

We are a Marxist-Leninist working-class party that unites Black, Brown and white, men and women, youth and seniors.

We are a Party that speaks out from a working-class point of view on every vital issue. *The People's Weekly World* is our voice and the voice of labor, of all militant movements for social progress.

We are a party of unity in action. We are an integral part of every struggle and movement for change to eliminate poverty and joblessness, against racism and for full equality. We are participants, initiators and leaders of every movement to make life better now and much better in a socialist future.

* Communist Party Ideological Conference

* About the Communist Party U.S.A.

* The Party's regional offices and contacts.

* CP-USA press releases.

* The *People's Weekly World* - weekly newspaper of the CP-USA

* Young Communist League website.

* *Political Affairs* - Theoretical Journal of the CP-USA.

* Important documents and position papers of the CP-USA

* On-line resources in support of the struggle for social progress.

* Reference Center for Marxist Studies, Inc. A resource for students, scholars and activists.

* The *Communist Manifesto* is the first expression of the modern working-class outlook. Originally written in 1848, this is a hypertext version of the English edition of 1888 published by Karl Marx and Frederick Engels.

Read the Peoples Weekly World !

For subscription info, e-mail: pww@pww.org
        or write to: 235 W. 23rd St. NYC 10011
        or telephone: (212) 989-4994

http://www.hartford-hwp.com/cp-usa/   Page 1 of 2

Figure 3.5. Communist Party USA Web Site, October 1999

an indication that the Web reflects the federalist nature of American government and electoral politics. In Maryland, for instance, Democratic Party sites dominated from January 1996 through the time of the Republican National Convention. The only statewide presence of Republicans, who were faring poorly in the real world of Maryland politics, was the Web site of the minority GOP House Caucus. In contrast, the Republican Party dominated the major party Web sites in Ohio. It had an extensive home page that solicited memberships, offered publications, a calendar of events, and links to Republican elected officials. By August, the Republicans had added a video clip with a welcome message from Robert Bennett, state party chairman. The Democratic Party of Ohio had no official page: Its only statewide sites were for the Ohio chapter of the Democratic Leadership Council and the Ohio State University College Democrats. The situation in California was mixed: The Democratic State Party had an official Web site that was central. The direct link from the RNC, however, was not to the state party's home page but to the California Republican Assembly, an officially recognized "progressive" party faction, which has been active since the early 1930s.

By summer 1998, the state organizations of both major parties had increased the number and quality of their sites on the WWW. The Democratic Party of Ohio, for instance, was now online and linked to the DNC via a "clickable" map. The Maryland Republicans also had an official party Web site, and the California GOP not only linked to the RNC but also had a cookie ready to send to each new visitor.[13] The national and state parties also had improved their site designs to download Web pages faster than in 1996.

This is not to claim that the major parties' efforts on the Web have gained them greater benefits than have those of the minor parties. Regardless of party, none of the contact persons or Webmasters at the national, state, and local levels reached by email or telephone from April through June 1996 and from January through March 1998 suggested that their Web sites had had a substantial electoral impact. No one claimed that the information they disseminated through their sites had made any important impact on people's actions or attitudes about questions of public policy. Several contacts suggested that the Web sites or associated newsgroups and mailing lists served as excellent means for communicating with their members and mobilizing or channeling the energies of their supporters, but none indicated that the sites had helped to raise substantial sums of money or to recruit large numbers of activists.[14]

Jesse Ventura's successful campaign for governor of Minnesota in fall 1998 may be the exception that proves the rule. Besides serving as a tool for organizing and communicating among his original supporters, Ventura did raise nearly a third of his campaign funds over the Net, and his Web site was critical for recruiting and mobilizing new supporters. In his Webmaster's estimate, the Internet was necessary though not sufficient for victory (Kamark, 1999). When minor party candidates who are neither celebrities like Ventura nor multimillionaires like Ross Perot begin to replicate Ventura's success, the Internet will have leveled the playing field.

Even though the minor party sites have the potential to draw more attention than their parties normally receive from the mass media, virtual party headquarters are no substitute for money and organization on the ground. The Republican and the Democratic parties and their candidates and public officeholders have used their superior resources to emerge as the dominant electoral presence on the Web. It is difficult to demonstrate that this dominance has produced substantial gains, however, beyond those of facilitating communication among party branches and candidate organizations. Although some Webmasters and party leaders expect them to have more impact in the year 2000 and beyond, party Web sites today serve mostly as demonstrations of modernity. They show mastery of the communications technology that is supposed to preponderate in the early years of the twenty-first century.

Candidates on the World Wide Web

As the quality and distribution of party sites on the Web have come to reflect their counterparts in the real world, so too have the quality and distribution of candidates' Web sites. Republican and Democratic candidates' sites outnumber those of minor party candidates. They also tend to overshadow them in terms of visual appeal, use of interactive multimedia, and links to party organizations, informational sources, and related interest groups.

True, the Web's open access provides unusual opportunities for minor candidates to present their ideas to a mass audience. In January 1996, for instance, visitors could browse Web pages of Bruce Daniels and Lyndon LaRouche seeking the Democratic presidential nomination, of Charles Collins and Tom Shellenberg seeking the Republican nomination, and even of Irwin Shiff and Rick Tompkins, who were battling it out with Harry Browne for the Libertarians' nod. Moreover, in addition to the official White House site put up for President (not candidate) Clinton and official campaign sites for the major Republican candidates, enthusiastic supporters and critics had put up everything from unofficial Web sites of their favorites to parodies of their rivals. There were Web sites exhorting Colin Powell to run as well as sites to draft Rush Limbaugh and Ross Perot. Even after candidates ceased active campaigning or had withdrawn from the race, in most cases their sites remained.

President Clinton was not presented on the Web as an official candidate until July 10, 1996, when Vice President Al Gore launched the official Clinton/Gore '96 Web site at http://www.cg96.org/main/index.htm (a Web site that is no longer functional). Instead, Clinton appeared as a statesman above the fray. The White House home page just happened to contain handsome images of the President and the Vice President, together with information on "their accomplishments, their families and how to send them electronic mail" (http://www2.whitehouse.gov/WH/Welcome.html). Other features included links to a virtual library where visitors could "listen to speeches, and view photos" and to a "White House [service] for Kids: Helping young people become more active and informed." As in the real world, Bill Clinton could also rely on his supporters to have established an elaborate presence, a series of unofficial pages linked to Democratic Party sites and to various partisan and nonpartisan information services.[15]

Not to be outdone, Bob Dole's official home page (http://www.dole96.com/) invited visitors to a wonderfully interactive presidential campaign site throughout the primary season (http://www.dole96.com/dole96/main.html; neither Dole site is now functional). Besides standard activities, such as signing the guest book or signing up to join the campaign, and ordinary collections of fact sheets and press releases, visitors could access a library that included search capabilities, sound bites, and videos. They could click on an interactive map to find which prominent politicians from each state supported Senator Dole. And, just for fun, they could test their "knowledge of trivia about Senator Dole!" and "download exciting screen savers and desktop images!" The site, which introduced customization and high-fidelity "real audio" shortly before the national convention, boasted of the senator's "commitment to staying on top of the latest technology" and to having "the most user-friendly, interactive and interesting page of any presidential campaign on the Internet."[16] Like President Clinton's unofficial sites, the Dole site provided links to party organizations, leaders, and selected groups that supported Dole's bid for the presidency. Also like President Clinton's White House site, it was remarkably free of reference to overtly ideological issues, such as censorship of the Internet or support for the family values of the Christian Coalition. Visitors had to dig into the Dole library to discover even a hint of his positions on matters of controversy.[17]

When the Web sites of major party candidates like Clinton and Dole were compared with lesser-known and minor party candidates, the contrasts mirrored the differences we found between the Web sites of major and minor parties. The minor candidates' sites displayed some attractive features—through what other media could citizens easily obtain pictures and information about Harry Browne, Lyndon LaRouche, or Tom Shellenberg? But they generally failed to approach the interactive capacities or the multitudinous organizational links of Clinton or Dole. Browne's links to some Libertarian Party sites were among the last items encountered on his home page. The lack of local party organization among the minor parties also meant that the great majority of candidate sites found below the state level belonged to either Republicans or Democrats.

Well-funded major party candidates dominate poorly funded and minor party candidates with the breadth and capacities of their sites. However, it is difficult to demonstrate that this dominance has produced substantial electoral gains. Students from Margolis's political parties course reported that the most substantial claim made by candidates' Webmasters or other knowledgeable spokespersons whom they interviewed by telephone in spring 1996 was that Pat Buchanan's site had recruited more than 1,200 volunteers to the "Buchanan Brigade." Lamar Alexander's contact rationalized that Alexander's Web site served mostly to establish him as the candidate for the twenty-first century, the man who had shown what technology and private enterprise could do. He pointed out that as the first major candidate to establish his site on the Web, Alexander had set the trend. Alexander's site succeeded in communicating with supporters: He received as many email messages as letters delivered by the U.S. Postal Service. Solicitations from the site, however, failed to raise substantial campaign funds. Buchanan's Webmaster also admitted that raising funds was not "part of the Home Page experience."

A further indication of the relative lack of impact of the Web on electoral outcomes was the sparsity of candidate sites for the 1998 federal elections compared to those in spring 1996. Even though reports indicated that candidates were spending more money earlier than ever, the lion's share of expenditures, as usual, was for advertising on television (Mitchell, 1998). Of 13

Republican stalwarts whom *The New York Times* listed as "desperately seeking attention," only Newt Gingrich maintained an active campaign site, ostensibly for reelection to the House of Representatives. Potential presidential candidates, such as Lamar Alexander, Steve Forbes, Dan Quayle, and Pat Robertson, did not have official campaign sites. A Knoxville newspaper tracked Alexander; Robertson had spawned an Anti-Robertson/Anti-Christian Coalition site; and several Usenet groups were devoted, with varying degrees of sincerity, to Gingrich and Quayle. Governors like George Pataki and Pete Wilson had Web sites in their public capacities, but none as candidates for the presidency. On the Democratic side, the pattern generally repeated: There were Web sites for potential candidates in their capacities as public officials but not as candidates per se. We found several unofficial campaign sites for Vice President Gore—one even offered him some new jokes to tell on the hustings—but none for Minority Leader Richard Gephardt.

Although campaign Web sites have not significantly affected many electoral outcomes as yet, candidates for major offices seem obliged to produce exciting interactive sites that demonstrate their commitment to the latest technology.[18] Moreover, if the growth of Web users continues at present rates, there will be enough voters online for political uses of the Net to have an important impact on the American presidential campaign in the year 2000. We expect that this impact will be limited mostly to campaigns with large constituencies, such as those for senator, governor, or chief executive of major counties or cities. We doubt that many candidates with smaller constituencies will invest heavily in campaigning on the Net.

Political Interest Groups on the Web

If the effectiveness of campaigning by parties and candidates on the WWW is hard to demonstrate, evidence of the effectiveness of interest groups' use of the Web for political purposes is even more elusive. There are few agreed-upon systems of identifying and classifying political interest groups on the Web, and there has been little systematic study of political interest groups' use of CMC. Whereas Yahoo indexed more than 1,000 sites for parties (538), elections (443), and political opinion (333) directly under U.S. Government and Politics (http://www1.yahoo.com/Government/U_S_Government/Politics/) in March 1999, far fewer political organizations

(125) and interest groups (24) turned up.[19] In 1996, the Web sites we visited were used mostly to disseminate information about each particular group, its projects, and how the visitor could participate. We make no claim of statistical representativeness for the interest groups whose sites we chose to visit, but the types of information posted and the types of participation urged were generally familiar: Learn more about the group and its public policy concerns; contact representatives or relevant public officials; join an electoral campaign and vote; contribute to the cause. In short, interest groups appeared to employ CMC to encourage an increase in traditional forms of political participation, not to stimulate new ones.

In 1996, the Institute for Legislative Action (ILA) of the National Rifle Association (NRA), for example, boasted of "electing 82% of NRA-endorsed candidates to office" in 1994 (http://www.nra.org/grassroots/vote96/vote96.html; no longer functional), but this success appeared to stem from traditional grassroots activity. The ILA asked visitors to call a toll-free number "to find out what you can do to help elect pro-gun lawmakers, or to request special voter registration posters, display boards, or stickers!" The Web site, which had won awards from Lycos, Magellan, and others, listed hundreds of local events sponsored by friendly organizations, but not one of these listings contained a URL or email address.

By spring 1998, the NRA had begun to use the Internet more systematically, but mostly it still relied on communication by fax and telephone. The organization had negotiated with NETCOM a special rate for its members with Windows-based computers, and it had established three mailing lists: legislative alerts, press releases, or both. Nevertheless, in mid-April 1998, only one of three of the NRA's regional offices and 6 of 37 area representatives listed an email address. Only 5 of 50 state organizations and only 11 of 100 state officers listed either a URL or an email address.

On a broader scale, in spring 1996, the MIT political participation project's (http://www.ai.mit.edu/projects/ppp/home.html; no longer functional) nonpartisan *Directory of Grassroots Organizations* listed "hundreds of grassroots organizations, including their name, address, phone numbers, purpose and budget," but it contained not one URL. As it turned out, however, the project atrophied in 1997 after its director, Mark S. Bonchek, finished his doctoral dissertation and joined the private sector instead of academia. In spring 1998, all that remained were a farewell message and some links to Bonchek's thesis, one academic paper, and his email address and URL at his new employer.

Out of a systematic sample of 52 political issue Web sites drawn from the *Vote Smart Web Yellow Pages* (Project Vote Smart, 1997b) and visited in April 1998, there was only a handful of quirky, radical, or otherwise dissident groups. The overwhelming majority belonged to interest groups that could be fairly described as part of what protesters of the 1960s and 1970s called "the political establishment." To begin with, 24 of the 52 sites contained articles or reports from U.S. government sources, print or online journals, universities, research foundations, or institutes. These sources included the White House, the Department of State, Cornell, Georgia Tech and West Virginia universities, the Brookings and Heritage Foundations, and the magazines *Policy Review, Mother Jones,* and *Feed.* The 28 groups in the sample included Care, Oxfam, the American Medical Association, the NRA, Friends of the Earth, the Federation of American Scientists, the League of Women Voters, the Child Welfare League, the National Organization of Women, the League of United Latin American Citizens, the Family Research Council, and three commercial law firms. The handful of less familiar—and arguably dissident—groups included a public access television producer group (Paper Tiger TV); a gay, lesbian, bisexual, and transgender group for Catholics (Dignity USA); a victims' rights organization that advocates more capital punishment and more pictures and descriptions of offenders on the Web (Justice For All); and a women's rights fund (Global Fund for Women). The sample also included the National Organization for the Reform of Marijuana Laws, a long-established group that advocates legalizing marijuana, and Aegis, a ".com" group that maintains an HIV/AIDS information network. In short, the interest groups associated with political issues on the WWW looked a lot like the groups associated with those issues in the real world.

Whereas politics and the Internet as a topic received modest coverage in the popular media, it received hardly any in scholarly books and journals of political science or public opinion prior to 1997.[20] What appeared usually emphasized the theoretical possibilities to increase citizen participation and achieve democratic reform but offered little about the impact of the use of the Net for political purposes by parties, candidates, or interest groups. Where thorough case studies have been carried out, the impact of political uses of the Net, even on matters concerning politics that affects the Net, has been mixed. Laura Gurak (1997) showed that mobilization against the proposed release of Lotus Marketplace, directed at a private company, was successful in having the product canceled. Mobilization against the U.S. government's proposed adoption of the clipper chip, however, was notably unsuccessful. Others have pointed out that although numerous groups staged an impressive protest following the passage of the Communications Decency Act, they were notably unsuccessful in stopping the bill's passage in the first place. Moreover, it was traditional civil liberties organizations, such as the American Civil Liberties Union, that sued to overturn the Act's most objectionable provisions (Sidlow & Henson, 1998).

As was discussed in Chapter 2, the systematic survey work that has been done indicates that those who use the Net for political purposes tend to be drawn from the same high-status demographic categories as those who show higher levels of traditional forms of participation (Fisher et al., 1996a; Georgia Tech, 1999, GVU Surveys). This work, coupled with the prominence of established parties and interest groups on the Web, suggests that the prime beneficiaries of CMC's increased informational efficiencies and reduced organizational costs most likely will be those parties, candidates, and interests that are already politically active and influential.

The Future of Political Web Sites

Notwithstanding the paucity of evidence regarding their impact on elections or public policy, party, candidate, and interest group Web sites will continue to grow in number and sophistication. They or their equivalents will play important roles in politics on whatever forms the Internet cum-Information Highway cum-World Wide Web eventually takes. It seems doubtful, however, that their impact will be to democratize or otherwise bring about fundamental change in American politics.

With regard to politics on the WWW, we must remember first of all that unless extraordinary events like wars or economic depressions impinge on their daily lives, most people do not actively participate in politics, and most neither know nor care very much about it. Even as the Internet lowers the information costs of learning about parties, candidates, and issues in a campaign, we cannot expect people to overcome their habitual indifference unless parties, candidates, or interests motivate them to follow electoral politics more closely and to care more about it. The same goes for encouraging citizens to engage regularly in the formation of public policy between elections. Democrats and Republicans have superior resources and ready-made organizations in nearly every voting precinct. They have an advantaged position from which to develop and link their organizational and candidate Web sites.

They are unlikely to advocate rules that limit their own expansion on the Web or that encourage or subsidize third parties or independent candidates to develop competitive Web sites in the name of democratization (Frendreis, 1994; Lowi, 1994).

Secondly, as discussed previously, the Internet is rapidly becoming a commercial medium. Concerns about democratic politics play only a small part in the hype about the Internet in the popular press. A Lexis-Nexis UNIVerse search of articles in major newspapers from May 1994 through April 1998 averaged more than 1,000 articles per month that mentioned "Internet" or "World Wide Web" or "Information Superhighway" (or "Highway"). But only 398 of these—fewer than 1%—also contained words with the roots "politic" or "democra" within 100 words of the aforementioned terms. In the tradition of American capitalism, the Information Highway is increasingly here to advertise and to sell products and services, not to improve the democratic quality of American politics and civic life (Caruso, 1996).

Political scientists have noted the difficulty of mobilizing ordinary citizens to realign the balance between the two major parties, let alone to challenge their electoral domination, especially when the social and political environment remains relatively stable (Conway, 1991, chap. 4). From 1995 through 1999, the economy flourished and crime rates declined. The public has accepted as politics as usual new Republican majorities in both houses of Congress, the "Contract With America," the momentous Monica Lewinsky scandal, and the subsequent impeachment and trial of President Clinton. The Web has arrived on the scene when divided government and sensational investigations have become routine (Ginsberg & Shefter, 1999). If we were living in more critical times, the Web's political features might attract and inspire a greater number of creative and talented citizens who currently do not participate in politics. In these times, however, it seems more likely that the established political patterns of the real world will predominate in cyberspace.

Creating sophisticated multimedia Web sites is expensive. In the future, flat text, simple scanned pictures, and graphics will have to compete with pages of true multimedia: moving graphics, three-dimensional renderings, videos, voice, music, interactive texts, and so forth. As we move from hypertext to multimedia, a move roughly comparable to the move from newspapers and magazines to television, the metaphor of Web "pages" will become less apt. Instead of screens dominated by print and static graphics, Web pages will resemble short television clips. As production values increase, so will the cost of production itself. Furthermore, even though professional training in the use of multimedia will become more common, expertise in this area will not come cheaply. In short, the price of cutting-edge Web pages will increase, and so will the cost of campaigns for candidates and for political issues on the Net.[21]

The Internet does have the potential to change the nature of American and even world politics, but the evidence does not indicate that it will. Instead, commercial interests and mainstream politics are likely to dominate the WWW or its successor in the way they presently exert dominance in other mass media.[22] Citizens who can afford it will have better access to information about products and services and about a multitude of subjects, including politics, and most people will act as high-tech consumers rather than as political activists.

Nevertheless, the Internet does promise to grow as a source of political information and a means of communication among individual citizens, interest groups, elected officials, and public and private bureaucrats. In the next chapter, we explore how government officials have begun to use cyberspace as a medium to provide information about themselves and their public policy concerns and to communicate with their constituents and clientele.

Notes

1. The superiority of resources and technical expertise available to Democratic and Republican party organizations and candidates for developing Web sites suggests that the proportion of sites reflects the proportion of actual "hits" on the sites. However, we are unable to measure the number of hits directly or the average time spent or pages browsed by visitors who hit each particular site.

2. Minor parties tend to let their Web sites atrophy more frequently than do the major parties (Margolis, Resnick, & Wolfe, 1999).

3. The advertisements themselves generated $53.2 million for Yahoo in 1997, a threefold increase from 1996. Similar advertising appears in Lycos, Infoseek, and Excite, the three most popular search engines after Yahoo. In summer 1996, Open Text, then a search engine, introduced a "preferred listing" procedure that allowed advertisers to pay for having their advertisement—labeled as such—appear among the first 10 results of a relevant search (http://chronicle.com; McMurray, 1996). Goto.com, a spinoff of Idealab of Los Angeles, will advance this concept one step further: It will sell prominent listings to the highest bidders. As long as a site meets general criteria of relevance, it will be listed near the top, regardless of its centrality to the client's inquiry (Flynn, 1998).

4. Early in 1999, Intel brought out the Pentium III chip, capable of transmitting a unique serial number to Web sites that request it to help verify a user's identity ("Intel Unveils Controversial Chip," 1999).

5. See section in Chapter 2 titled "Political Consequences of Popularization."

6. Indeed, companies like I/Pro market software and services that monitor exposure and click-through rates and will even analyze demographic data collected about users. Ultimately, these companies aim to establish themselves as the Web's equivalent of A. C. Nielsen for television or Arbitron for radio. Recognizing the potential of the Web, Nielsen has invested in I/Pro. I/Pro is also partnered with DoubleClick, a media placement company that specializes in advertising on the Internet (see Reid, 1997, pp. 221, 227-232).

7. Selections were made on the basis of browsing using standard Internet search engines, supplemented by the observations and WWW listings provided by students in Margolis's undergraduate class on political parties during winter quarter 1996 and by the authors and a research assistant in winter and spring quarters of 1998. No claim is made that the data represent an unbiased sample of the electoral activities of parties, candidates, or interest groups. On the difficulties of collecting such a sample, see Fisher et al. (1995) and Fisher et al. (1996a).

8. In March 1999, the RNC home page featured a montage of multiracial youth in wholesome recreational settings or using a desktop computer.

9. Telephone and email interviews with party Webmasters, summer 1998.

10. http://www.democrats.org, ttp://www.lp.org/, and http://www.hartford-hwp.com/cp-usa/.

11. Compare the prominence of Libertarian links, for instance, with those associated with the Democratic and Republican parties on sources like Agora (http://www.agora. stm.it/politic/home.htm) or Allpolitics (http://allpolitics.com/1998/index.html). We also note that Agora offers commercial services, such as Web site design and marketing, and Allpolitics is a partnership of *CNN* and *Time Magazine.*

12. The Communist Party site is maintained by Hartford Web Publishing, apparently at cost. "We create pro bono web pages that: promote social progress; serve the people of Hartford; support education; relate to historiography" (http://www.hartford-hwp.com/). See Margolis, Resnick, and Wolfe (1999) for statistical details on minor parties' presence on the Web.

13. Again, quality and linkage varied across states and parties. The New Mexico Democrats, for instance, still had no Web site. The RNC did not provide a clickable map that linked directly to information on state parties. Visitors had to employ the "search" facility to find the links. For a listing of party sites by state, see Project Vote Smart (1998).

14. Gibson and Ward (1998), Margolis, Resnick, and Wolfe (1999), and Roper (1998) showed similar findings for parties in the United Kingdom and New Zealand.

15. These included Clinton, Yes! (http://www.av.qnet.com/yes/) and Clinton/Gore '96 (http://www2.linknet.net/lsufan/politics; no longer functional).

16. There is a certain irony here. Dole the senator had no presence on the Internet, not even an email address (Casey, 1996, pp. 201-202).

17. For example, "As Commander-in-Chief, President Dole will reinstate the long-standing military policy regarding homosexuals in the military," that is, President Bob Dole would forbid homosexuals from serving in the armed forces, period. With similar circumlocution, Senator Dole promised to end governmental affirmative action programs for women and minorities and to limit citizens' rights of habeas corpus. More straightforwardly, he supported constitutional amendments "requiring a 60% majority in Congress to raise income tax rates, . . . [to allow] student-led voluntary school prayer . . . [and] to prohibit physical desecration of the flag. . . . The Dole Administration will actively support a constitutional amendment protecting the flag."

18. Politicians share a similar faith with business interests in the yet-to-be-demonstrated power of the Web to provide most online operations with substantial real-world benefits (Levin, 1995). Bonchek (1996) argued that ineffectiveness of campaigning on the Web may stem from candidates treating the WWW as a broadcast medium rather than using its potential as a many-to-many medium.

19. The ratios of the Yahoo listings have remained much the same since 1996. Search engines differ in the manner in which they classify interest groups. Lycos and Magellan, for example, present more high-level links to categories such as parties, elections, government agencies, politicians, or campaign '96 than to political interest groups, activism, or issues. Excite's initial level of politics and law is more balanced. It lists parties and groups under one category, although most "social and activist organizations" are then classified under "life and style" rather than "politics and law." Project Vote Smart (1997b) *Web Yellow Pages* list URLs for more than 1,300 political "issue" sites, but nearly half of these contain articles or reports issued by governmental authorities, universities, established journals, or research centers.

20. A word search of the "periodical abstracts" reveals no mention of the words "Interne*" and "Politi*" in articles appearing in the *American Political Science Review* (1988-June 1996), *American Journal of Political Science* (1989-May 1996), *Journal of Politics* (1988-May 1996), or *Public Opinion Quarterly* (1988-Spring 1996). Except for Computer-assisted Survey Methods (CSM), Finifter (1993), Miller and Shanks (1996), and Verba, Schlozman, and Brady (1995) contain no prominent mention (if any) of CMC. Articles like Klass and Cooley (1994) and Fisher et al. (1996a, 1996b) remained uncommon in social science journals.

21. Advertised prices on the WWW in 1996 indicated that developing a plain vanilla Web site—one page of text and one link to another site—could start as low as $100. To create a low-end scanned image, links to three sites, and one or two index entries costs about $250, at minimum. Multiple scanned images, multiple links, and multiple search engine entries bring the minimum cost closer to $1,000. Developers like Town Hall charged up to $25,000 for customized Web sites with multiple pages, dynamic graphics, audio files, guest books, email, tables, maps, statistics on access, and so forth. To these costs, add domain registration, monthly maintenance charges, customized forms, morphing, database design, data entry, data storage, special updates, and other services. Alternatively, consider the cost of buying your own host computer(s) and hiring or training your own Webmaster(s).

22. See Chapter 5, this volume. See also the special theme issue of *The Nation, 262*(22) (June 3, 1996; see particularly Miller, 1996; Miller & Biden, 1996; Schiffrin, 1996).

4

Elected Officials and Government Bureaucracy in Cyberspace

One of the authors had a part-time job during his junior year of high school looking up tax records for his uncle, a suburban real estate developer. He spent Saturday mornings in a dimly lit records room of the Cook County courthouse, where he sat at long tables with other researchers, poring over and copying information from the large public ledgers. (The room closed at noon on Saturdays and 4:45 p.m. on weekdays, too early to make a trip downtown worthwhile after school.) A few years later, as an Oberlin College student council representative, he put this experience to use to dig through similar books of the town's court records for citations issued to bicycle riders for license and traffic violations. (The records demonstrated that local police had cited college students at disproportionately high rates compared to those of high school students and other "townies.") By then, of course, he had learned to use public records like the *Statistical Abstract of the United States, Congressional Directory, Congressional Record, United States Government Organization Manual,* and various volumes of federal and state statutes, regulations, and court decisions that are found in the reference department of most research libraries.

Much of the information, though publicly available, was still difficult to obtain. Voter registration lists, official election results, lists of political party precinct leaders, rosters of candidates' committees, reports of campaign expenditures, and the like, not to mention information on licensure, public safety, and other routine activities, usually required a trip to the appropriate governmental office and payment for the costs of reproduction. In addition, consider the time and effort required to secure other materials, such as governmental forms for everything from applications for food stamps and unemployment compensation to reservations for picnic shelters, athletic fields, and parade routes. How much easier it would be if all those records and forms were freely available on the Internet!

Accessing Government Via the Internet

We argued in Chapter 3 that the burgeoning presence of parties, candidates, and interest groups on the Internet seems more likely to reinforce the status quo than to overturn the established order. Even so, easy access to governmental records and forms, combined with the ability to use the Internet to communicate with public officials over issues of personal and public concern, could increase citizens' interest and participation in the established processes of governance and politics.

In the subsequent sections, we examine the extent to which U.S. governmental agencies and elected officials have used cyberspace to provide citizens with information about matters of public concern. We also take note of references to this information available from other sources on the Internet. In addition, we consider the content of the information, how it is organized, and the ease of finding it. Finally, we speculate on the ramifications of moving governmental information onto the Internet and the implications for the development of public policy and the conduct of democratic politics. In keeping with our general model, we consider mainly politics that affects the Net and political uses of the Net. These considerations lead us to anticipate problems of regulation and privacy, which we take up in Chapters 6 and 7.

As we begin, however, let us keep in mind that the availability of information about government online does not mean that citizens will access it. Indeed, the more that the interests of Internet users resemble those of people in the real world, the more we should expect that they will use the Net to acquire information about topics other than governmental policies and political issues. We have seen that commercial sites outnumber and generally are more popular than governmental sites. Given citizens' ignorance or indifference regarding most questions of public policy, we expect that most governmental sites will focus on providing information and services rather than on soliciting input about policy. Providing information and services caters to citizens mostly as audiences or consumers. Soliciting input about policy, in contrast, encourages more active political participation.

The Executive on the Net

The growth of the mass media as primary sources of political information, particularly the emergence of radio and then television, generally has served to increase the power of the executive relative to that of the legislature. The executive is organized hierarchically, usually with a single person at the top. Even though they cannot always control what their subordinates say, chief executives in the United States—presidents, governors, county commissioners, mayors—normally can count on their principal officers to stick to their administration's agenda and to speak more or less compatibly, if not with one voice.

Legislatures and councils may have partisan or nonpartisan leaders, but they rarely present a united front. The legislative process is a complex, messy business, and power is often dispersed among various leaders. With summaries and "soundbites" as the common form for reporting political news on commercial radio and television, broadcast news directors ordinarily find it simpler and easier to cover American executives more thoroughly than American legislators. Chief executives, their staff, agency heads, and high-level bureaucrats are far more likely to offer coherent viewpoints than are legislators. Even newspapers tend to assign their political reporters to cover the executive more heavily than the legislature. This is a prudent business decision. Major American newspapers and magazines get most of their income from advertising, and advertising rates are based largely on readership. Most readers are interested neither in the complexities of legislation nor in the arcane process by which it is passed.

Executives and their spokespersons have become sophisticated in using the mass media to their advantage. By and large, the executive branch has more and better sources of information about public problems than have the legislative branch or the mass media. Chief executives and top-level bureaucrats supply exclusive information to friendly broadcasters and journalists. They initiate policy proposals and plans, and they call on their respective legislatures or councils to pass them. They draw public attention to their policy agenda by coordinating press releases and conferences, speeches, photo opportunities, and the like among executive officers and functionaries. Even when real-world events intrude on their best-laid plans, executives normally are better positioned than their legislative counterparts to produce a unified response (Diamond & Silverman, 1995; Kernell, 1997).

By the same token, the bureaucracies of private corporations have more and better sources of information concerning their commercial and political interests than do individual citizens, their representatives, their governments, or the media. These private bureaucracies provide government and the media with much of the information that forms the basis for public policy regarding commerce and business.

Notwithstanding periodic assertions of legislative prerogatives, Americans have come to expect the executive rather than the legislature to take the lead on most issues of public concern. The executive has used its superior resources to fulfill these expectations. At the national and state levels and in most counties and municipalities, the executive drafts the budget, provides data to justify it, and proposes legislation to implement it. Even so, legislatures in the United States remain among the most powerful in the world, and American executives also must contend with an independent judiciary. It follows that the primacy of the executive over other branches of government in most other countries is greater still.

Because most theories of democratic governance postulate that citizens or their elected representatives ultimately should control government, these developments are worrisome. Some critics have argued that to realize democratic control, it is necessary to restore the balance among branches of government. Computer-mediated communication (CMC) via the Internet could be the vehicle for this. It can provide citizens and their representatives with access to the same documentary information as bureaucrats. It even can provide access to the documents upon which powerful interest groups—corporate bureaucracies in particular—base their claims on government (Barber, 1984; Davis, 1999; Margolis, 1979).[1] Is it realistic, however, to expect this to happen?

The short answer is "No."

Why not? Let us begin by considering nongovernmental bureaucracies. On what basis would corporate entities, the largest private bureaucracies, allow citizens or their representatives direct access to their electronic files? Under American law, corporations are legal persons who enjoy essentially the same rights and obligations as do their fellow citizens. Personal privacy is among these rights, and this includes the right to proprietary information. Government must demonstrate a lawful need to search and seize such information before it can force corporations to release it. How many years, for instance, did it take to require the tobacco corporations to release documents that described the effects that cigarettes had on their customers' health? That corporations hardly resemble ordinary people makes little difference. The principle of personal privacy applies to them, sometimes more strictly than it applies to individuals.

Information placed on commercial Web sites is proprietary. Users are granted access at the discretion of the providers, not as a matter of right. Politically sensitive information can be kept behind so-called firewalls, accessible only to users authorized by the providers' organization. The ostensive purposes of most Web sites are commercial, not political, and the primary interests of most Web users are business, commerce, sports, entertainment, education, family, or personal matters, not politics. Normally, the users' curiosity about, let alone their demand for, such politically sensitive information remains low. Indeed, the more common concern is not to facilitate access to such information but to protect it from the purview of citizens, their representatives, or their government (Dyson, 1997, 1998).[2]

When it comes to governmental Web sites, the executive generally has outshone other branches of government in much the same way that we found mainstream interest groups and political parties to outshine lesser interests and political parties. Although no single indicator is conclusive, several indicators corroborate this relative dominance. First of all, the federal executive maintains more numerous and more prominent sites than do the other branches. The *Vote Smart Web Yellow Pages* (1998), for instance, listed 171 executive sites but only 48 for the judiciary and 147 for Congress. Similarly, Yahoo listed 1,712 Web sites for the executive branch, in comparison to 239 for the federal judiciary and 789 for the Congress.[3] The pattern repeated at the state level. With few exceptions, the *Vote Smart Web Yellow Pages* listed more sites for the executive and legislative branches than for the judiciary, and more for the executive than for the legislative. At the state level, the Yahoo search hierarchy also lists more executive than legislative sites.

A second indicator is the relative sophistication of the Web site. The executive's Web sites are more likely to have higher-quality graphics, more attrac-

tive "hot buttons," and easier-to-use tables of contents and search paradigms than those found among the Web sites of the legislatures and the
courts. At the federal level, the cabinet departments, White House offices,
and myriad federal agencies accessible from the White House home page
(http://www.whitehouse.gov; see Figure 4.1) generally contain more advanced features, such as hot buttons that reveal a list of underlying links
(Agriculture), cookies to track users (Veterans Affairs), or animated graphics
or texts (Justice) than are found on congressional sites. Although use of the
Web grew under Newt Gingrich's leadership, Congress was notoriously
slow in moving into cyberspace (Casey, 1996). By fall 1998, however, the
Library of Congress ("Thomas," http://Thomas.loc.gov), the House
(http://www.house.gov/), and the Senate (http://www.Senate.gov/) had developed sophisticated sites like those of the White House and Cabinet (see
Figures 4.2, 4.3, and 4.4). Congressional committees also had Web sites and
email, but the pages below each chamber's home page often contained pon-
derous texts that failed to take good advantage of the Web's capacity to organize information hierarchically through hyperlinks.[4]

Although the Supreme Court has no official site, an extensive Web site
is maintained by Cornell University's Legal Information Institute
(http://supct.law.cornell.edu:8080/supct/; see Figure 4.5). Sites for circuit
courts of appeal are maintained regionally by law schools at Emory,
Georgetown, Pace, and Villanova universities and at the Universities of Texas
and Washington (Project Vote Smart, 1997b). These research sites are laden
with textual information that is useful for scholars, journalists, lawyers, and
citizens with an abiding interest in the law, but they are not designed for
casual visitors. Although we can expect them to improve their sites in the future, Congress and the judiciary do not as yet have Web sites that match the
executive's in attractiveness and user-friendliness, especially for visitors
who might discover them through passing interest or perhaps just by chance.

A third indicator is not merely numbers of sites but "Web presence." Web
presence or prominence of a Web site can be measured as a function of the
number of links from external sites to that site (Hill & Hughes, 1998, p. 143).[5]
It is one thing to have a Web site; it is another to have a Web site that users are
likely to visit. Once again, the general pattern is that the executive's Web
sites are more prominent than those of the legislature, especially at the state
and local levels. Although all the national executive and legislative Web sites
in Figures 4.2 through 4.5 are heavily trafficked, Alexa ranked the White

(text continued on page 88)

Figure 4.1. White House Web Site, October 1999

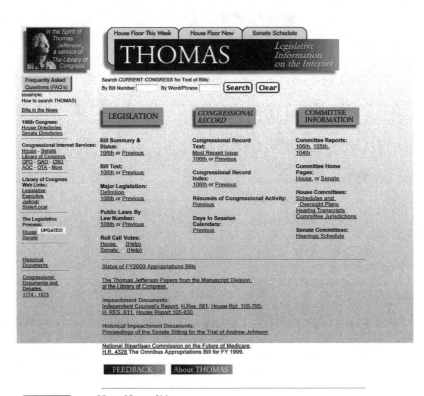

Figure 4.2. Thomas Legislative Information Web Site, October 1999

U.S. House of Representatives
106th Congress, 1st Session

House Operations

House Directory

Search House Sites

United States House of Representatives
Washington, D.C. 20515
(202) 224-3121

**House
Office
Web Sites**

Member Offices

Committee Offices

Leadership Offices

Other House Organizations,
Commissions, and Task Forces

Media Galleries

This Week on the House Floor
The schedule the House intends to consider this week.

Currently on the House Floor
Up-to-date events on the House floor as they happen.

Annual Congressional Schedule

The Legislative Process
Access to information about bills and resolutions being
considered in the Congress.

Roll Call Votes
As compiled through the electronic voting machine by the House Tally
Clerks under the direction of Jeff Trandahl, Clerk of the House.

House Committee Hearing Schedules and Oversight Plans
Each committee maintains its own schedule of hearings on the web. A
committee's oversight plan describes its agenda for the 106th Congress,
based on the jurisdiction of the committee. The public can attend any open
committee meeting listed, and some hearings are televised by C-SPAN.

THOMAS

In the spirit of THOMAS Jefferson, the Library of Congress provides you
with searchable information about the U.S. Congress and the legislative
process. Search bills, by topic , bill number, or title. Search through and
read the text of the Congressional Record for the 104th, 105th, and 106th
Congresses. Search and find committee reports by topic or committee
name.

Write Your Representative

Constituents may identify and/or contact their elected
Member to the U.S. House of Representatives.

United States Code

Free, public, full-text searchable and downloadable access to the U.S.
Federal statutes of a general and permanent nature, organized by subject.

**Educational
Links**

**Visiting
the Nation's
Capital**

**Government
Links**

Comments

To comment on how to improve this site, use this form or send e-mail to the Webmaster.

Privacy and Security Notice

Figure 4.3. U.S. House of Representatives Web Site, October 1999

Figure 4.4. U.S. Senate Web Site, October 1999

Supreme Court Collection

collection home   search   tell me more   lii home

contents & context

ways to access material

Decisions from 1990 to the present:

The Legal Information Institute offers Supreme Court opinions under the auspices of Project Hermes, the court's electronic-dissemination project. This archive contains nearly all opinions of the court issued since May of 1990. In addition, our collection of over 600 of the most important historical decisions of the Court is available on CD-ROM and (with reduced functionality) over the Net.

During our first four years of operation, the LII simply built finding aids -- such as tables of party names and searching tools -- which in turn pointed to the Hermes archive at Case Western Reserve University. In 1997, we acquired our own Hermes subscription and began streamed conversion of the decisions into HTML at the time of release. We have also converted the entire CWRU backlist to HTML.

As the foregoing implies, there are still some omissions and errata in this collection, and a high likelihood that in the process of conversion we've missed a few links here and there. If you run into a problem which is not mentioned in our list of errata and items under construction, do let us know.

At the start of the October 1997 term, the Court changed the file formats used in its Hermes distribution. Previously, opinions, syllabi, and order lists were distributed in WordPerfect 5.1 and flat ASCII formats. Current practice is to distribute the opinions in Adobe Acrobat (PDF) format and in a special, SGML-ish tagged ASCII format which is a hybrid of structural and presentational markup. The Court no longer distributes files in any word-processing format. In order to view the opinions in the proprietary Acrobat format, you will need to get Acrobat Reader software from Adobe.

Decisions before 1990:

The LII collection of historic decisions of the US Supreme Court contains over 600 of the court's most important decisions through the whole period of its existence. The decisions can be accessed by party name, by topic, and by opinion author. The full collection can be purchased on CD-ROM.

Other collections of decisions prior to 1990 are available on the Net sources, in a variety of formats. FedWorld provides pointers to various uses of the FLITE database, including one at Villanova; FLITE only covers the period from 1937 to 1975, but does so comprehensively. The Findlaw collection also reaching back to 1937 is comprehensive without the post-1975 gap. The USSC+ service from Infosynthesis provides full coverage from 1945 onward, and some 450 older cases dating back to 1793. Finally, the fee-based WestDoc service provides full coverage of all the court's decisions. There are other sources for the opinions; this is not a comprehensive list.

- Quick search:

  Go
- This month's decisions (Court is in recess until Oct. 1999)
- This month's order lists
- Looking ahead:
  - Court calendar
  - Oral argument schedule
  - Questions presented in cases to be heard
- Historic decisions
  - Online
  - Purchase CD
- For the 1998-99 term:
  - Highlights
  - Decisions arrayed by date
- Arrayed by topic:
  - Decisions from 1990-present
  - Historic decisions
- Arrayed by party name:
  - 1999 -- 1st. party, 2nd. party
  - 1998 -- 1st. party, 2nd. party
  - 1997 -- 1st. party, 2nd. party
  - 1996 -- 1st. party, 2nd. party
  - 1995 -- 1st. party, 2nd. party
  - 1994 -- 1st. party, 2nd. party
  - 1993 -- 1st. party, 2nd. party
  - 1992 -- 1st. party, 2nd. party
  - 1991 -- 1st. party, 2nd. party
  - 1990 -- 1st. party, 2nd. party
  - Historic decisions

Figure 4.5. U.S. Supreme Court Web Site, Cornell University, October 1999

House in the top 1,000 for numbers of "hits," but it ranked Thomas, the House, and the Senate in the top 10,000.[6]

As we hypothesized previously, we expected that service-oriented governmental Web sites would tend to have more traffic than would policy-oriented sites. Although we do not have the resources to examine every federal government site or even to compile a reliable sampling frame for those sites, the Web sites of the service-oriented departments and commissions that we have examined do show considerable traffic. For example, even though the Departments of Agriculture and Veterans Affairs, the National Science Foundation, and the Social Security Administration had fewer links than the houses of Congress, all of them nonetheless ranked in the top 10,000. In contrast, the Federal Election Commission, which contains slogs of data, did not even make the top 100,000. In general, the popular executive and legislative sites tend to be those that provide information about accessing governmental services or programs or those that provide forms or other means for accessing them, not those that provide information mostly on questions of public policy.[7] Even the home pages of the House and Senate Web sites follow this pattern: Service and information links are more prominently displayed than are links to policymaking.

The information-laden Web sites of the federal courts are used less frequently than those of the Executive and Congress. The Legal Information Institute at Cornell had 50,602 links and ranked in the top 5,000 for traffic, but the Web site for the Supreme Court had only 4,565 links pointing to it, and its traffic ranked in the top 50,000. The sites for the circuit courts of appeal were less popular. The Fifth and the Eighth Circuits, with Web sites at the University of Texas and Washington Law Schools, for instance, had only 1,895 and 996 links, respectively, and both ranked somewhere between the top 100,000 and the top million in visits. The Web sites of the Third and Ninth Circuits at Villanova University Law School had 11,230 links combined and ranked in the top 50,000. The Web sites of the Fourth, Sixth, Tenth, and Eleventh Circuits at Emory University Law School had 10,253 links combined and also ranked in the top 50,000 (see Project Vote Smart, 1997b, pp. 17-18, for URLs).

We found similar patterns but generally starker differences for Web presence of governors' and big city mayors' home pages in comparison to those of state legislatures and city councils. Almost invariably, the state's home page, prepared by a Webmaster who works under state administration, touts the governor and departments, agencies, and services that fall under the aegis of the executive. The legislature and judiciary receive short shrift, their relatively few first-level links mixed in with the myriad links to state services and agencies. New York's home page, which contained no direct links to the legislature or courts, (http://www.state.ny.us/; see Figure 4.6), provides one of the more elaborate examples of executive dominance. Although visitors could hardly ignore Governor Pataki's presence and the executive's departments, agencies, and services, they could easily overlook links to the legislature and judiciary, which were found on pages two levels down, under "government agencies." The measures of Web presence were consistent with this impression. The Executive's Web site had 3,787 links pointing to it and ranked in the top 50,000 for hits. The Web site of the New York State Assembly, despite the nice search capabilities in its Legislative Information System, had only 1,460 links and ranked only in the top 100,000.

Alabama's home page (http://www.state.al.us/; see Figure 4.7), redesigned under Governor Don Siegelman early in 1999, displayed a similar pattern. The state executive, with its own search capacity, had the most prominence. Links to the state's home page jumped to 1,677, up from 341 in the previous administration, and traffic remained in the top 50,000. Even though visitors could link directly to the legislature and courts, the sites are registered to the state executive's Information Services Division. The Alabama Legislative Information System provided information about state legislators and ways to contact them. It also added its first search capacity for pending bills in 1999. But it still had only 10 links and received only moderate (below top-100,000) traffic. Alalinc, a service provided by the Alabama Supreme Court and state law Library, was highly sophisticated, with excellent Boolean search capabilities, but it had only 167 links, and it also received only moderate traffic.

The City of Chicago serves as a third example (http://www.ci.chi.il.us/). Once again, visitors could hardly miss Mayor Daley's administration, but they had to dig under the City Clerk's Office to discover anything about the Chicago City Council (http://www.chicityclerk.com/citycouncil/ about.html; see Figure 4.8). The council was listed among "related agencies," and its Web site's only search capability was to find the name and address of each ward alderman. Legislation was listed under the home page of the Mayor's Office. The city's "Chicago Mosaic" home page had 2,804 external links and ranked in the top 10,000 in traffic. As was the case for the Alabama legislature, the city council's Web site was registered on the executive's server, so Alexa could provide no separate count of its links or its traffic.

(Text continued on page 93)

Figure 4.6. New York State Web Site, October 1999

Figure 4.7. State of Alabama Web Site, October 1999

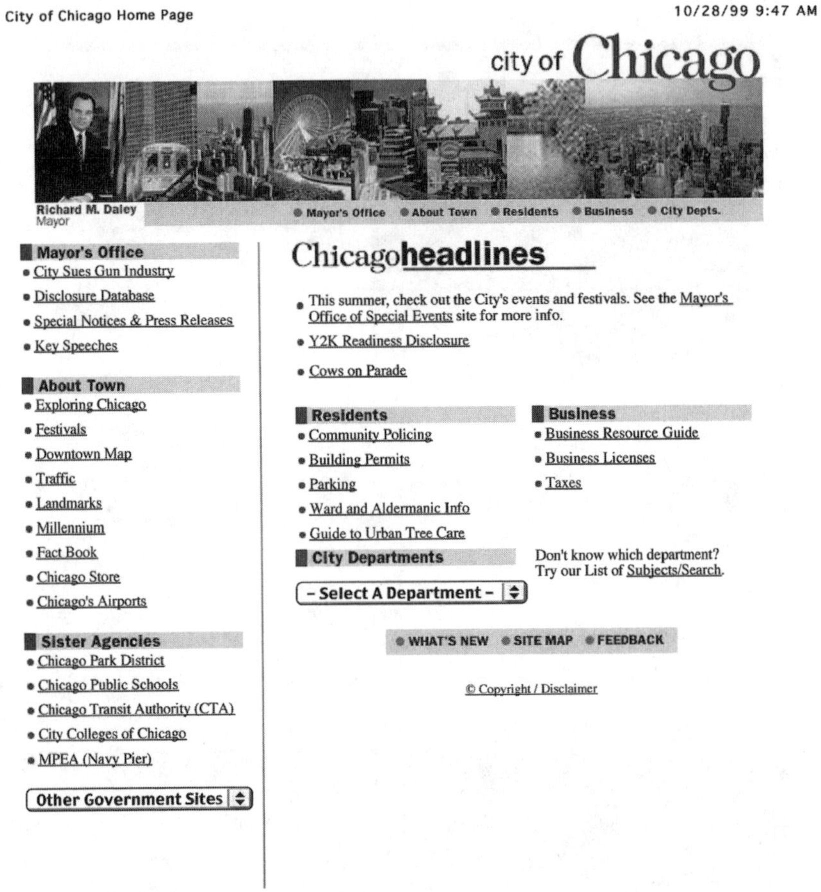

City of Chicago Home Page 10/28/99 9:47 AM

city of Chicago

Richard M. Daley
Mayor

Mayor's Office · About Town · Residents · Business · City Depts.

Mayor's Office
- City Sues Gun Industry
- Disclosure Database
- Special Notices & Press Releases
- Key Speeches

About Town
- Exploring Chicago
- Festivals
- Downtown Map
- Traffic
- Landmarks
- Millennium
- Fact Book
- Chicago Store
- Chicago's Airports

Sister Agencies
- Chicago Park District
- Chicago Public Schools
- Chicago Transit Authority (CTA)
- City Colleges of Chicago
- MPEA (Navy Pier)

Other Government Sites

Chicagoheadlines
- This summer, check out the City's events and festivals. See the Mayor's Office of Special Events site for more info.
- Y2K Readiness Disclosure
- Cows on Parade

Residents
- Community Policing
- Building Permits
- Parking
- Ward and Aldermanic Info
- Guide to Urban Tree Care

Business
- Business Resource Guide
- Business Licenses
- Taxes

City Departments

- Select A Department -

Don't know which department? Try our List of Subjects/Search.

WHAT'S NEW · SITE MAP · FEEDBACK

© Copyright / Disclaimer

Figure 4.8. City of Chicago Web Site, August 1999

None of this should be surprising. Just as the major parties generally have more resources than do the minor parties, the executive generally has greater budgetary and personnel resources than does the legislature or judiciary. And just as these superior resources tend to make major parties' Web sites graphics, tables of contents, search capabilities, and so forth better than those of minor parties, so they tend to make the executives' sites better than those of rival branches.

Finally, it should be noted that many of the prime listings of state and city home pages related to establishing businesses in the state or city, doing business with the government, or tourism. To reiterate the point: State and local governments in cyberspace—as in the real world—are highly interested in attracting and facilitating business (Lindblom, 1977; Wade, 1998). Using Web sites to encourage netizens to participate in formulating public policy is of secondary importance, at best. As can be seen in the next section, this is even the case for the Web sites of congressional committees.

Legislatures on the Net

Lawmakers have been slower than executives in getting up on the Net, especially below the federal level. Until Newt Gingrich became House Speaker, however, even the congressional leadership had not encouraged members to use the Web to facilitate communicating information to constituents or to provide a means for constituents to communicate with representatives and senators. As late as November 1994, Senator Edward Kennedy was the only member of Congress with a personal Web site. In November 1995, barely more than 100 representatives had developed anything beyond the generic home page that the House Information Resources (HIR) Office had provided them at the beginning of the year (Casey, 1996). Although nearly every senator listed an email address by November 1998, almost 20% of House members still did not. More significantly, 29 members did not even maintain their generic Web site.[8]

For what do members of Congress use their Web sites? They are largely used as extensions of their home offices. We drew systematic probability samples of 32 representatives and 20 senators in October 1998 and examined their use of the Web. Most Web sites emphasized constituent services and provided information about government programs, the realization of what Chris Casey (1996) characterized as "a 24-hour-a-day info booth and service center" (p. 85). Only one representative in our sample had no Web site. Although every Web site provided information on how to contact the representative or senator by telephone and by post, nearly one quarter of the representatives did not list an email address. Six linked to a "Write your Representative" page provided by the HIR that only permitted constituents (as determined by zip code + four) to email the representative. Replies from these pages and from those who write directly by email are normally sent by ordinary post using the congressional franking privilege. Three representatives employed new Constituent Communication Centers. These centers allow constituents to establish personal Web mailboxes so they can receive replies from their representative via email. Of the Senate sample, only Ben Nighthorse Campbell listed neither an email address nor any other electronic communication link on his home page. Four senators filtered their email through a Senate service similar to "Write your Representative" on the House side. The remaining 15 permitted immediate access via email.

Even though some Web sites were rich with information about the legislative interests and accomplishments of the senators and representatives, none of the sites sampled contained explicit requests for input from constituents about pending questions of public policy. Like ordinary congressional offices, they provided a means for constituents to access information about government services; to request help of their representatives for these services; and to learn how their representatives are working for them, their interests, and also for the public good. In short, they fulfilled the related purposes of providing services to constituents and producing the good will necessary to ensure their reelection.

That the individual Web sites emphasized distribution of information about matters of public policy rather than solicitation of citizen input should not surprise us. After all, in their quest for reelection, most senators and representatives spend more time dealing with how administration of current legislation affects individuals and groups in their states or districts than they do working on new legislation (Fenno, 1978; Mayhew, 1974). Most legislation is crafted in congressional committees, not in the members' offices. That the Web sites of standing committees of Congress also do little to solicit citizen input about pending legislation, however, suggests that the potential for the Internet to democratize the legislative process through increased participation by interested and informed citizens does not have a high priority. Committee Web sites we reviewed in fall 1998 resembled interactive press releases more than legislative forums open to citizens' input. Indeed, savvy committee chairs know that many reporters have begun to surf the Net as part of their daily routine. Placing information on their Web sites for reporters and other interested individuals to uncover actually gives committee chairs greater control of the flow of information than does holding a press conference or a public hearing (see Davis, 1999, especially chap. 5; also see Project Vote Smart, 1997a).

As previously noted, the Web sites of state legislatures and city councils we have visited generally have less sophisticated features than do those of the state or city executive. These sites, often administered by the executive, usually contain generic information about the legislative body and its members. Most have not as yet developed individual or committee Web sites that are comparable to those of Congress. As a majority of their constituents come to use the Internet, however, we expect that most legislative bodies and individual legislators will produce independent sites. Even though ordinary citizens have a greater chance statistically of playing a critical role in electing or otherwise influencing most legislators at the state and local levels than they do at the national level, we nonetheless expect legislative Web sites will be modeled on those of Congress, placing far greater emphasis on conveying information than on seeking citizen input.

In sum, there is good reason to expect that the Web, like the frank, will be used largely as a communications device to protect and to enhance the advantages of incumbents. Just as those who "own" a Web site, in contrast to an open newsgroup or listserv, can control the information posted, legislative Web sites can be expected to reinforce support for the dominant political attitudes and established political parties. There are ethical questions involved in linking legislators' official Web sites to campaign Web sites, but it is safe to predict that as the Web grows in importance for recruitment, organization, and mobilization of supporters, the links will be made.

This is not to ignore that the Web will improve the opportunities for interested citizens to participate in the legislative process. Along with the growth of individual legislators' Web sites, we will see the emergence of Thomas-like Web sites at the state, county, and municipal levels. Those who are interested in legislative process will access these sites to acquire information and otherwise to follow legislation as it develops. These interested groups and individuals will use their own Web sites to distribute information among like-minded allies who share their legislative interests and to organize and mobilize support or opposition. We do not expect a significant growth in the number of citizens or the varieties of interest groups that participate in the legislative process, however, unless popular interest in the everyday routine of politics increases. Instead, we expect that those individuals and groups who already participate in legislative politics will take the best advantage of the Web's improved opportunities to enhance the effectiveness of their participation.

Far from availing themselves of greater opportunities to participate in the legislative process, we expect that most citizens will prefer to make use of forms and publications regarding government services and information provided by various executive agencies. For example, we suspect that most netizens have more interest in finding out about the lowest airfares from their nearby airports (e.g., http://ostpxweb.dot.gov/aviation/domfares/domfares. htm) than about current legislation regarding airline regulation (e.g., http://www.dot.gov/legandreg.htm). It is easy to envision future uses of the Internet as extending to mundane activities, such as voter registration, license renewal, tax filing, consumer complaints, and feedback about quality of government services (Demchak & Colón, 1998; U.S. Internet Council, 1998). Similarly, we can envision established groups increasing the efficiency (and perhaps the numbers) of their members who engage in sophisticated activities, such as providing testimony on pending legislation or responding to pending rules and regulations for implementing legislation (Worth, 1998b).[9] But, barring a crisis that greatly increases citizen interest in politics, it is difficult to envision many new groups of citizens engaging in these activities.

Keeping Government on the Web in Perspective

Although the direct presence of government through Web pages, Web traffic, and links into and resources devoted to its sites has grown, it pales next to the presence of commercial Web sites. People use the Web and most other features of the Internet largely to pursue their own private purposes, not to participate as netizens in a more open political order. The Web is marketed as an enhancement of private life—better shopping, better information, better entertainment. The Web also provides a better means for businesses to communicate with one another and with the government. If the style of governmental Web sites is any indicator, however, business communication with the government is first and foremost about doing business with the government, either directly through contracts or indirectly through taking advantage of various programs that governments provide to attract businesses to particular locations or, indeed, even to some virtual locations on the Internet.

The role of government on the Internet is likely to remain that of information provider and, to some extent, regulator. It will make certain rules that inevitably will affect politics on the Net. The governmental policy-making process is unlikely to be affected directly by hoards of new activists using the Web to facilitate their participation in politics. Rather, if current trends continue as we expect, established interests will master the intricacies of Web communications and will extend their real-world dominance of everyday politics to cyberspace. Their efforts in these matters will be aided by the dominant presence of established news media.

Where once it was expected that alternative news media—Usenet newsgroups, listserv mailing lists, or various "underground" newspapers and journals—would compete with or possibly dominate the established media in cyberspace, the advent of the WWW has helped turn cyberspace into yet another media market. The dominant news media in cyberspace increasingly are those that supply most of the information in the real world. In the next chapter, we take a closer look at this phenomenon.

Notes

1. Barber is critical of representative democracy per se. He prefers a "strong democracy" in which citizens in community groups participate directly in political decision making.

2. A similar argument applies to keeping unauthorized individuals and government from accessing proprietary information on the Web sites of other individuals, nonprofit organizations, and noncommercial interest groups.

3. http://dir.yahoo.com/Government/U_S_Government/ (March 5, 1999). This count excludes more than 2,900 Web sites that belong to the military. Both the *Web Yellow Pages* (Project Vote Smart, 1998) and Yahoo listings (1999) indicated a substantial increase in the number of Web sites for all branches compared to the previous year.

4. Congressman Christopher Cox's Web site was a notable exception. This attractive, well-organized site featured an exemplary guide to the Internet Tax Freedom Bill (successfully passed in October 1998) linked to commentary and testimony on the bill. As of March 5, 1999, the site had its own search capabilities and was regularly updated so that visitors could obtain further information about tax policy (http://www.house.gov/chriscox/nettax/).

5. We use statistics given by AlexaPPC (http://www.Alexa.com). Alexa automatically counts the number of links to the designated Web page. Hill and Hughes (1998) enter URLs in Infoseek's "advanced search" function to count the number of external links to any given site (http://www.infoseek.com). Hill and Hughes then multiply the links by the number of Web pages that comprise the Web site. Although the measures are different, both usually produce the same order regarding numbers of links. Alexa, however, provides additional information about the sites, such as number of Web pages and currency of updates.

6. For comparison, Alexa ranked Yahoo's site in the top 10. In late September 1998, we found 46,777 sites with direct links to the White House Web site. This compared to a substantial but still considerably smaller 30,269 links to the Library of Congress's "Thomas" site, the most sophisticated of the legislative Web sites. The House site had 46,120 links, and the Senate 26,748.

7. The figures, based on visits in mid-July 1998, were:

U.S. Department of Agriculture (http://www.usda.gov): Top 10,000, links = 16,057
Veterans Affairs (http://www.va.gov): Top 10,000, links = 4,376
Social Security Administration (http://www.ssa.gov): Top 10,000, links = 7,968
National Science Foundation (http://www.nsf.gov): Top 10,000, links = 23,130
Federal Election Commission (http://www.fec.gov): Not in top 100,000,
    links = 1,717

8. For email addresses, see http://www.lib.umich.edu/libhome/Documents.center/congress/conemail.txt. Some prominent members have reasons other than "technophobia" for not maintaining a public email address. Barney Frank's home page, for instance, displays the following message:

To WWW Surfers: I do not maintain an E-mail address. The significant increase in mail volume that would result would place too great a strain on my resources and my staff's ability to keep up with their already heavy work load. However, I will, as always, gladly respond to any question, comment or inquiry received by letter or phone call. Thank you.

Henry Hyde, David Obey, and Dick Armey, among others, also do not list email addresses.

9. Congressional committees post schedules of hearings and lists of witnesses on their Web sites. The *Federal Register,* which contains proposed rules and regulations, also is available online (http://clio.nara.gov:70/register/toc).

5

The Internet, Mass Media, and Public Opinion

People online are excited, and this is not an exaggeration. The various discussion forums connected to the Net are the prototype for a new public form of communication. This new form of human communication will either supplement the current forms of news or replace them. . . . The very concept of news is being reinvented as people begin to realize that they can provide the news about the environment they live in . . . and this information proves worthwhile to others.

Hauben and Hauben, 1997, p. 227

There was a time when starry-eyed Netizens envisioned a counterculture media universe flowering with a million small, personal, way cool Web sites. . . . [A]fter all . . . the humblest home page is as accessible as the slickest corporate site. Now that the Web has reached its toddler stage, those one-person sites and little zines are still there. But they're mostly leading a lonely digital existence. . . . Sandy Reed, editor-in-chief of the computer trade journal *Infoworld*, . . . agrees: "The Net is changing. There will always be outposts of ideology, but the majority of the Net is putting on a suit."

"Who's on the Playing Field," 1996

The Great Democratic Hope

Citizen interaction in cyberspace has the potential to affect both the formation of public opinion and the conduct of democratic politics. The Net provides new ways for citizens to connect with each other. It has fostered "virtual communities," groups whose members meet only in cyberspace, and some of these communities carry on a lively civic life. The Internet provides a new public space—an electronic agora, if you will—that facilitates participation in democratic politics adapted to advanced postindustrial societies.

Communication in cyberspace differs from broadcasting in that there is no central cluster of studios from which most information on the network gets distributed. Each netizen can be both a receiving node and an originator. The Internet makes it feasible for political agendas to emerge through interaction among participants who share equal powers to communicate. Moreover, as the Internet extends across national boundaries, virtual communities provide opportunities for everyone who desires to participate in the emerging politics of the global village. Here is a worldwide network, accessible from a computer terminal. To provide that access, the terminal needs nothing more complicated than an ordinary telephone line and a modem.

For optimists, political participation in cyberspace approximates an ideal type of communitarian democracy that emphasizes mutuality. Not only do the netizens share equal powers for receiving and sending, but they also share equal access to vast stores of data. The time and money needed to become informed about any topic drop substantially when anyone can surf the Web to locate and retrieve desired information on a vast variety of topics, including matters of public policy that comprise the formal business of government. Whether politics involves resolution of differences among competing interests, unitary processes for building consensus, or some combination of the two, the Internet provides the means for realizing democratic participation in the policy-making process.

Civic life, of course, extends beyond formal matters of public policy. People can interact with one another over a variety of matters, and such interactions can build a sense of community among those who discover shared interests. This sense of community has led to thousands of virtual communities that run Usenet newsgroups, listserv mailing lists, or even separate community networks, such as the Cleveland Free-Net or Seattle Community Network. In some cases, virtual communities may choose to form distinct conferential networks, such as the WELL. Some of these communities may operate as cooperative societies, that is, members may participate for one another's mutual benefit without the expectation of a quid pro quo for each particular contribution or service they provide. The civic life of the virtual community may resemble the mutuality of a barn raising or a potluck supper (Anderson et al., 1995, chap. 5 and appendix B; Barber, 1984, pp. 229-233; Hauben & Hauben, 1997; Mansbridge, 1980, pp. 8-10; Rheingold, 1993, pp. 12-13).

The civic life of cyberspace may have an advantage over the ordinary interactions of civil society. Because people usually interact with one another mainly by exchanging texts or documents, the common prejudices they hold against particular genders, races, ethnic or religious groups, or the like may remain irrelevant.[1] In theory, civic life in cyberspace may consist of purer, less bigoted interactions than those that commonly take place in the real world, where citizens interact face to face. In this regard, cyberspace has the potential to foster a higher order of democracy than has been achieved elsewhere.

Those who consider notions of virtual communities based on mutuality too idealistic still may perceive cyberspace as an environment that facilitates a more traditional civic life that involves organization, mobilization, and bargaining among interest groups. Mailing lists and interactive Web pages that serve as electronic bulletin boards represent two powerful means of communication among group members. They can be used to increase the efficiency and lessen the overall costs of traditional participation in adversarial politics. Positions can be developed, strategies devised, bargains and compromises achieved.

Whereas traditional democratic politics involves the resolution of group conflict through combinations of pressures, bargaining, and compromise, some like-minded citizens of cyberspace may develop a type of civic life that involves little or no exchange among those who hold different opinions. The Internet allows virtual communities to develop that resemble the semiprivate spaces of modern health clubs more than the public spaces of agoras. Instead of meeting to discuss and debate issues of common concern to the society, members of these virtual communities meet largely to promote their own interests (whether or not these are political) and to reinforce their own like-mindedness. These communities, however, tend to exclude those who disagree. As a consequence, some fear that they also reinforce the fragmentation and factionalism of modern society (Hill & Hughes, 1998, pp. 71-75).

In any case, many observers have expected that the Internet's powerful communications capabilities would provide tools for citizens to alter the public policy process radically. Before the growth of access to the Internet, the information sources available to ordinary citizens through the mass media were rather limited. As their name indicated, mass media were for the masses, and they focused mostly on news and information of interest to a general audience. Because this audience ordinarily had little interest in any particular policy issue and only passing interest in politics in general, most newspapers and newscasts tended to cover topics that their editors judged to have greater popular appeal than politics. Coverage of politics in depth was the exception, not the norm. Even those who cared enough to read about a particular aspect of politics in newsmagazines like *Newsweek* or *The Economist* were unlikely to acquire much new information by turning to the local or national newspapers or to competing journals like *Time.* They would acquire even less from radio or television newscasts. To get more thorough information, they would have to seek out specialized private or governmental publications housed in libraries or available only from the original sources.

For coverage of events outside their local circulation or broadcast territory, most news organizations relied on a limited number of news services, such as the Associated Press or Reuters, or the news bureaus of a few broadcast networks or of large daily newspapers. But these news services in turn devoted only modest portions of their reporters' time and resources to cover politics. Indeed, the U.S. government itself devoted more money and personnel to gathering and disseminating political information than did major American newspapers, news agencies, and radio and television networks. Although the actual resources major corporations devoted to politics are not a matter of public record, it is safe to wager that they also deployed more resources in their own areas of political interest than did the mass media. We do know that government and corporate offices and spokespersons became the sources for much of what reporters wrote or broadcast about political events (Bennett, 1996; Fulbright, 1971; Parenti, 1993).

Consolidation of ownership of the mass media exacerbated the problem. When World War II ended, more than 80% of American daily newspapers were still independently owned. By the late 1980s, more than 80% belonged to corporations that owned other newspapers and mass media. Similar patterns of consolidation occurred as large corporations gobbled up magazines and publishing houses, broadcast radio and television stations, and then cable TV systems. By the late 1970s, competition among daily newspapers had dis-

appeared from all but 36 major American cities, and 20 conglomerates accounted for more than half the magazine revenue in the United States. By the
early 1990s, just preceding the explosion of the WWW, cross-media ownership had become commonplace. Half the magazine revenues then flowed to
two conglomerates, and 6 of the top 12 cable television companies derived
substantial portions of their revenues from other media enterprises (Alger,
1996, p. 90; Bagdikian, 1989; Graber, 1997, pp. 39-49; Sussman, 1997,
p. 125).

Would access to the Internet really change all this? Are the public forums
of the Haubens' "excited" people online (Hauben & Hauben, 1997, p. 227)
likely to compete successfully with the established media by presenting alternative sources and interpretations of political and civic affairs? For reasons
given subsequently, we believe the answer is "No."

This chapter traces the evolution of the Internet as a medium for informing
the public about political and civic affairs. In the next section, we argue that
the democratic hopes attached to the Internet resemble those that have been
hitched to other communications media when they were new. From the popular press to community access cable television, each of these media has made
its impact on political and civic life, but none has fostered the enlightened
democratic participation that its ardent boosters expected. Before the Web
took hold, an unusually high proportion of those who followed politics online
may have acted as independent information providers by accessing email,
bulletin boards, Usenet newsgroups, or listservs. Today, their participation is
less active. They use the Web more to acquire political information than to
generate it. Mostly, however, they use the Web to acquire information about
subjects other than politics, to entertain themselves, or to conduct commercial transactions. The movement from textually based forums to multimedia
Web sites, coupled with the advent of search engines that have popularized
the Internet, has brought about this transformation. These developments also
have given rise to a formidable presence of mainstream media in cyberspace.

In the third and final section, we examine the extent to which mainstream
news media have extended their real-world operations into cyberspace and
have captured major portions of users who seek information about public affairs. Nevertheless, as other new information media did, the Internet is having
an impact on politics and civic life, although hardly the revolutionary one that
some democrats expected. Once again, we should keep in mind that, as in the
real world, seeking information in cyberspace about public affairs comprises
but a small proportion of most people's time and energy.

Media and Democracy

Mass media in Western society have always been used for propaganda. From early times until literacy became common, pictures were an important medium for propagating support for both secular and spiritual authorities. Ancient coins contained the likenesses of rulers; prescribed renderings of Jesus and the Virgin Mary could be found anywhere from church walls and altars to portable triptychs used by itinerant priests. To the extent possible, control of information about affairs of state and church was exercised from the top down. Emperors and popes, kings, lords, and their vassals, bishops and priests managed to hold onto legitimate authority throughout most of the Middle Ages in Western Europe.

Dissent within the Roman church, the rise of nation-states, the humanistic learning of newly established universities, and the expansion of the merchant class were harbingers of the Protestant Reformation and the Renaissance. The introduction of moveable metal plates for printing in the mid-fifteenth century hastened the change by spreading the new ideas. By the end of the century, printers' guilds had been established, as had the publishing and book-selling businesses. The established orders no longer controlled the mass media. Information was democratized. By the early 1500s, literate individuals, though still an elite, could acquire and examine information on their own. Reformed churches, though hardly democratic in their internal governance, nonetheless could publish their own doctrines separate from the church of Rome. And nationalistic princes and kings could ally themselves with these churches to buttress their own independence from centralized secular and spiritual authorities.[2]

Although Latin remained the primary language for the published works of scholars and priests (the two groups overlapped), the new technology for print also supported the development of national languages. Books, newspapers, tracts, documents, and other materials that appeared in the vernacular encouraged the spread of literacy among ordinary people. As early as 1539, the first printing press was established in Mexico City. Even though there are no hard figures on the exact rates of literacy, by the time of the American Revolution, the power of the printed word to reach broad portions of the population was well established. In addition to including religious freedom, the Northwest Ordinance of 1787 included the promotion of education as a goal, and the First Amendment to the United States Constitution included freedom of the press as well as freedom of religion.

The newspapers that became common in European cities in the sixteenth century did not have mass circulation. They were printed on hand presses and were still relatively expensive to produce. The first daily newspaper was not established in England until 1702, and the birth of the popular press had to await the invention of continuous roll papermaking machines and steam-driven presses in the first decades of the nineteenth century. In the latter half of that century, the development of cheap newsprint, coupled with the urbanization of the Industrial Revolution, provided new opportunities for newspapers, magazines, and books to succeed in reaching the general populace. The democratic dream of an informed citizenry with access to cheap and plentiful sources of information on public affairs seemed possible (Mill, 1861/1991, chap. 2; Mill, 1863/1998, chap. 1).

Booksellers and subscription-based newspapers and journals had to make their profits largely from the price readers paid for their products, but popular newspapers and magazines could make money by selling advertisers access to their readers. To attract advertisers, the popular press sought to maximize its readership rather than cater to subscribers or sponsors like political parties who tended to share particular points of view. This was accomplished by providing sensational news: information designed to amuse, amaze, or entertain the readers as much as to inform them about public affairs. Studies affirm that mass audiences of today prefer light and simple presentations to grave or complex analyses of public affairs—indeed, they are hardly interested in most public affairs. It is unlikely that the public of the late nineteenth century, who were less educated than today's citizens, were any more interested in or concerned about public affairs (Graber, 1997, pp. 207-212).

Suffice it to say that the popular press did not produce a vitalized democracy. It did affect public consciousness, however, making information about civic and political affairs available more widely—albeit often more shallowly—than previously. For better or for worse, the quest for large circulation fostered the development of great newspaper chains, such as those of Hearst, Pulitzer, and Beaverbrook, and eventually encouraged the consolidation of media ownership mentioned in the first section of this chapter. Yet, the growth of newspaper chains also expanded the market for news agencies, such as the Associated Press, founded in 1870, and thus broadened the coverage of national and foreign affairs. As the news agencies distributed information to a variety of newspapers with disparate editorial interests, they encouraged their reporters to develop objective rather than analytic styles of reporting. The professional reporter who focused on factual questions of who, what, when, where, and why in an ostensibly objective manner became the norm. At the same time, the reliance on advertising revenue increased the leverage of large advertisers, mostly businesses, to influence the content—or even the presence or absence—of particular stories that affected their interests.

A general pattern repeats itself for each new mass medium that emerged after the onset of the Industrial Revolution. Political philosophers and theorists proclaim that the new medium provides the means to realize an active and informed citizenry. Film, radio, and television, for example, are seen not merely to convey information on public affairs to the general populace but to allow them to experience the cultures of faraway places, the performances of great drama, dance, and music, even the pleasures of great literature. As the pioneer producers and broadcasters break new ground, the medium also will provide channels for new and diverse ideas to take hold. By the time a majority of the population begins to use the medium regularly, however, these lofty aims largely have been cast aside. The economic imperatives of high production costs force not merely growth but also consolidation. Powerful producer groups draw as many citizens as possible into a mass audience, access to whom can be sold to investors, advertisers, or sponsors. This mass audience is assembled mostly by responding to popular tastes, not by attempting to raise cultural and educational standards. Although the process by which popular tastes arise is complex, the tastes themselves reflect the existing norms of society. In nearly all societies, particularly in those that purport to be democratic, these norms include the familiar and often vulgar intellectual and artistic preferences that the optimistic philosophers and theorists proclaimed the new medium would elevate (Hacker, 1967; Mill, 1863/1998; Neuman, 1998).

For a short period after the passage of the Public Broadcasting Act of 1967, it appeared that public radio and television in the United States might challenge the dominance of commercial networks. The Corporation for Public Broadcasting (CPB), flush with new money from Congress, began to underwrite production of programs that sometimes presented new voices that were critical of the values and assumptions of established groups. From 1968 through 1972, the Public Broadcasting Service (PBS) also had the aid of massive grants from the Ford Foundation to produce regular television news coverage that was comparable in scope to the network news operations. The American tradition is that public corporations should largely earn their own keep, however. Having provided seed money, the Ford Foundation turned most of its attention to other causes after 1972. The federal government continued to fund almost one third of the cost of public radio and television throughout the 1970s, despite mounting opposition from conservatives. Besides objecting to the PBS using federal subsidies to produce programs critical of governmental policy, conservatives also objected to programs that violated what they saw as community standards. When the expansion of cable television channels indicated that market forces alone might weaken the network domination of broadcasting, serious moves were made to close down public broadcasting altogether. In any case, during the Reagan administration, Congress reduced federal funding to 16% of the public broadcasting budget, forcing the local PBS affiliates to raise ever larger portions of their budgets from other sources. Although Congress restored some federal money (it provided about 20% of the funding in the late 1990s), public broadcasters today raise as much as half their budgets from private businesses, universities, and private foundations, often selling them sponsorship of "noncommercial" air time in ways that hardly differ from how commercial channels and stations sell air time to their sponsors and advertisers. They raise nearly another 25% from membership drives and other fund-raising events that must attract a popular audience. Finally, by "paying for some programs and refusing to pay for others," the sponsors and the conservative appointees to the CPB provide additional guidance for public broadcasters as to what is acceptable fare (Graber, 1997, p. 37; see also Alger, 1996, pp. 98-100; Sussman, 1997, 38-42).

In the 1970s and 1980s, preceding the phenomenal growth of the Internet, cable television was expected to provide the technological means to achieve intelligent participation of the general public in democratic politics. Local cable companies were required to maintain community access channels and to train ordinary citizens to use them so that they could broadcast to their peers. The meetings of local councils and other governmental bodies could be broadcast live, as could other meetings of other groups concerned with civic affairs, such as local housing or parent-teacher associations. Community meetings could combine telephone and cable technology to widen community participation. As had happened with previous technologies, however, people proved to be interested in using cable television more for recreation than for edification, and less for political and civic matters than for other matters (Arterton, 1987, chap. 9).

With the passage of the Cable Communications Policy Act of 1984, nearly all federal requirements for public service cable programming were eliminated. Moreover, as cable viewership grew, owners of broadcast and print media began to seize control of cable systems. By 1993, broadcast companies held substantial stakes in 23 of the 50 largest cable systems, and newspaper and magazine companies held substantial interests in 17 (Graber, 1997, pp. 395-396). With important exceptions, such as C-Span and local community access or governmental channels, the multiplicity of cable channels brings viewers mostly popular fare, from network reruns to movie first runs (often for a premium). It does offer at least three 24-hour news networks (CNN, MSNBC, and Fox News), which are good sources for breaking news, and specialized channels that provide something for nearly every interest: sports, weather, hobbies, shopping, stock markets, comedy, cartoons, pop music, history, even arts (albeit paired with entertainment). Although very few cable channels attract large shares of viewers, their combined viewership has broken the network oligopoly and is expected to exceed the combined NBC-ABC-CBS-Fox-PBS share early in this century. Cross-ownership helps to mitigate the financial effects of this competition with broadcast networks, but it certainly does not provide many new incentives to develop substantial increases in public affairs programming, either on broadcast or on more narrowly focused cable channels and stations.

The incentive it does provide is to present politics as entertainment. The success of nationally syndicated talk radio shows provocatively hosted by intellectual giants like Rush Limbaugh, G. Gordon Liddy, and Oliver North, not to mention the popularity of television talk shows like those of Jerry Springer or Larry King—which are more explicitly entertainment-oriented—has inspired many local imitators. Candidates have begun to use national and local talk shows as venues to present themselves directly to voters. Although some critics have complained that such appearances are negotiated to avoid so-called hardball questions from seasoned reporters at televised press conferences or on established shows like *Meet the Press,* others have argued that appearances on these shows sometimes reach audiences who would not otherwise pay much attention to electoral politics. Moreover, many of these new shows invite audiences to call in, so they are certainly more genuine than Richard Nixon's controlled appearances to answer questions before live audiences in 1968 (McGinnis, 1969). Soft news programs like *Today* and *Good Morning America* also have begun to invite more candidates and public officeholders to explain controversial policies, respond to attacks, or reveal hitherto unannounced plans, especially when circumstances indicate that such appearances are likely to draw larger than normal audiences (Alger, 1996, pp. 328-329; Graber, 1997, pp. 238-240).

Cable television ownership is useful not merely for reaching suitable audiences directly and then selling advertisers access to them but also for selling third parties demographic information about cable subscribers. The Cable Television Consumer Protection and Competition Act of 1992 forbids cable operators from disclosing the content of viewer habits or the nature of transactions viewers make over the cable system. But it does allow cable providers to collect, sell, or otherwise disseminate various pieces of information:

> Your name, service address, billing address, . . . telephone numbers (business and home), credit card information, account number, installation, billing, payment, deposits, complaint and service records, . . . records of information you have furnished . . . such as locations and number of television sets and service options you have chosen. Such records may include your place of employment, whether you lease or own your residence, name and address of your landlord, identification card numbers (such as driver's license and/or social security number) and other personally identifiable information. (Intermedia, 1998)

The only major requirement is that the companies notify you in advance of the opportunity to contact them if you wish to stop the distribution of the personal information they hold about you.[3]

None of this is to deny the impact these media have made on politics: The interested citizen undoubtedly can find more and better information about political and civic affairs in various mass media than could be found in the past. We do argue, however, that the average citizen's relatively low demand for information about such affairs, coupled with the imperatives of the market, tends to discourage efforts to devote larger proportions of the media's limited resources to these matters. Why should we expect the proportion of resources devoted to political and civic affairs on the Internet to be any larger? Indeed, why should we expect that the most prominent sources of information about political and civic affairs on the Internet should be much different from those already found in other mass media?

News of Public Affairs on the Internet

When we conducted an online survey of the politics and civic life of Internet users in July 1994 (Fisher et al., 1996a), the most common sources of news and information online were Usenet newsgroups; listserv mailing lists using Bitnet protocols; and proprietary networks, such as CompuServe and AOL. Versions of the Mosaic browser for Windows and Macintosh were barely more than 9 months old, and Netscape Navigator 1.0 would not be introduced until December. Though numerous, the user population was a highly educated and wealthy elite that was disproportionately youthful, white, and male. Few respondents described themselves as novice computer users.

Users spent a median of 6 hours weekly using email or perusing bulletin boards, newsgroups, or mailing lists. Their perusal generally involved more than simply gathering information: 33% reported that they posted or responded to a message at least weekly, whereas only 19% reported never having done so before responding to our survey. Not surprisingly, they also reported above-average rates of ordinary political participation, such as petitioning or otherwise contacting public officials. Respondents were not political junkies, however. They reported using the Internet more for amusement, for information on subjects of interest (some possibly concerning public affairs), or for work-related or professional purposes than for expressing their opinions, ideas, or arguments about any or all subjects. Although many private companies had their own intranets, using the Internet's backbone for commercial transactions was virtually unknown (Fisher et al., 1996a, 1996b; see also Pitkow & Kehoe, 1995).[4]

What a difference 5 years has made! Today's users, though still more affluent, educated, and politically active than their fellow citizens, resemble the general population more closely than did their predecessors. Like their predecessors, however, they use the Internet mostly for purposes other than learning about or participating in public and civic affairs. More than two thirds have now carried out commercial transactions over the Net (see Chapter 2, this volume). Instead of subscribing to a number of Usenet newsgroups or mailing lists to obtain new information, they normally jump onto the Web and use a search engine to direct their browser (almost always either Netscape or Internet Explorer) to the relevant Web pages. When they do wish to obtain news about political or civic affairs, it usually concerns breaking news, and their usual interest is to obtain a quick summary rather than an analysis in depth. According to a 1998 study, nearly half of all Americans who use the Internet regularly access news online. That amounts to approximately 13% of American citizens who get news online. The news they seek, however, is not necessarily about politics. Moreover, they normally spend less than 10 minutes on this activity, and they favor "sites that aggregate headline-driven news" (Jupiter Communications, 1998).

The Internet that they encounter, of course, is no longer the poorly mapped plain that requires sophisticated skills to find fertile fields of information.

Most users now enter cyberspace through a well-marked "portal" (a default starting point for a browser) that places them on a well-mapped site of the World Wide Web. There, they generally can follow the signs that lead to Web pages with information relevant to their subject of inquiry. Instead of leading nowhere, there is a danger that following the signs will uncover too much information—a daunting list of URLs that threatens to exhaust all but the most determined. A rational strategy, therefore, is to have one's browser remember the pages that have contained useful information, the portals through which the user has passed, and/or the search engine(s) whose signs the user has followed.

Information, as we have observed, is not a free commodity. Someone has to pay to collect, organize, and display it. As governments of industrialized nations have diminished tax subsidies and turned over operation of the Internet to private hands, this cost has to be borne by donations, by users' fees, by profits from online transactions, by advertisements that stimulate such transactions, or by other effective means, such as online advertisements that generate business offline.

The upshot of all this is that just as market pressures have shaped the structures of mass media offline, they are shaping their structures online. True, there are millions of Web sites that offer more choices than any user can contemplate. But, in fact, a majority of Americans who use the Web now employ fewer than 10 as their portals. Table 5.1 presents a snapshot of these portals taken in July 1998 by Media Metrix (Kerstetter, 1998, p. 18).

There are several observations to make about these data:

1. All of the portals are commercial domains. That means that they must make money by attracting "customers" or "traffic" who either will buy products or services directly from them (Microsoft, Netscape, America Online) or will click through to buy the products or services of advertisers.[5]
2. Advertising agreements often represent exclusive arrangements or alliances with major corporations. For instance, in July 1998, Office Depot was heavily invested in Excite, Barnes & Noble was allied with AOL, and its rival Amazon Books advertised on Yahoo.[6]
3. Most of these sites have added features to make themselves the final destination for many visitors, as opposed to serving merely as the portal.
4. The cost of advertising to maintain visibility, coupled with the cost of maintaining glitzy, heavily trafficked Web sites, decreases the likelihood that users will notice smaller, less well-funded sites.
5. In late 1998, an industry shakeout was in progress that appeared likely to concentrate the number of portals even more. For example, between July and December

Table 5.1   Most Popular Web Portals Used by Americans Who Access the Web

Name	Percentage of Users Who Employ
Top Web Domains From Home	
1. America Online	46.0
2. Yahoo	40.5
3. Microsoft	27.3
4. Geocities	25.9
5. Netscape	25.4
6. Excite	23.2
7. Infoseek	15.6
8. Angelfire	15.1
9. Lycos	14.5
Top Web Domains From Work	
1. Yahoo	49.0
2. Netscape	40.0
3. America Online	34.1
4. Microsoft	33.0
5. Excite	30.3
6. Infoseek	22.8
7. Geocities	22.1
8. Altavista	19.9
9. Lycos	19.7
10. MSN	14.3

SOURCE: Media Metrix (Kerstetter, 1998, p. 18).

1998, AOL agreed to buy out Netscape, and Infoseek allied with Disney to launch a new portal called "Go Network" that would link more than 300 Disney sites and incorporate several others. (Hansell, 1998)

When we examine news media on the Web, the picture is not much different from what we find in the real world. Whereas unusual Web newspapers and magazines once had the jump on established mass media, the Web is now dominated by the same news providers that are prominent in the real world. This includes the major radio and television networks, as well as the print media. These powerful news organizations simply have the expertise and wherewithal to gather, organize, and display more information more attractively than most upstart rivals. They also can pay more to advertise online and offline to direct traffic to their sites. Moreover, they have better name recognition and more good will to draw on than do new parties who might challenge them. Most users, who are not very interested in public affairs to begin with, are likely to turn to familiar names for the headline news they desire.

The numbers bear this out. In December 1998, Alexa ranked the Web sites of nationally distributed dailies—*The New York Times, The Washington Post,* and *USA Today*—in the top 100 in volume of traffic. CNN and ABC-TV News also ranked as among the top 100 in traffic. The Web site of every broadcast network news operation—CBS, PBS, and NBC—all ranked in the top 1,000, and even C-Span and Fox News ranked in the top 5,000. A sample of major metropolitan dailies selected at random from the American Journalism Review's "Newslink" (http://AJR.Newslink.Org) produced rankings that ranged from top 500 (*Los Angeles Times*) to top 50,000 (*Cincinnati Enquirer, Hartford Courant, Sacramento Bee*). On the other hand, none of the nondaily regional newspapers selected ranked higher than the top 100,000. High rankings, like high circulation figures, allow a newspaper to sell ads on its Web site. The *Los Angeles Times* Web site, for instance, was sponsored by United Airlines, GTE, and Barnes & Noble.

Although the major news media of cyberspace have come to resemble the major news media of the real world, important differences remain. News online is digital. It can be updated more quickly than hard copy, and because consumers can select which stories to access, it even can rival cable television for providing instantaneous coverage, especially when several stories are breaking at once. It also can be searched automatically, copied, downloaded, and transmitted to other consumers (Negroponte, 1995; Neuman, 1998). Although relatively few online journals, such as *Salon* magazine, have succeeded in attracting a large readership (top 500 in traffic in December 1998), any of the standard search engines will provide immediate access to many more obscure publications on any given subject online than are normally available in most libraries or media outlets in the real world. Access to foreign publications is also far more comprehensive on the Web than in the real world.

For better or for worse, however, you can present a variety of news about public affairs, but you cannot force citizens to pay attention. In its biennial study of news consumption, the Pew Research Center for the People and the Press (1998) found that the American audience for news had become highly fragmented. The Center's findings agreed with the Jupiter Communications (1998) study that Americans' interest in breaking news was growing. This meant a fragmentation of the news audience, as an estimated 40% of adults got their news primarily from one of the cable TV news channels. Although this compared to 57% who regularly watched some type of network broadcast news—morning, evening, or news magazine—the cable news audience was growing while the broadcast news audience was shrinking. Pew estimates of the online news audience were even larger than Jupiter's: 36 million who logged on for news at least weekly. Nonetheless, this audience sought news about science, health, finance, and technology more frequently than about political and civic affairs. They also had more interest in local events than in national events. Forty-six percent paid little attention to national news except when a major story was breaking; 63% similarly paid little attention to international news except in times of crisis. Adults under age 30 showed the least interest in news (33% vs. the 68% of adults over age 60 who follow it regularly), but they liked its availability on diverse outlets (77% vs. 52% for adults over age 60). This also suggests that the cable and online audience will grow.

The Pew (1998) study employed a cluster analysis to classify the fragmented audience into six categories: *mainstream, basically broadcast, very occasional, constant, serious,* and *tabloid.* Those in each category differed in both the sources they used for news and the levels of interest they had (see Table 5.2).

Even though everyone professed some interest in news about local events, crime, and health, only those in the "constant" and "serious" categories regularly followed national political news. Serious types were the only ones who followed international events on a regular basis or who paid attention to cultural news. Constant and tabloid types valued the personalities of the anchors who deliver the news, and the latter tended to seek stirring or entertaining news. Notwithstanding this diversity, there was general agreement, even among tabloid types, that the mainstream press, CNN, and regular broadcast news had more credibility than journals like *The National Enquirer* or soft news programs like *Inside Edition.* These judgments suggest that as online news sources become more popular, netizens will have the ability to make critical distinctions as to the credibility of diverse news sources. Public opinion may not be easy to manipulate.

The danger, however, is that the high cost of news operations, coupled with the reluctance of netizens to pay for news that they have become accustomed to accessing without a subscription fee, will force news operations online to pander to the lowest common denominator to attract nearly all types of news consumers: sensational coverage of breaking events. America's 1998 obsession with the Clinton-Lewinsky affair, not to mention the growing effort to expose the sexual peccadilloes of members of Congress, may portend the future of online journalism. Matt Drudge, the Walter Winchell of the

Table 5.2   Pew Research Center News Consumer Typology

Type	Characteristics
1. Mainstream (20%)	Regular audience for newspaper, cable, network, and local TV news in moderate amounts
2. Basically broadcast (17%)	Same as mainstream, but no cable news
3. Very occasional (18%)	Ignores news except when major stories break
4. Constant (13%)	News junkies: Indiscriminate consumers of everything from soft news to National Public Radio (NPR)
5. Serious (12%)	Selective: Heavy use of NPR, Newshour with Jim Lehrer on PBS, *The New York Times, Wall Street Journal,* and the like
6. Tabloid (14%)	*The National Enquirer,* tabloid TV news; rejects broadcast news

SOURCE: Pew Research Center for the People and the Press (1998).

Internet, has broken into the mainstream of news coverage. New stories about Monica Lewinsky consistently raised the ratings of cable TV networks. Only the serious types, a mere 12% of the news audience, professed an active dislike for this sort of coverage.

The Internet is a new and growing medium for the presentation of news in the twenty-first century. As has been the case with its twentieth-century predecessors—print journalism, radio, and television—the major news providers are businesses that must make a profit; they are not public services. Unless news media on the Web can convince their consumers to pay for the costs of gathering and preparing the news for presentation through subscriptions or access fees, the pressure to present news in a manner that panders to low tastes of both advertisers and audience may cancel out the opportunities the Web provides to voice opinions and present information that is not common in the real world.

The financial aspects of the operation of news media are but a piece of the more general problem of financing, regulating, and taxing the business operations of the Internet. The next chapter turns to a discussion of these problems.

Notes

1. A widely circulated cartoon about cyberspace depicts a terrier on its hind legs working a desk computer. The terrier declares to its canine companion, "On the Internet, no one knows you're a dog!"

2. The historical discussion is based on material in Harris and Levey (1975) and Grun (1982).

3. By late 1998, there were even fewer restrictions on the use of such information made available through various registration procedures and business transactions over the Internet. Demographic information, information on searching habits revealed by cookies, and the capacity of the Pentium III chip to transmit its unique serial number open a whole new world for marketers and raise enormous problems of privacy (see Chapters 2 and 6, this volume).

4. The survey was posted to a stratified sample of 100 newsgroups and 100 mailing lists. Fifty of each group were selected because they had something overtly political in their title; thus, we expected respondents to report higher-than-average levels of political activity (see Fisher et al., 1996a; see also Fisher et al., 1996b, pp. 405-411).

5. On any given day, Alexa ranks most of these portals as among the 10 most heavily trafficked sites and rarely less than among the top 100.

6. Rivals Barnes & Noble and Amazon Books had exclusive advertising arrangements with major portals that effectively limited the ability of other booksellers, such as Borders Books, to compete with them on the Web.

6

Doing Business on the Web

New Rules and New Taxes?

The "normalization of cyberspace" thesis we outlined in Chapter 1 implies that as virtual reality evolves it loses its strangeness and comes to resemble the real world. We see cyberspace as maturing from a virtual state of nature into an extension of civil society. Our lives have not been radically transformed, and the excessive hopes and fears of early observers of cyberspace have not been fulfilled. Rather than becoming a postindustrial totalitarian menace or the means for a utopian transformation of society, the Internet has become integrated into our existing reality. Cyberspace has not transformed the multitudes. The millions of new netizens and the political and commercial interests they attracted changed cyberspace to fit themselves. In Chapter 3, we showed that when people and organizations with a political agenda went online, they did not absorb the early Internet political culture. The Internet became just one more means to pursue their customary political activities and strategies. Most of the politically astute treated it as simply a new medium of mass communication with potential, but one that still had to prove itself.

Our analysis of government on the Net in Chapter 4 showed that government was primarily there to provide information and services to clientele, not to encourage ordinary citizens to participate in the process of policy formation. Nor was government reaching out through the computer screen to manipulate and dominate clientele. Rather, the main impact of the government's use of the new medium was to upgrade its performance of mundane tasks—no mean accomplishment, but hardly one that promised to expand popular control of the policy-making process. Chapter 5 took a realistic look at the potential for the Internet to become a liberating medium for news and political information. Although greater choice was available in cyberspace than in the real world, we nonetheless found that news on the World Wide Web was becoming dominated by familiar commercial news media—major newspapers, magazines, and broadcast and cable news providers—that have transferred some of their resources and operations to the Net. Thus, a major restructuring of the sources from which most citizens get their information about public affairs also appeared unlikely. The dominant news media online increasingly resemble the dominant news media offline.

Today, it is hard to believe that there was once a strong social norm against advertising and commercial activity in cyberspace. Cyberspace could not resist the pressure to change once its commercial potential was recognized. In this chapter, we extend our normalization thesis by examining the changes in cyberspace that accompany its metamorphosis into a space for doing business. Business on the Net has attracted the attention of government because electronic commerce promises to be a major growth area for the world economy in the new century. With its tendency to control, regulate, and tax, government could not long ignore such a potentially significant aspect of civil society.

Commercial interests do not present a united front against all government interference in cyberspace. There is an increasing awareness on the part of business that government should play a role in cyberspace. The future growth of the online commercial sector requires that government establish a predictable, secure, legal framework for conducting business online and provide solutions to the problem of protecting privacy and intellectual property.

The entry of government into cyberspace is also part of the process of normalization. At this time, politics that affects the Net already has become more significant than intra-Net politics. Indeed, it has made the old form of intra-Net politics almost irrelevant for this sector of cyberspace. Those doing business on the Net cannot determine their fate for themselves. They must now engage in a process of negotiation with a host of powerful players offline. The future of the Internet will be shaped by the political struggles that occur offline involving powerful interests in civil society.

Electronic Commerce

Cyberspace has become a commercial space, and the Internet has the potential to transform the way the world does business. Electronic commerce is older than the Internet, but it primarily has involved electronic data interchanges and transfers of funds between businesses using dedicated private networks. This early form of electronic commerce involved complex expensive custom-made systems developed for large firms. Electronic commerce really took off with the creation of the WWW, which significantly lowered the costs of doing business electronically. It made it possible for small and medium-sized firms to engage in types of economic activity that had been restricted to well-capitalized, established corporations. Electronic commerce has now proliferated around the world. It no longer involves specific interactions between parties who know each other; it has evolved into a complex system of interactions involving numerous parties who have never met but who want to do business with each other.

Electronic commerce is now big business. Businesses are expected to spend $954 billion on information technology by 2002 to maintain and support their online activities, up from $211 billion in 1998 ("Europe Said to Embrace Internet," 1998). It is estimated that the total revenue from electronic commerce in 1997 was around $26 billion and is projected to reach $1 trillion by 2005 (Organization for Economic Cooperation and Development, 1998). "Electronic commerce" now refers to myriad forms of commercial activity that employ the transmission of digitized data. It involves consumers buying goods and services from businesses, governments procuring goods and services, and business-to-business transactions. It encompasses activities such as selling and buying goods and services online, online advertising and promotion, the delivery of digitized goods such as software and music via the Internet, electronic transfer of funds, and providing after-sale services to consumers. Advocates foresee it as a significant vehicle for furthering economic growth in the twenty-first century. It holds forth the promise of easy and cheap access to worldwide markets for consumers and producers. It will create new types of economic enterprises and new markets and increase worldwide employment.

Although the average new surfer notices the commercialization of cyber-space in terms of the increase of advertisements and the profusion of sites offering to sell just about anything, the business-to-consumer sector of the Internet is not as significant as one might think. It is only a small fraction of the business-to-business sector, which now accounts for at least 80% of the total electronic commerce activity. Electronic commerce in the business-to-business sector is expected to grow because of its direct effect on costs and productivity. Businesses employ the Internet to lower transaction costs, reduce inventories and cycle times, and lower purchasing costs. It has the potential to increase international trade significantly by lowering the cost of doing business internationally. It is estimated that generating and transmitting information on paper for a typical cross-border purchase and sale is up to 28% of transaction costs (Sutin, 1998). The cost of operating a storefront in cyberspace is significantly less than operating one offline. The business is open 24 hours a day, has a worldwide reach, and duplicate inventories are eliminated because only one cyber-storefront is needed instead of many. Needless to say, the distribution costs for products such as financial services, software, and entertainment that can be delivered electronically are significantly reduced (Organization for Economic Cooperation and Development, 1998).

The future looks bright for a steady increase in business on the Net, yet such predictions are based on the assumption that the conditions for future growth will be in place. A secure and predictable legal environment is necessary, but what that means in practice is up to the political process. Business in cyberspace will require modification of existing rules and the creation of new ones. There is significant political controversy about the content of such rules and about who should be responsible for creating them. Government has a role to play, but exactly what this role is to be is subject to ongoing contentious debate. The increase of commercial activity also has sparked intense interest among those who see it as generating new wealth that should be subject to taxation. Commercial activity is subject to taxation offline, but how—or even if—it should be taxed online is now being decided by governments around the world. In this chapter, we first investigate problems generated by the need to create new rules for commercial activity in cyberspace and then turn to an analysis of the controversial subject of taxing the Internet.

Establishing a Legal Framework
for Electronic Commerce

As commercial activity increases on the Internet, government is inevitably drawn in. Those who desire to realize the economic potential of electronic commerce are well aware that more needs to be done to ensure continued growth. The regulations that apply to commercial activity offline have to be rethought and modified for electronic commerce. Rules have to be established that provide a workable framework for conducting commercial activity, but political issues surround the question of who is to frame the rules for cyberspace. The two big contenders are government and private business. At present, there is agreement between the U.S. government, the European Union, and organized international business interests that the private sector should take the lead in establishing new rules and standards for the future growth of the Internet. Governments are to step in where necessary, but they always should seek the participation and support of private business.[1]

The Clinton administration champions a market approach to electronic commerce on the Internet. They point out that many Internet users fear that as electronic commerce comes to play a larger role in the world economy, there will be increasing pressures on government to regulate it in ways that restrict its commercial potential. This fear should be taken seriously. Their warnings against the dangers of regulation are directed against other nations that are not as committed to free market principles as are Americans:

> Potential areas of problematic regulation include taxes and duties, restrictions on the type of information transmitted, control over standards development, licensing requirements and rate regulation of service providers. Indeed, signs of these types of commerce-inhibiting actions already are appearing in many nations. (White House, 1997)

The Clinton administration has been pursuing this policy in a number of international forums, attempting to get other countries to go along with its view of the need for government restraint when it comes to regulating the Internet. In place of government regulation, the preferred strategy is industrial self-regulation.

The proper role of government is to provide a simple, safe, and secure legal framework for conducting business. Like traditional commerce, electronic commerce requires the creation of trust among the parties to a transaction, and trust cannot be established in a lawless environment. One of the basic barriers to the increased use of the Internet for both businesses and consumers is uncertainty about the legal framework. Many fear that cyberspace may be too much of a frontier, lacking the ordinary protections of the law. Offline, there are traditional background legal conditions that secure economic transactions, but these may be nonexistent or inadequate for doing business on the Internet. Uncertainty is a particular problem when it comes to international transactions. It is not only lawyers who worry about things like the enforcement of contracts, legal liability, protection for intellectual property, privacy, and taxes.

One of the technical legal difficulties encountered by those wishing to promote electronic commerce is that there is now no generally agreed-upon method to verify that messages sent on the Internet are sent by the persons who appear to have sent them. Rules have to be developed for "electronic signatures" and other certification requirements. Many countries are developing or already have implemented such rules. They vary from those that are fairly liberal to those that are fairly detailed and burdensome (Global Information Infrastructure Commission, 1998).

The European Commission of the European Union also has studied the problem of implementing new rules to foster electronic commerce. Member states of the European Union are attempting to create a single market. They have found that just as differences in regulatory national policies have created difficulties offline, they have the potential to thwart the development of electronic commerce as well. Rules developed by many states to govern contracts are creating uncertainties because they were not developed for an electronic environment. For example, there are requirements for written documents and for handwritten signatures. New rules have to be created for accounting and auditing that recognize electronic invoices. As various nations move to update their commercial code, the European Union is concerned that new rules not impede the creation of a single market (European Union, 1997). The United Nations, through its Commission on International Trade Law, also is involved in developing such technical rules for international electronic commerce.

The Clinton administration's preference for what it refers to as "a predictable, minimalist, consistent and simple legal environment for commerce" implies more than the provision of agreed-upon legal rules of the technical sort so that legally binding contracts can be created in cyberspace, parties can be clear about their legal liabilities, and legal disputes can be adjudicated. The legal environment proposed is also one that ensures market competition. The administration prefers a "simple legal environment based on a decentralized, contractual model of law rather than one based on top-down regulation" (White House, 1997). Yet, we must remember that the so-called top-down type of regulation emerged for a reason. It arose because of market failure and the resultant public perception that the contractual model did not sufficiently protect the public interest. There is no guarantee that electronic commerce will not suffer a similar fate.

The U.S. hostility to top-down regulation is not shared by many governments around the world, nor has it disappeared from all aspects of American commercial life. Many people worry not that commercial activity on the Internet will be stifled but that the process of unregulated and unrestrained growth will have severe negative consequences on society. In addition, calls for regulation often arise, not from those who want to regulate all commercial activity on the Internet, but from opponents of particular types of commercial activities involving pornography, gambling, and invasions of privacy, among others.

If regulation is required, the administration would like it to be neutral between electronic and other forms of commerce. The problem is that not all commercial activity is treated the same around the world. Electronic commerce has the potential to run afoul of the attempts of nation-states to apply their own view of what is proper regulation to activity that transcends national borders. The views of the United States on free speech, gambling, pornography, advertising to children, and financial securities are not shared by many countries around the world. The current free market approach to the Internet is sure to generate political opposition in the future, both in the United States and around the world.

There is another important technical problem that supports arguments for leaving to the private sector the process of developing rules and standards for electronic commerce. The Internet is undergoing radical changes due to technological advances. Experience teaches that the political process is slower than the pace of change in cyberspace. Regulations that are technologically specific and that require a particular solution to a perceived problem are in danger of being rapidly outmoded by new technology. Rules and standards that are developed by private markets are easier to change and more likely to be appropriate for a rapidly developing sector of the world economy than are those enshrined in national and international law.

Intellectual Property Protection

The old mantra of the early netizens—"information must be free"—has little place in the new world of electronic commerce. To those whose livelihood depends on their intellectual products, their "information" is private property. The position of the U.S. government is that intellectual property is one of the most important areas that needs protection and government intervention. Those who own and sell such property have to be assured that it will not be stolen. Buyers of intellectual property need the assurance that they are receiving authentic goods and not some second-rate or defective imitation. Actually, because it is so easy in the digital age to make perfect copies, the costs of forgery are borne much more by the owner than by the end user.

International agreements are necessary to protect copyrights and trademarks. In December 1996, efforts were made to update intellectual property protections for the digital age by the World Intellectual Property Organization (WIPO), under whose auspices two new treaties were drafted—the WIPO Copyright Treaty and the WIPO Performances and Phonograms Treaty. These treaties require that 30 countries ratify them before they come into force. The Clinton administration submitted them to Congress for ratification and implementation, and it has encouraged other countries to ratify the treaties. The bill introduced by the administration, titled the "World Intellectual Property Organization Copyright Treaties Implementation Act" (Dart, 1997), became the subject of much political controversy.

The controversy over the passage of the WIPO copyright treaties carried over into cyberspace a long-standing debate about how to balance the rights of authors, composers, and producers of intellectual property with the general public's right to fair use. The music recording industry long has been worried about the impact of new home recording technology on the value of its copyrights. Movie studios have been concerned about videotapes, and publishers about photocopying. The existence of the Internet has only exacerbated these worries. Previously, only those engaged in criminal copying theft and sale were able to reproduce thousands of copies of copyrighted materials. The Internet poses a new challenge. As a digital medium, it partakes of the advantage of digital technology over analog. Each copy of a digital original is, for all practical purposes, identical to the original. Moreover, the Internet allows a person to upload a piece of recorded music or a copyrighted document on their Web site and make it available to millions of persons around the world.

The entertainment industry pressed for quick passage of the treaties because they foresaw the loss of billions of dollars of revenue. Rich Taylor, a spokesperson for the Motion Picture Association of America, argued that the day will soon arrive when it will be possible to download a movie from the Internet. "We need copyright protection so operators of foreign Websites will not be able to provide [American] movies with the click of a mouse to anyone with a computer and a credit card." The entertainment industry saw the protection the new treaties would afford intellectual property as crucial for promoting electronic commerce and protecting against the pirating of copyrighted materials. The Internet is also a good vehicle for the easy distribution of pirated software, and software publishers have joined with the entertainment industry to push for the ratification of the new treaties. "Strong copyright protection for creative works . . . is a critical component to a flourishing Internet," said Robert Holley, president of the Business Software Alliance, the organization that represents Microsoft and other software companies (Dart, 1997).

Educators, librarians, consumers groups, and sections of the computer industry opposed quick passage of the ratification bills, arguing that the bills went beyond what is required in the two WIPO treaties. Attempts to introduce stronger protections of copyrights from piracy threatened to tip the balance against consumers. They feared that language in some versions of the bills would alter current fair use practices. For example, there were provisions that would outlaw devices that circumvent encryption, which is used to protect copyrighted digital material. Computer developers and researchers argued that this would prevent them from making sure that new software would be compatible with existing products. There was also a danger that it would be a criminal offense for a student to circumvent a technical protection device to copy a map for a school project. Libraries were afraid that electronic encryption would be used to create pay-per-use works that they could no longer freely lend to their patrons (Clausing, 1998b; Jaszi, 1998).

The House version of the implementation bill had grafted onto it an independent piece of legislation known as the Collections of Information Antipiracy Act (Green, 1997). This bill was designed to create a new type of copyright protection for electronic databases, because, under existing U.S. law, most databases containing factual information do not receive strong protection. Protecting databases would go beyond implementing the WIPO treaties. Such provisions were considered at the time that the other two international treaties were drafted. A treaty covering databases was one of the three treaties considered by the WIPO treaties, but eventually it was tabled. Compilers of databases argued that because of the ease of simply copying data collected by others, the absence of copyright protection would discourage companies from investing in the creation of new ones for fear that their work would be stolen. The issue was brought to the attention of the international community, in part because the European Community issued a directive to member countries requiring them to have their own database protection laws in place by the end of 1997. Databases created by companies outside the European Community would not be accorded legal protection. This caused American companies to worry that their databases could be subject to wholesale duplication by Europeans (Green, 1997).

Opponents of creating such new copyright protections for electronic databases argued that existing protections and incentives are sufficient, and that such a law would upset the traditional balance between the creators and users of information. It would hinder the development of electronic commerce and impose new costs on universities, libraries, and consumers. The provision to protect databases did not survive the conference committee, although it was introduced in the 106th Congress as a separate piece of legislation (H.R. 354, sponsored by Rep. Howard Coble).

The need to pass the WIPO treaties provided an opportunity for Congress to consider another difficult political problem raised by the need to update the copyright laws for the digital age. Internet service providers (ISPs) were pressing for an exemption from traditional copyright law. They felt they should not be held liable for material transmitted by their subscribers that infringed on copyright laws. This pitted the software, entertainment, and publishing industries against the ISPs and the telephone companies. The position of copyright industries, supported by the Clinton administration, was that ISPs should be treated like any other type of business under existing law. This meant that they could be held liable for copyright violations that they abetted even if they did not make any money from the violations. Going after the ISPs was much easier than trying to prosecute individual copyright violators. The ISPs argued that monitoring the postings of all their subscribers would be very difficult and would be prohibitively expensive. Holding the ISPs liable would place the primary burden of policing copyright violations in cyberspace on them (Band & Kennedy, 1998).

In spring 1998, the copyright industries and the ISPs reached a compromise. The parties hammered out a compromise because neither side was willing to let Congress decide on the new copyright language. Under the accord, the ISPs agreed that if they learned of a violation, they would stop it, but they would not be held liable for violations about which they had no knowledge. Although originally the ISPs wanted to limit the agreement to domestic violators, they eventually agreed that they would shut down transmissions by violators even if they are located outside the United States. They also agreed to be held liable if a suspected violation were brought to their attention and they did not thoroughly investigate it; they would have preferred to have a lower standard—to simply wait until it is absolutely clear that a violation has taken place before they are obliged to act (Richtel, 1998a). The final bill, which incorporated the compromise, was passed by Congress on October 12, 1998 ("Copyright Bill Clears Congress," 1998).

Protecting Privacy

A Business Week/Harris Poll taken in spring 1998 identified concern about privacy as the main reason Americans were not using the Net, ranking it above cost and ease of use. Of those who were using the Net, 57% reported that Web site policies that guarantee the security of their personal data affect their decision to purchase things online (Green, Yang, & Judge, 1998). Industry has attempted to ease these fears by various self-regulation schemes and proposed technology-based privacy protection standards. The Clinton administration has backed industry efforts, but pressure has increased for legislation and new privacy regulations. Efforts at self-regulation so far have not been very effective in the United States, and there is pressure from interest groups and regulatory authorities, as well as from the European Union, to raise the U.S. standards of privacy protection.

The Federal Trade Commission (FTC) has broken with the Clinton administration's self-regulation approach to Internet privacy. The FTC originally had put its hopes in the promises of industry representatives that there was no need for regulatory action. At a 3-day public workshop on consumer privacy run by the FTC in June 1997, firms engaged in electronic commerce and database companies gave assurances that business would have no problem in safeguarding sensitive personal information, and that there was no need for government regulation. Industry assurances were not taken at face value. Workshops and hearings continued at the FTC, and complaints about privacy were registered by members of Congress and interest groups. In June 1998, the FTC released a scathing report (Federal Trade Commission, 1998) that documented the failure of self-regulation and called for new legislation to protect privacy.

The FTC report was supported by data gathered at the agency in what was called at the agency "the Big Surf." Dozens of agency lawyers were specially trained and equipped with PCs and fast Internet connections and spent 2 weeks surfing the Web looking for privacy problems. In their random sample of more than 1,400 commercial Web sites, they found that more than 85% collected personal information but that only 14% notified customers how the information would be used, and only 2% announced a comprehensive privacy policy.

The privacy issue has become especially politically sensitive because it involves the protection of children. An investigation of children's Web sites conducted by the Center for Media Education (Montgomery, 1998) found that sites were using such techniques as contests, surveys, and offers of free gifts to get children to supply email addresses, street addresses, purchasing preferences, and information about other family members. According to polls conducted by Georgia Tech and Louis Harris and Associates, the majority of parents want stronger laws to protect Internet privacy for children (Montgomery, 1998).

The FTC also surveyed children's sites and found that 89% collected information from children, whereas only 54% reported how the information would be used, and few sites sought parental involvement in the information-gathering process. The FTC concluded that the self-regulation efforts undertaken on behalf of online businesses had proved ineffective. New incentives were necessary to spur effective self-regulation by industry, and new legislation was necessary to place parents in control of information collection and to establish basic standards for the use of such information from children to protect their privacy online (Brinkley, 1998; Federal Trade Commission, 1998).

Prior to the release of the FTC report, there had been various attempts at voluntary self-regulation through seal systems. One of the first was promulgated by TRUSTe, a nonprofit organization created by CommerceNet and the Electronic Frontier Foundation. Those who affix the TRUSTe seal to their Web site pledge to reveal how the information that they gather will be used. The Better Business Bureau also announced a plan to develop its own privacy seal. At the time of the FTC report, these voluntary attempts at self-regulation had not made much progress (O'Harrow, 1998). After the report was released, a new coalition named Online Privacy Alliance was formed to press for self-regulation and preclude the growing threat of government regulation. This organization included such industrial heavyweights as America Online, Disney, Microsoft, Netscape, and IBM.

The guidelines for members (http://www.privacyalliance.org/) require that they implement policies that deal with notice and disclosure, choice, data security, data quality, and access, as well as a privacy seal and third-party enforcement programs to monitor and verify compliance. They try to address the most serious problem the FTC identified, protecting the online privacy of children, by requiring parental consent to gather information from any person under age 13 and notifying parents of how the information will be used. The alliance also intends to foster the development of technologies to protect privacy, such as the Privacy Preferences Project and the Open Profiling Standard. These standards would be incorporated in Web browsers and make it possible for individual computer users to determine by themselves how much personal information to disclose to a Web site. Lacking confidence that this new coalition will be any more effective in implementing privacy protections than other industry self-regulation efforts have been, consumer advocates called for new legislation (Borland, 1998; Glave, 1998c).

Ira Magaziner, President Clinton's point man on Internet issues, did not agree with the FTC's approach. He reiterated his faith in industry self-regulation and warned against proposed federal legislation to protect privacy on the Internet. He referred to the call for new legislation as a "knee jerk reaction of the industrial age when government was expected to protect you. In the digital age, there are new paradigms; one of them is to empower people by giving them the tools to protect themselves" (Scobilionkov & Glave, 1998). Though recognizing that the existing situation in respect to online privacy was unacceptable, he praised the efforts of the Online Privacy Alliance and expressed hope that its efforts at industry self-regulation would succeed (Scobilionkov & Glave, 1998). Magaziner also hoped that the American self-regulation approach to dealing with privacy would triumph over the regulatory approach in the international arena. He discussed the issue with industry groups in Europe, Japan, and Australia and advocated the use of privacy seals around the world. What he advocated was an international system with identical privacy seals guaranteeing that those who earn the seal have conformed to the same privacy code but allowing for different enforcement mechanisms in different countries (Glave, 1998b).

Europe is now ahead of the United States in passing legislation to protect privacy. According to Peter Swire (Kaplan, 1998b), a law professor at Ohio

State University and coauthor of a recent book on European law, the reasons for this are historical and cultural. He believes that the experience of World War II and the Nazis left many Europeans deeply afraid of government surveillance. Europeans also are more suspicious of the private sector than are Americans, and there is less support for a laissez-faire approach to the protection of personal privacy. On the other hand, Joel Reidenberg (Kaplan, 1998b), a law professor at Fordham University and an expert on international privacy law, argues that Americans value privacy as much as Europeans do. He points out that Europeans started to become seriously interested in passing privacy legislation as a result of American innovations like the passage of the landmark Fair Credit Reporting Act (see Kaplan, 1998b) in the early 1970s, which afforded privacy protection for consumer credit information. Reidenberg predicts that within 5 to 10 years, the United States will pass a comprehensive privacy law that will be the rough equivalent of European privacy standards. Other observers doubt that there is the political will to pass such comprehensive legislation (Kaplan, 1998b).

The fact that Europe has pursued legislative solutions to the problem of protecting privacy more vigorously than has the United States is not simply a matter of academic interest. The European Union has adopted the Data Protection Directive (Markoff, 1998), which is based on the idea that privacy is a fundamental human right. It requires that member countries adopt national legislation to ensure that they conform to minimum standards for the protection of personal data. Of particular concern to the United States is Article 25, which forbids the transfer of personal data to countries outside the European Union that do not guarantee protection of such data. This directive went into effect on October 25, 1998. Most observers agree that the United States does not meet the standards for data protection of the European Union. The fear is that it could disrupt international commerce by blocking all transactions involving the transfer of personal data. Some have hoped that new software would solve the problem of online privacy without the need for legislation, but the European Union issued a report in June 1998 that attacked the technological standards approach as inadequate and in possible violation of European privacy laws. The proposed standards do not require that information be provided about sanctions and remedies available to users. Such standards would be illegal for a European Web site (Markoff, 1998).

The Clinton administration has been negotiating with the European Union, but in testimony at the House Commerce Committee hearing on global electronic commerce in July 1998, U.S. Commerce Secretary William Daley said that the stalemate between the United States and the European Union over online privacy protection is the most important issue threatening worldwide electronic commerce. Despite this situation, Daley expressed optimism that, by the October 1998 deadline, they would meet the standard of adequate protection of privacy (Wasserman, 1998). Not all observers were so confident and warned that individual businesses dealing with Europe should familiarize themselves with the European directive and be prepared to develop their own strategies for complying with European standards for privacy protection (Gidari & Aglion, 1998).

Taxing the Internet

The Internet originally was created and nurtured at taxpayer expense. There were no farsighted government bureaucrats who conceived of it as an infant industry to be nurtured until it could make a substantial contribution to the economy and, through taxation, to government coffers. Using government money to subsidize the creation of what came to be known as cyberspace was not a political issue. There were no debates in the press about whether it was wise to spend public money in this way; the Treasury Department was not devoting time and energy trying to develop an Internet policy; Congress was not besieged by lobbyists eager for their share of revenues from this new information technology. As we have seen, it was created by government bureaucrats in collaboration with nonprofit organizations and a few relatively obscure private businesses. At the time, it was almost inconceivable that the Internet would come to be the linchpin of the new information economy and, as such, a fitting target for government regulation and taxation.

The majority of those who were involved in creating the Internet worked either for the government or for the nonprofit sector, and those who populated cyberspace in the early days evinced a strong anticommercial spirit. The Internet was a space for the free exchange of ideas, not the exchange of e-cash for goods and services. Yet, as cyberspace became populated with millions of ordinary citizens around the world, it took on the attributes of a mass medium and a commercial market. The marketplace of ideas so beloved by political theorists became somewhat crowded out by the "real" marketplace of economic theory. Those who saw cyberspace as a great democratic agora that would give birth to a new vibrant participatory democracy might recall that the much-vaunted real agora, the public space of Athenian democracy, was actually a commercial market.

The explosion of commercial activity in cyberspace attracted the attention of government. Where there was money to be made, it was only natural to expect the arrival of the tax man. Tax policy has the potential to generate intense political controversy. Although the primary purpose of taxation is to raise revenue, all sorts of secondary policies can accompany it: Imposing taxes has both intended and unintended consequences. Taxes need to be justified. It is not enough to say that government needs money. Governments always claim to need money. There are delicate political questions involved. Is the tax falling on those who deserve to bear it or can afford to bear it? For what are the moneys to be used? What individuals and industries will it affect, and how will it affect them?

On July 1, 1997, President Clinton issued a government report titled "A Framework for Global Electronic Commerce" (White House, 1997). This report set forth the administration's guiding principles for commerce on the Internet. It asserted that for the Internet to develop and prosper, government must know when to render assistance and when to withdraw. The framework stated that for the Internet to flourish, "Governments must adopt a non-regulatory, market-oriented approach to electronic commerce, one that facilitates the emergence of a transparent and predictable legal environment to support global business and commerce" (White House, 1997).

The framework pointed out that many companies fear that governments will impose onerous regulatory and tax burdens on the Internet. Already there are serious policy proposals in many nations around the globe that would have an adverse impact on Internet commerce, and the administration intended to prevent such proposals from being implemented. The framework argued that nations have been reducing tariffs for about the past 50 years, and it makes no sense to reverse this trend and impose new tariffs on global commerce on the Internet. The United States takes the position that cyberspace should be a duty-free environment for products and services that are delivered via the Internet, and that governments should apply only existing tax concepts and principles to electronic commerce. This policy position puts the administration at loggerheads with many Europeans, who are in favor of a new type of Internet tax called the "bit tax." It also puts the federal government at odds with the tax policies of several states and localities.

To analyze the politics of Internet taxation, we begin by asking how a new tax will affect the bottom line, who stands to benefit, and who stands to be harmed. Two reasonable assumptions can be made about the Internet that explain a great deal of the politics surrounding taxation:

1. There is now, for all practical purposes, no tax on Internet commerce.
2. If there are no significant changes in the political environment, there will be a great increase in the volume of Internet commerce in the near future.

These assumptions are widely accepted both by those in favor of Internet taxes and by those opposing them. Given these assumptions, who believes they would be harmed, and who believes they would benefit from the growth of the Internet? Governments that want to impose new taxes believe that such taxes are necessary to compensate them for the loss of tax revenue that would result from increasing commerce on the Internet. They foresee that commercial activity, which currently is taxed, will migrate out of their jurisdiction, either because firms will be able to conduct their business in ways that enable them to evade taxes or because local businesses will be forced to close due to competition from firms in cyberspace. Those who believe that the increasing electronic commerce will harm them will favor new taxes; those who, like the U.S. federal government, believe they will be helped by the future growth of the Internet in an environment free of new taxes will oppose them.

The official administrative position as stated in the framework is that "only existing tax regimes should be applied to Internet commerce. No new taxes should be imposed on Internet commerce" (White House, 1997). Soon after the release of this position paper, Ira Magaziner gave an interview explaining the government's Internet policies. In answer to a question about taxing electronic commerce, he stated the rationale for the fact that the federal government has chosen not to seek new Internet taxes: "Well, first of all, at the federal level, we have a corporate income tax, and we believe that as electronic commerce really takes off, more businesses will do more business and make more money, and we'll get our share from the corporate profits tax, and we won't need to do anything else" ("Talking Internet Commerce," 1997).[2]

Much of the political debate about taxes and the Internet in the United States has surrounded a bill called the "Internet Tax Freedom Act" (U.S. House of Representatives, 1998). The original bill proposed a tax moratorium for 6 years, preventing state and local governments from taxing the access fees that ISPs charge users. This would have had a significant impact on tax policies already in place. The proposed legislation also would prevent state and local governments from imposing any special taxes on Internet commerce during the moratorium, requiring them instead to treat Internet transactions for tax purposes in the same way that they now treat interstate commercial transactions conducted by mail and the telephone.

There were already signs of the desire of states and localities to assert their authority to tax Internet purchases in ways beyond their treatment of ordinary catalog purchases in Interstate commerce. The state of Texas claimed tax jurisdiction over online purchases if any part of a transaction flows through telecommunications lines or servers that are located in Texas. Thus, at least in theory, if a shopper in Denver buys something on the Web from a company located in New Orleans, and the transaction information is zapped through lines located in Texas, the purchase is subject to Texas sales tax (Lassman & O'Donnell, 1997). Although it is hard to imagine how to collect such a tax, the fear of this sort of claim by taxing authorities prompted the call for federal legislation.

Proponents of the Internet Tax Freedom Act believe that it is necessary to make sure Internet sales are free of state and local taxes to ensure that the Internet fully realizes its great economic potential. There are now thousands of separate taxing jurisdictions in the United States, and the prospect of a significant number of them turning to the Internet as a source of revenue creates fear of multiple and overlapping taxes and collection and record-keeping problems that could choke off future growth of the Internet as a commercial vehicle. Senator Ron Wyden (D-OR), one of the sponsors of the bill, pointed out this danger:

> There are more than 30,000 taxing jurisdictions in the United States, and already more than a dozen states have exacted tolls on electronic commerce over the Internet. Congressman Chris Cox [who sponsored the bill in the House] and I are concerned that the growth of Internet taxes could kill the goose that is starting to lay golden eggs. (Clausing, 1997c)

The major problem with this bill from the point of view of states and localities is that they already lose an estimated $3 billion to $4 billion in mail-order purchases due to a loophole in the U.S. tax system. As it is now, if you live in Ohio and order boots from L. L. Bean in Maine, L. L. Bean is not required to collect Ohio sales tax. You still owe the tax, but no real attempt is made to collect it. The U.S. Supreme Court has declared that a state cannot force a retailer to collect sales taxes on items purchased by residents out of state unless the retailers have a significant physical presence in the purchaser's state.

Sales taxes are an increasingly important source of money for state and local governments, providing $132.2 billion for states in 1995, about one third of their $399 billion tax revenue. The monetary loss through the loophole, although high in absolute terms, is not yet a significant portion of their overall revenue (Johnston, 1997). But the potential growth of electronic commerce and the consequent severe drain on revenues is worrisome. The National Governors' Association came out against the Internet tax moratorium. Governor (now Senator) George Voinovich of Ohio, chair of the Association, asserted that the proposed law would have severe effects:

> [It would] represent the most significant challenge to state sovereignty that we have witnessed over the last 20 years. If enacted, the legislation coming out of the House would undercut state and local taxes and lead to a virtual sales tax collapse over the next 10 years that would be felt by every American community. (Tanouye, 1997)

He went on to claim that the law would hurt local merchants, who would not be able to compete with tax-free sales on the Internet, and that it would be unfair to those who do not have access to the Internet, especially those who cannot afford computers (Tanouye, 1997).

Most states believed that they had more to lose than gain by allowing the Internet to develop without new taxes, but the Internet does not affect all states the same. Governors Pete Wilson of California, Paul Cellucci of Massachusetts, George Pataki of New York, and George Allen of Virginia disagreed with the position taken by the National Governors' Association. They wished to limit taxes on the Internet. Not surprisingly, all of these states have significant computer-related industries (Tanouye, 1997).

The National League of Cities, the U.S. Conference of Mayors, and the International City/County Management Association also came out in opposition to the House and Senate bills. Local legislators came to Capitol Hill to lobby against the bill. Brian O'Neill, vice president of the National League of Cities and member of the Philadelphia City Council, testified at a hearing of the House Judiciary Subcommittee on Commercial and Administrative Law. He stated that any proposed tax moratorium "would be a significant infringement on state and local sovereignty, put hundreds of state and local budgets in a deficit, create considerable budgetary problems for local governments, and lead to unfair competition in the marketplace" (Vesely, 1997). The state and local officials received little or no support from lobbyists for retail industries and unions, even though there is the potential that increased Internet commerce could adversely affect many of their members (Munro, 1998).

The state and local officials were opposed not only by the White House but also by antitax groups, the Communications Workers of America (a powerful union), Internet advocates, and a great number of high-tech companies with interests in the Internet. Backers of the bill formed the Internet Tax Fairness Coalition. The members of the coalition included such heavyweights as the U.S. Chamber of Commerce, the National Retail Federation, Microsoft, IBM, America Online (the largest ISP, with more than 11 million subscribers), Charles Schwab & Co., Inc. (the financial services company that has the largest share of the online brokerage business), the National Association of Realtors, the American Hotel and Motel Association, and Ticketmaster, among many others.

The Internet Tax Fairness Coalition has its own elaborate Web site that, in addition to presenting a defense of its position against Internet taxes, provides general position papers, papers on the effect of Internet taxation on specific industries, media news articles, and a press kit. It also urges political action on behalf of anti-Internet tax legislation. It suggests sending email, phoning and writing officials, and writing letters to the editor. If you do not feel up to drafting a letter yourself, they will do it for you:

> Uncomfortable writing a letter to your elected officials? Check out our Internet Letter Desk. By completing the Letter Desk form, you will provide Coalition workers with enough information to write a personalized letter for you. We will forward the letter to you so you can review—perhaps add a P.S.—and forward to your Senators and Representatives. (Internet Tax Fairness Coalition Web site)

Needless to say, the Coalition is well funded, and there is money behind this Web site.

In February 1998, the National Governors' Association proposed a permanent prohibition on taxing Internet access (a minor source of revenue) in return for an agreement to establish a single nationwide consolidated tax on out-of-state purchases both for electronic commerce and mail order (Munro, 1998). In *Quill Corp. v. North Dakota* (1992), the U.S. Supreme Court left in place the loophole enabling most mail-order customers to avoid paying state sales taxes, but it did permit Congress to close it by enacting legislation that would allow states to levy sales taxes on remote purchases effectively. Despite heavy lobbying by the states in the past, Congress has so far refused to do this. The governors' offer satisfies the ISPs but would entangle Internet tax legislation with the very unpopular attempt by the states to force mail-order businesses to collect sales taxes on out-of-state purchases.

After intense negotiations, a compromise was reached, and in March 1998, Representative Cox (R-CA) held a press conference to announce that the National Governors' Association, the National Conference of Mayors, the National Conference of State Legislatures, the National Association of Counties, and the National League of Cities would now support the bill. The revised bill included shortening the moratorium from 6 to 3 years, providing for a more targeted moratorium instead of a prohibition on all Internet-related taxes, and creating a commission to study state and local tax issues and recommend legislation to Congress. The bill also called on the Clinton administration to seek bilateral and multilateral agreements with foreign countries to ensure that the Internet would be free of tariffs and discriminatory taxes. In June 1998, the House of Representatives voted unanimously to approve the Internet Tax Freedom Act (U.S. House of Representatives, 1998). Representative Cox, the bill's sponsor, joked, "Read my email, no new Net taxes" (Glave, 1998a).

Although the moratorium provision of the revised bill forbids any new taxes on Internet access for 3 years, it does contain a provision that would "grandfather" in eight states that presently collect such taxes. The states are Connecticut, Wisconsin, Iowa, North Dakota, South Dakota, New Mexico, Tennessee, and Ohio, but these states each must pass a law within 1 year of the passage of the Internet Tax Freedom Act indicating that they wish to continue taxing Internet access. Two states that currently have such taxes, Texas and South Carolina, opted not to be included in the grandfather provision because their governors did not support taxes on Internet access. The 3-year moratorium also covers "bit taxes," that is, taxes that would be imposed on the volume of information transmitted electronically, as well as multiple or discriminatory taxes on the Internet (National League of Cities, n.d.; U.S. House of Representatives, 1998).

The moratorium preserves the tax-free treatment of remote purchases to the extent that it exists now by prohibiting the creation of new collection obligations. It also prohibits the creation of any new "nexus" for establishing jurisdiction for tax purposes. This provision is intended to support the *Quill* decision and ensure that Internet commerce is treated the same as mail-order business. The rationale for this is that any change would place Internet businesses at a competitive disadvantage and would discourage the continued growth of electronic commerce. The alternative method of ensuring fair competition—imposing an effective uniform state sales tax on both Internet commerce and mail-order and catalog commerce—was rejected. This was the method favored by most of the states. The states, however, did receive a minor concession. The bill calls for the creation of a temporary advisory commission that would study the issue of state and local taxation and make legislative recommendations about sales taxes on both electronic and mail-order transactions. The commission would have 31 members, 3 federal officials, 14 state and local representatives, and 14 business and consumer representatives. The commission would give the states a forum for continuing to pressure Congress for the right to tax remote-sales transactions (Hardesty, 1998b).

Lawrence Summers, deputy secretary of the Treasury Department, said the administration "strongly supports" a temporary moratorium but warned that the Internet must not become a tax haven that would drain state and local revenues that would be needed to build schools and prevent crime. He said that the administrations intends to offer suggestions to improve the bill if and when a House and Senate panel meets to reconcile different versions of the bill ("Net Tax Moratorium Passed," 1998).

On the Senate side, Senator Ron Wyden (D-OR), who previously had collaborated with Cox on the passage of the Internet Freedom and Family Empowerment Act of 1966, introduced the Internet Tax Freedom Act (U.S. House of Representatives, 1998). The bill passed the Senate by an overwhelming majority of 96-2 on October 8, 1998. In addition to a tax moratorium itself, the bill also provides for a temporary 19-member Advisory Commission on Electronic Commerce, which is to explore the impact of Internet commerce on the tax-gathering ability of the states and localities and report back to Congress within 18 months. There was debate in the Senate about the scope of the commission. Some, such as the chair of the Senate Commerce Committee, John McCain (R-AZ), wanted to limit it to studying Internet tax issues, but by a vote of 68-30, the Senate yielded to the pressure of the state governors and agreed to widen the mandate to include the problem of taxing mail-order and catalog sales. The language of the Senate bill was incorporated into the Omnibus Appropriation Bill, which was approved by Congress on October 20, 1998, and signed by the president on October 21. The new law established a tax moratorium on the Internet from October 1, 1998, until October 21, 2001, but the issue of taxing the Internet is by no means settled (Fram, 1998; "Net Tax Bill Nears Final Hurdle," 1998).

Although passage of the bill was greeted with almost universal praise, there still were those who criticized it. An editorial in the *Industry Standard,* which bills itself as "the newsmagazine of the Internet economy," took the overwhelming support for the bill in Congress as a sign that significant issues had been ignored. It observed that Internet commerce is now carried out as an elite activity and "to carve out a duty-free zone that is largely inaccessible to the poor (and the information poor) could be seen not only as regressive, but much worse" ("Duty-Free Net?" 1998). In addition to issues of tax equity, they argued that it is fantasy to believe that the Internet can remain a tax-free zone forever. Taxes will come eventually, and they hope that the advisory commission will do a better job than Congress has in devising new workable forms of taxation ("Duty-Free Net?" 1998).

We have no way of knowing whether the commission will come up with a more constructive tax plan than Congress has, but we do agree that it will play an important role in keeping the issue alive. The fact that the commission has a broad mandate to consider the general issue of collecting sales taxes on interstate commerce almost guarantees that the issue of collecting taxes on electronic commerce will be subject to renewed political controversy, especially if it is seen as one aspect of a broader problem of state tax collection. The question of whether to tax commerce on the Internet is now settled, at least until the Commission presents its report to Congress. We expect at that time that the question will be reopened and subject to a new round of political debate.

The debate surrounding the Internet Tax Freedom Act in the United States raises important political and economic issues regarding state and local sovereignty, the dangers of multiple and overlapping taxes, and the differing effects of the Internet on economic activity located within specific geographical regions of the United States. Many officials fear that the loss of state and local revenue due to the shift from main street commerce to Internet commerce will have a greater negative impact than any potential increase in revenues resulting from the growth of computer-related industries. The United States is a large and diverse economy, and, as we would expect, those jurisdictions that believe that they would lose out in a relatively tax-free Internet economy are in favor of new taxes; those who believe the contrary are opposed.

One complex of problems involving the avoidance of state taxes is not addressed by the Internet Tax Freedom Act. Although the law permits the states to try to collect existing sales tax, it does not address the special problems of tax and regulation avoidance raised by the growth of mail-order beer and wine clubs on the Internet. State alcohol regulators claim that these clubs are costing the states millions of dollars in revenue and that they are, in effect, "Internet bootleggers" whose operations violate state liquor control laws. Unlike the diffuse opposition to untaxed online commerce by states and localities that fear the loss of general sales tax revenue, the prospect of direct Internet sales of alcohol has mobilized specific bureaucratic and commercial interests (Gay, 1997).

Aaron Stansbury, assistant director of Maryland's alcohol and tobacco tax unit and treasurer of the National Conference of State Liquor Administrators, stated that direct shipments of alcohol are clearly affecting state liquor revenues. He explained that in the United States liquor is not treated like other commodities offered for sale. Each state has its own law regulating the sale of alcohol. The 21st Amendment repealed Prohibition, but it left it up to the states to regulate alcohol as they wished. Section 2 of the Amendment prohibited the importation or transportation of liquor into any state in violation of that state's laws. This section was implemented by the Webb-Kenyon Act of 1935, which made such shipments into a state a federal crime. This statute was intended to protect "dry" states.

After the repeal of Prohibition, there arose a three-tiered system of alcohol distribution in the United States, from producer to wholesaler to retailer. There are 34 states in which alcohol can be distributed only from producers to licensed wholesalers, who, in turn, sell to licensed retailers and restaurants. This is the system by which states collect their taxes and enforce their drinking laws. This time-honored and cozy relationship between state regulators and wholesale liquor interests apparently cuts little ice with Internet users. Stansbury complained that such users have little regard for state liquor laws: "They just see a product for sale and order it like a pair of stockings" (Gay, 1997). New York State Attorney General Dennis C. Vacco pointed out another dire consequence of Internet alcohol sales; it provides an easy way for teenagers to get booze: "Teenagers who can't legally buy a can of beer at the corner store can get virtually any type of alcohol beverage delivered right to their doorstep" (Gay, 1997). He asserted that we must not let technology be a vehicle for evading state laws: "How far are we going to allow technology and expedience to usurp safeguards against underage access and state revenues?"

Needless to say, those engaged in the online sale of alcohol see the matter differently. They claim that vested commercial and bureaucratic interests are refusing to adapt to the way modern small businesses are using new technology. The liquor wholesalers acknowledge that their interests are threatened by Internet direct sales—some industry estimates put the loss at $1 billion—but they claim that there are also other public policy concerns raised by Internet sales that circumvent the traditional licensed wholesale distribution system. They assert that protecting the public from unregulated alcohol sales is an important reason for stopping direct Internet sales. David Dickerson, a spokesperson for the Wine and Spirits Wholesalers of America trade association, agrees that direct sales to underage drinkers is a problem. Selling alcohol on the Internet would permit sellers to evade state laws that implement public policy decisions on how alcohol should be regulated. Presumably, he means, among other things, that the state policy of granting a monopoly to licensed wholesalers is an important element in this public policy. "If it's not through our hands, it's a concern to us," he asserted. "This is at the center of a public policy argument about how the public wants to handle alcohol" (Gay, 1997). Wine wholesalers are also asking Congress to act now "to catch a massive problem early" before it gets out of control.

Direct Internet distributors believe that the underage drinking issue is a "red herring." One prominent Internet businessman, Louis Amoroso, president of Merchant Direct, which operates the Web site "Beer Across America," offering beer from a range of small regional microbreweries, explained that they charge by credit card, ask for customers' ages, do not provide immediate delivery, and require that shippers get signatures of adults when making deliveries (Gay, 1997).

However the issue of interstate sale of alcohol via the Internet is eventually resolved, this debate demonstrates the potential for the Internet to challenge the ability of governments to collect taxes and regulate retail sales using traditional means. Cyberspace is inherently difficult to regulate, and new technologies have the potential to make government control and regulation much more complicated in the future.

Although the Clinton administration opposed any new taxes on the Internet, political controversy arose over the administration's intention to use moneys raised by existing taxes on telecommunications companies to subsidize certain classes of Internet users. The Telecommunications Act of 1996 updated the concept of universal service that previously had been designed to provide a cross-subsidy to ensure that phone service was available at reasonable rates in areas where it was expensive. The money was provided by contributions to a universal service fund by telephone companies, and the cost was passed through to telephone users. The new law extended the concept of universal service to cover more than just telephones by redefining it as an "evolving level of telecommunication services" (available at http://www.fcc. gov/Reports/tcom1996.txt). It also explicitly included schools, libraries, and rural health facilities, but left the amount of the subsidy program to be determined later. The subsidy for schools and libraries came to be known as the "e-rate," for education rate.

To administer the subsidy program called for by the new law, the Federal Communications Commission (FCC) established two nonprofit entities: the Schools and Libraries Corporation (SLC) and the Rural Health Care Corporation. The FCC originally sought $2.25 billion for 1998. The program seemed to be popular and raised little public controversy, until two long distance phone companies, AT&T and MCI, announced in May 1998 that they would begin to add a charge to customers' telephone bills to pass along the cost of the subsidy to consumers.

The FCC had expected that planned reductions in the access fees long distance companies must pay to local phone carriers would go a long way toward compensating them for the new subsidies. Both supporters and opponents of the FCC were caught by surprise when long distance companies decided to make the subsidies explicit by putting them on customers' phone bills. At a congressional hearing, Representative Ed Bryant (R-TN) brandished a telephone bill sent to him by an upset citizen in his district and said, "How shall I explain this tax to my constituent? Do I tell him I voted to place that tax on him to support schools and libraries on the other side of the continent?" (Tumulty & Dickerson, 1988). Opponents complained that the companies were to blame for adding the surcharges. Senator Bob Kerrey (D-NE) vowed to introduce legislation requiring the companies to list their profits on customers' bills along with the new surcharges ("School-Wiring Subsidy in Peril," 1998).

The program also got embroiled in presidential politics when congressional Republicans labeled these fees the "Gore Tax." Other embarrassing aspects of the program started hitting the popular press. It was reported that the General Accounting Office had declared that the FCC had exceeded its authority and perhaps acted illegally in setting up the two quasi-independent corporations. Opposition also was raised to the $200,000 salary paid to Ira Fishman, a former White House aid, as the chief executive of the SLC.

In early June, four key members of Congress—two Republicans, Senator John McCain, chairman of the Senate Commerce Committee, and Representative Thomas Bliley, chairman of the House Commerce Committee, and two Democrats, Senator Ernest Hollings and Representative John Dingell, ranking minority members of the Commerce Committee—wrote to the FCC complaining that phone bills were about to be increased and "this is not what we intended when Congress passed the Telecommunications Act of 1996." Their letter went on to say, "The commission's efforts to implement the universal service provisions of the act have been a spectacular failure, and—more importantly—a raw deal for consumers" (Schiesel, 1998; "School-Wiring Subsidy in Peril," 1998). John Dingell, a staunch liberal, is also reported to have said, "We did not vote to have the FCC set up a giant bureaucracy headed by someone paid as much as the President" (Tumulty & Dickerson, 1998).

In response to the criticisms calling for the end of the program, the FCC on June 12 voted 3-2 to cut back on the subsidies. They agreed to provide $650 million in the second half of the program's first year, thus bringing the total for 1998 to $1.275 billion, a 43% cut from the original $2.25 billion requested by the FCC. After receiving 30,000 initial requests for subsidies totaling $2.2 billion, they planned to pay out the moneys in 18 months rather than in a year. This would slow down the program and reduce the amount of subsidy they would have to collect in the first year. Internet subsidies for rural health care providers, a much smaller program, would continue to be subsidized at $100 million for 1998. They also agreed to cut Fishman's pay to $150,000, and, rather than a first-come, first-served policy they originally had announced, they now would give disadvantaged schools priority. Even after the vote, congressional opposition to the plan continued. President Clinton, who previously had announced that connecting all U.S. schools to the Internet by the year 2000 was a national educational priority, weighed into the debate and came out in support of the FCC. He stated, "I will steadfastly oppose any effort to pull the plug on the [subsidies] and our children's future, or to thwart the FCC's ability to move forward with this initiative" ("Net Subsidies Frozen," 1998).

In late June, House Speaker Newt Gingrich suggested that the entire e-rate program needed to be overhauled. He argued that Congress should remove oversight authority from the FCC and establish a block grant system that would provide money to the states, which would decide for themselves how to administer the program and award subsidies (Macavinta, 1998b). In July, Senator Conrad Burns (R-MT) and Representative Billy Tauzin (R-LA) introduced legislation to eliminate the e-rate and the FCC control and replace them with money from existing federal excise taxes, which would be block-granted to the states (Macavinta, 1998a). The National Taxpayers

Union set up an elaborate Web site dedicated to opposing the e-rate. In a banner headline, next to a dollar bill with Gore's face on it, it shouted: "The Hidden Tax in your Telephone Bill, Unmasking the e-rate, Gore Tax.com" (Gore Tax.com Web site, http://www.goretax.com).

The administration did not remain idle in the face of a frontal challenge to one of its pet high-tech projects. In late July, the Commerce Department released a report titled "Falling Through the Net II" (National Telecommunications and Information Administration, 1998), which was requested by Vice President Gore. It examined telephone and computer penetration rates to determine who is and who is not connected to the information infrastructure. It concluded that the gap between the digital haves and the digital have-nots has been growing. There is a significant gap between the races. Whites are more than twice as likely to own computers than are African Americans or Latinos. Among the least connected are the rural poor, rural and central city minorities, young households, and single-parent female-headed households. Despite an overall increase in access to the information infrastructure among all groups of Americans in the past 3 years, the report concluded, "It is still essential that schools, libraries, and other community access centers ('CACs') provide computer access to connect significant portions of our population" (National Telecommunications and Information Administration, 1998).

After the report was issued, White House officials used it to round up political support for the e-rate. Education Secretary Riley, in his first speech devoted solely to technology and education, spoke to the National Young Leaders Conference (available at http://www.broadcast.com/news/dc/ram/riley072998.ram). The speech to high school students also was intended to meet the increasing volume of criticism directed against the policy goal of connecting every classroom to the Internet. He cited the Commerce Department report and argued that the time has come to "break the cycle" of technological inequity. To achieve a bright future "requires a real commitment by this nation to end the race disparity between those who have and those who do not have these exciting tools for learning. . . . The ['e' in] 'e-rate' could also stand for equality or equal access." Larry Irving, assistant Secretary of Commerce and administrator of the National Telecommunication and Information Administration, also made the rounds of Congress and the press, urging the country to rally around the administration's effort to ensure support for the subsidy (Macavinta, 1998a; Mendels, 1998).

A grassroots campaign on the Internet was organized to save the e-rate. Pamela Fielding, advocacy coordinator for the National Education Association, one of the country's largest teachers' unions, believes that this campaign was instrumental in saving the e-rate. The NEA set up a Web site for a little more than $1,000, which, according to her, generated about 22,000 email messages to Congress in 2 months in support of the e-rate (Mukherjee, 1998a; NEA e-rate Web site, n.d.; Save the E-rate Now Web site, n.d.).

Despite the attack on the e-rate and the resignation in August "for personal reasons" of Ira Fishman, the chief executive of the SLC, the SLC issued the first wave of e-rate funding commitment decision letters to schools and libraries on November 23, 1998 (E-ratecentral.com, 1998). The Burns-Tauzin plan to eliminate the "Gore tax" died with the end of the congressional session, but it surfaced again in the next Congress (Macavinta, 1998c; Goretax.com Web site).

These challenges to the e-rate are prompted by a general concern about the appropriateness of using public money to subsidize new social programs. In an article with the provocative title "Feds Hate the Web," James Freeman (1997) in *Forbes ASAP* argued that this policy is an example of the attempt to impose twentieth-century-style utilities regulation on the Internet. He cites a statement from the previous FCC head who explained how the policy of subsidizing Internet connections would be paid for: "Probably the most equitable way that you could raise money for a national purpose would be through contributions by communications companies, because they cover the whole country." Freeman commented, "Bit tax, anyone?" (Freeman, 1997).

This remark is a polemical dig against the administration's subsidy policy. Yet using money raised from telecommunication companies for such purposes does not entail anything as radical as a bit tax. The bit tax idea has been floated seriously in European political circles and has been greeted with general hostility by the Internet community. The administration's rationale for using tax money raised on the Internet for social purposes, though, does echo the European idea of using a new general Internet information tax to deal with social and economic problems raised by the creation of the Internet. The debate in the United States about money collected by telecommunication companies only involves subsidies for inexpensive Internet connections and money for wiring educational institutions and health care facilities. The argument assumes that ordinary state and local tax revenues need to be augmented so that worthy public institutions can take advantage of the new technology. There are also worries that electronic commerce will undermine local tax revenues. In Europe, the issues surrounding Internet taxation arouse deeper core fears about the long-term employment effects of the new information society.

The Bit Tax

Compared to the tax controversy in the United States, the discussion of taxing the Internet in Europe focused more on the broader implications of the transformation of the modern industrial economy by new information technologies. Although in the United States there have been rumblings that the Internet might be bad for certain local businesses because of new competition, in general, the response to the economic implications of the Internet has been almost uniformly positive. In Europe, the possible negative impact of the growth of electronic commerce has been taken more seriously. With near-record unemployment rates in France and Germany, observers feared that the jobs issue would be raised as a reason for resisting the growth of the Internet itself or for taxing it for social welfare purposes.

The potential employment consequences in Europe are much greater than in the United States. The majority of the jobs in Europe are in medium-tech manufacturing concerns, which have not yet been affected by the new information technologies. A larger share of U.S. jobs are in high-tech or other industries that are likely to be stimulated by electronic commerce or, at least, not affected negatively. Europe's retail distribution system is particularly vulnerable to the cost-cutting and consolidation that Internet commerce can bring. Although electronic commerce is just getting off the ground, it already has stimulated dire predictions of job loss. In December 1997, the British think tank Demos issued a report that concluded that electronic commerce would eliminate thousands of jobs in downtown shopping districts without creating new ones. "Anyone who has just started work as a sales assistant who intends to work his way up to become a store manager has just had his future curtailed," claimed Wingham Rown, the report author. He explained further that "Online companies do not pay rents. They have no shoplifting problem, minimal overheads and need only employ a few computer operators and people to move boxes" (McGuire, 1997).

Those who feel they cannot stop the introduction of new technology often turn to the political process to blunt its impact. In Europe, predictions of the impact of the Internet on future employment lie at the heart of the argument for imposing the bit tax. Although in the United States the main political controversy has surrounded taxing Internet purchases and ISPs, the bit tax has potentially more far-reaching effects on cyberspace in general. Discussion of the bit tax also raises more explicitly the regulatory and redistributive policy implications of Internet taxation.

The bit tax is simply a tax on the bits flowing through the Internet. The idea of taxing information by means of a bit tax was first proposed by the Canadian economist Arthur Cordell in his 1994 Club of Rome report. It was developed in his subsequent papers and became the basis of a proposal by Luc Soete and Karin Kamp in their report for the High Level Group of Experts created to advise the European Commission on the social aspects of the new Information Society (Soete & Kamp, 1996).[3] Cordell (1996) tied his proposal of a bit tax to the assumption that the Internet is a core component of an emerging new economy based on information technologies. According to him, the new economy will be energy saving, capital saving, and labor saving. Jobs will grow, but very slowly. We will see what he refers to as "jobless growth." The challenge is to tap the productivity and wealth created by this new economy. A bit tax on the flow of information on the Internet will deal with the problem of increasing productivity and declining employment:

> It represents a new tax base that is at the heart of the new economy. It is also a new tax base that is growing. It is a tax base that can be easily identified, one where collection is in a few hands. In the New Economy it would be a tax that is difficult to avoid. (Cordell, 1996)

Soete and Kamp (1996) noted that adjusting the tax system to take into account the impact of the Internet is much more important for Europe than for the United States. European countries rely primarily on the value-added tax (VAT). In the United States, the main taxes that would be avoided in a tax-free Internet are local and state sales taxes on merchandise ordered through the Internet. In Europe, the VAT is charged on both goods and services. Most importantly, Europe would lose revenue from taxes on the service sector (such as banking, insurance, telephones, and the like) on a tax-free Internet. Sales on the Internet also would mean less physical distribution of goods and, therefore, fewer VAT taxes on goods in transit. It is argued that the VAT, which was designed to tax the value added at various stages in the production and distribution of material goods and services, cannot meaningfully be applied in the case of information and communication services. The bit tax, which would be levied on the intensity of the information transmitted, is intended to replace the value added in the area of immaterial goods and services.

Clearly, the Internet has a different impact on tax collecting in Europe than in the United States. Soete was asked to comment on the U.S. government's draft report on global electronic commerce that suggested that the Internet be declared a duty-free environment:

> While in the U.S. additional revenues generated by the growth stimulated by the duty-free zone would probably be more substantial than those lost on sales tax, in Europe—where sales taxes are twice as high—such a scheme could be devastating to the government's ability to raise money. (Guissani, 1997b)

Thus, the Europeans and other countries with a VAT are placed in the same political situation as the states and localities in the United States. Because they rely on a type of sales tax to collect substantial portions of their revenue, they view the growth of electronic commerce on the Internet as a threat. Because the U.S. government relies on individual and corporate income taxes, and federal excise taxes are not such a significant source of revenue, it can look to the future growth of electronic commerce as a golden opportunity to increase revenue.

Soete and Kamp (1996) suggested that the bit tax would have a number of significant policy implications beyond simply raising revenue from a new stream of wealth, each of which is politically sensitive and prone to political controversy. For example, they suggested that the new bit tax would have the advantage of reducing congestion on the Internet. It would be a way of dealing with the "increasing amount of 'junk' and irrelevant information transmitted." For many libertarians and other advocates of the Internet as an arena for freedom of expression, the prospect of governments adopting tax policies to eliminate junk information violates the basic spirit of cyberspace. The authors even go so far as to suggest that taxing the Internet might increase worker productivity because raising the cost would provide an incentive to eliminate using the Internet to send personal email or engaging in time-wasting Net surfing unrelated to business (Soete & Kamp, 1996).

Who will benefit from the moneys raised is another significant policy issue posed by the prospect of new taxes. Are they to be earmarked for the general revenue or for specific purposes? Many on the left perceive a new tax on the Internet as fair if the proceeds are directed to compensate those who have been forced to bear the cost of the new economy. It is even better, they feel, if the money is to be used to generate new jobs. Free market proponents, on the other hand, find it axiomatic that taxing the Internet is not a good way to increase employment in the high-tech sector and in the economy in general. Soete and Kamp (1996) suggested that a bit tax could stimulate job growth. They assumed that because the new information technologies will put additional strain on the already overburdened European social welfare system, it is appropriate that the taxes be used to fund the welfare state and, in the process, stimulate employment and economic development:

> On a priori grounds the use of the additional "bit tax" revenues to fund, for instance, the employers' social security contributions in countries like Belgium, the Netherlands, France, Italy or Germany should bring about a substantial reduction in labour costs, hence provide at least new incentives for job creation and improved competitiveness. (Soete & Kamp, 1996)[4]

They also argued that a bit tax could be a way to redistribute the benefits of the new information economy by exempting public hospitals, schools, and libraries from the tax. Finally, because it requires that usage be "itemized" in some way, they suggested that a bit tax could be used as a way to solve problems of intellectual property by assisting in collecting intellectual property right fees.

Politics is a complicated business, and new tax proposals have the potential to engage unexpected political passions and interests. Although the debate about the Internet Tax Freedom Act in the United States has not gotten entangled in racial and ethnic politics, the claim that it may prevent local governments, such as large cities, from meeting their revenue needs has at least the potential to mobilize such political forces. In Europe, this possibility already has been realized. In 1996, Elio Di Rupo, Belgium's vice premier and minister of economic affairs and telecommunications, proposed a bit tax. Revenue from the new tax was to be distributed as social security rebates to assist industries dependent on manual labor. Historically, much political controversy in Belgium has involved conflicts between the two major ethnic groups, the Flemish speakers of the north and the French speakers of the south. The bill was attacked immediately on the grounds that the tax was likely to affect the technically advanced northern Flemish community much more heavily than the French, because the French community contains more labor-intensive industry. Political cynics observed that it is no coincidence that Di Rupo is from the southern French-speaking region and that the proposed tax was merely a way of aiding the largely rural south. The proposed tax was shelved (Mendler, 1996).

The bit tax, an example of politics affecting the Net, has generated its own opposition politics on the Net—a clear case of what we refer to as "political uses of the Net." The draft proposal by Soete and Kamp (1996) for a bit tax to be adopted by the European Union was posted on the Net, prompting a lot of opposition in newsgroups and email responses to the authors. It even resulted in the creation of a Web page dedicated to its defeat, titled "Oppose the Euro Bit Tax." The page urges netizens to use the Net to voice their opposition, and, assuming you are a citizen of a country in the European Union, it urges you to contact your Euro member of parliament and your parliamentary representative and write to newspapers and magazines. It also advocates a type of lobbying unique to the Web. It asks you to create a link to the "Oppose the Euro Bit Tax" home page, copy a graphic banner opposing the tax, and add it to your own Web page (Oppose the Euro Bit Tax Web site, n.d.).

So far, the bit tax proposal that was before the European Commission, the policy body for the European Union, has not been implemented due to fear that a new tax would stifle the growth of the Internet. Although the tax was backed by Belgium and Italy, Mario Monti, the commissioner responsible for taxation, vetoed the plan. The argument was made that Europe needs to wait until the industry matures before attempting to impose such a tax. Other factors that influenced the decision related to problems of implementation. There is no practical method of metering Internet wire traffic, and it is possible that digital broadcasting in the future may replace existing networks ("European Commission Vetoes Bit Tax," 1997).

International Politics and Taxation

Taxing Internet commerce has implications for international politics. Given the globalization of the economy and the increasing ease with which firms can relocate to escape high taxes, the prospect arises that if any country or group of countries taxes cyberspace, firms will simply take the exit option and relocate offshore. In addition, nation-states face the same problem of multiple taxes that is created by the specter of innumerable state and local taxes in the United States. By defining the Internet as a tax-free zone, the U.S. government is, in effect, sandwiched between two levels of multiple tax jurisdictions. On the one hand, it is faced with state and local taxation and, on the other, the power of national governments to tax international commerce. Given the constitutional powers of the federal government, despite cries that it is invading the sovereignty of the states, it is clear that the national government can impose a single tax regime or a no-tax regime on the entire country. Despite Pax Americana, it is not possible for the U.S. government to solve the problem of multiple tax jurisdictions in the international arena by unilateral action.

Solving the problem of multiple taxation and overlapping jurisdictions on the international level requires negotiations and treaties. Tax lawyers have argued that U.S. firms are particularly vulnerable: "One of the dangers of a global tax environment that can create multiple taxation of the same income is that it very often harms U.S. multinationals more than others" ("Global Co-operation Needed," 1996). The U.S. government has recognized this problem and, in the white paper "The Framework for Global Electronic Commerce," observed that many countries concerned to acquire new sources of revenue are looking toward the Internet to solve their problems. It concluded:

> Therefore, the United States will advocate that the World Trade Organization (WTO) and other appropriate international fora declare the Internet a duty-free environment whenever products or services are delivered across the Internet. This principle should be negotiated quickly so that it can be established before nations impose tariffs and before vested interests form to protect those tariffs. (White House, 1997)

Some progress has been made in implementing the framework since it was first publicly announced in July 1997. On December 9, 1997, the United States and the European Union reached an agreement on guidelines for electronic commerce, including a commitment not to impose any new tariffs on goods that are delivered over the Internet (Lohr, 1997). On May 15, 1997, President Clinton and Japanese Prime Minister Ryutaro Hashimoto issued a joint communique that pledged both governments to "avoid imposing unnecessary regulations or restrictions on electronic commerce." They also agreed to work for the realization of an Internet free from tariffs and special taxes ("U.S., Japan Agree," 1998).

In February 1998, the United States formally proposed to the 132-member World Trade Organization (WTO) that they agree to continue to keep electronic commerce on the Internet free of customs duty. Some emerging market economies were not enthusiastic, fearing they would lose a significant source of new tax revenue. Several European countries, opposed to continued U.S. cultural expansionism, felt that any agreement should not cover the transmission of music or films ("U.S. Seeks Accord on Internet Free Trade," 1998). President Clinton attended the WTO's Ministerial Conference in Geneva and on May 18, 1998, gave a speech that reiterated the American position that the Internet should be a tax-free zone:

I ask the nations of the world to join the United States in a standstill on any tariffs to electronic transmissions sent across borders. We cannot allow discriminatory barriers to stunt the development of the most promising new economic opportunity in decades. (Available at http://dns.usis-israel.org.il/publish/press/whouse/archive/1998/may/wh7519.htm)

None of the 132 countries has custom duties on electronic goods purchased and transmitted on the Internet. The U.S. proposal was for a permanent bar on the imposition of tariffs on such electronic commerce, but the emerging market economies, led by Pakistan, forced a compromise. On May 20, 1998, the WTO announced agreement on a 1-year moratorium on Internet tariffs. The deal covered tariffs on items ordered and delivered via the Internet; it did not cover "hard goods"—products ordered on the Internet but shipped by normal means across international borders. The ministers also agreed to continue to discuss policy issues raised by electronic commerce and suggested that during their meeting in November 1999 in the United States, they might consider extending the tariff ban ("WTO: No Net Taxes," 1998).

Hopes were raised when Secretary William Daley expressed confidence that the global moratorium on electronic commerce customs duties would be extended by 18 months to 2 years (Jones 1999). But this prediction proved premature. Electronic commerce was buried as conflicts about agricultural subsidies, attempts to link labor standards and trade, and anti-dumping rules tore apart the conference. According to some ministers, the complexity of the subject matter and the refusal of delegates to compromise on politically sensitive issues doomed the talks. The conference collapsed without even issuing a final communiqué (Pearlstein 1999).

The political atmosphere inside the conference was exacerbated by street protests carried on by hosts of groups with grievances against the WTO. Former Italian trade minister and WTO director-general Renato Ruggiero pointed out the irony in the way the protestors organized themselves: "Evidently the protesters used the Internet to organize the protest. They used the very globalization they say they want to combat" (Associated Press, 1999). Notwithstanding the lack of progress in Seattle, issues of electronic commerce will undoubtedly appear on the agenda of future WTO meetings.

Despite doubts about the appropriateness of applying the VAT to Internet transactions, a new proposal is before the European Union that would require European consumers to pay the VAT on goods and services they order and receive over the Internet. The European Commission released a paper in June 1998 stating that the sale of all Internet digital products, such as downloaded software, should be taxed as services ("EU Seeks to Tax E-Commerce,"

1998). The proposal is being considered by the 15-member governments of the European Union. The policy would not violate the European Union agreement with the United States not to impose new tariffs on electronic commerce because it is not considered a "new" tax. The Commission agreed that purchases over the Internet should not be subject to new taxes but maintained they should not escape existing taxes either.

Although the recommended policy does not involve imposing new taxes, the paper did note that it still would mark "a significant change in executing European Union tax practices" because private individuals or businesses inside the European Union who purchase services outside the Union now do not usually have to pay the VAT. Even those who purchase services online within the Union, and even within the purchaser's own country, usually avoid the VAT because of the lack of enforcement. In the past, CompuServe exploited this loophole in Union regulations by claiming that the services it delivered were from its headquarters in the United States and thus were not subject to the VAT. European ISPs found themselves at a competitive disadvantage because they had to add the VAT at the local rate to each customer's bill.

The proposed policy would close this tax loophole, but it would go further. It would treat products such as software and music CDs that are delivered via the Internet as services for the purpose of the VAT. Ordinary goods are taxed where they are purchased, services where they are performed. Because virtual goods are treated as services, such goods are to be taxed where they are downloaded. Thus, for example, if software is purchased from a firm outside the European Union but delivered via the Internet to a customer residing within the European Union, that customer must pay the tax. The argument is that if the customer bought it in a box off a shelf within the Union, it would be taxed, and thus the existing practice of not taxing such virtual goods creates unfair competition for European Union businesses. The VAT need not be applied if a customer outside the Union purchases a good or service delivered via the Internet from a Union supplier. The Commission also noted that this policy would be difficult to implement, and it would consult with national governments and business groups to devise ways to make it work efficiently ("EU Seeks to Tax E-Commerce," 1998; Hardesty, 1998a; Lavin, 1998).

Despite the rejection of new Internet tax proposals by both the Clinton administration and the European Commission, it would be very premature to conclude that the antitax forces have won. Vint Cerf, one of the founders of the modern Internet, when addressing a meeting of the Internet Society, argued that Internet taxes are coming despite recent actions by the United States and the Europeans. According to him, there is no way of avoiding them. He called for planning and again warned of the desire of governments to tax the Internet: "If the Internet becomes a major tool for electronic commerce, every major taxing jurisdiction in the world will be interested in using that as a revenue stream" (Hayward, 1997). These are wise words. As of now, electronic commerce is in its infancy. There is a real danger of killing the goose in its infancy, before it starts really laying the golden eggs. Most observers believe that it is really not worth plucking now. When it matures and starts really producing, then the temptation to tax and pluck will be extraordinarily hard to resist.

Conclusion

As cyberspace becomes a place for doing business, it can no longer remain an isolated autonomous realm. As we have seen, the realization of the full commercial potential of the Internet requires the establishment of a framework of rules, and business and government are the two major contenders to author such rules. For now, it appears that online business has been given the green light to develop its own rules, with government playing a supporting role.

The dangers inherent in the unintended and unforeseen consequences of premature overregulation are taken seriously. Governments are wary because the rapid pace of technological change may make a regulatory regime irrelevant—or even counterproductive—by the time it is set in place (though this is not to say that governments have given up their right to intervene). Not all countries around the world share America's values and faith in free markets. It is difficult to know how the struggle between regulators and believers in free markets will turn out as cyberspace continues to evolve.

Even staunch advocates of a free market approach to Internet commerce in general recognize that there is a place for government in cyberspace, especially when their profits are threatened. You cannot have markets without private property, and cyberspace has turned out to be particularly dangerous to holders of intellectual property. The old struggle between the rights of the owners and of the consumers of intellectual property is being replayed in a new medium. New international copyright protections have been hammered out for cyberspace, but there are still issues to be resolved, such as the protection of databases.

Although business interests are in favor of laws to protect property, most are not in favor of laws to protect privacy. Personal information might seem like a form of property owned by each individual. Yet, most commercial interests operate under the assumption that, though collecting information about customers and potential customers is a valuable commercial advantage, netizens should treat that form of property as of little or no value and routinely give it away for the privilege of doing business online. There has been significant opposition to this view from online activists, public interest groups, and government officials. In line with its overall approach, the U.S. government has tried to let industry develop its own form of voluntary online privacy guidelines and codes, but these have so far proven ineffective. More vigorous governmental measures to protect online privacy are in the offing. The European Union already has taken such action, and the differing approaches to privacy in Europe and America have the potential to disrupt international commerce.

As the commercial potential of the Internet became evident, the issues of taxes arose, and, as we have seen, tax policy mobilizes a great variety of political interests. It also illustrates the increasing importance of politics that affects the Net. Those who fear the Internet will cost them tax revenues from traditional sources want to tax the Internet; others believe that a moratorium on such taxes would be in the long-range interest of society. So far, governments have resisted the temptation to impose new Internet taxes. Despite worry about job losses from the rise of Internet commerce, the European Union has rejected a proposal to impose a bit tax on the Internet. A 3-year moratorium on new Internet taxes is in place in the United States. This involved a struggle between state and local governments, which feared a loss of tax revenue, and those who feared that imposing taxes would severely hinder the future of electronic commerce. The moratorium solved the problem of the burden of multiple taxing jurisdictions within the United States—at least temporarily—but the potential still exists on the international level. We certainly have not heard the last from those who want to tax the Internet.

The problem of regulating the Internet discussed in a general way in this chapter has focused on politics that affects the Net. Intra-Net politics played no role in our analysis. Yet, it has been claimed that intra-Net politics and self-regulation do have an important role to play in cyberspace, even in the commercial sphere. In the next chapter, we turn to a case study of Internet gambling. This enables us to investigate the importance of self-regulation and delve more deeply into the complex issues of different national values and jurisdictions that are raised when governments attempt to regulate cyberspace, a space without national borders.

Notes

1. For the position taken by international businesses, see Global Information Infrastructure Commission (1998). The principles in this document are supported by the International Chamber of Commerce and the Business Industry Advisory Council of the Organization for Economic Cooperation and Development, among others. For the official U.S. government position, see White House (1997); see also the "Joint E.U.-U.S. Statement on Electronic Commerce" (E.U.-U.S., 1997).

2. He expressed similar sentiments in an earlier press conference in Brussels, Belgium (U.S. Mission to the European Union, 1997).

3. The bit tax also has been discussed in government circles outside Europe. The Australian Taxation Office is reported to be interested in the possibility of imposing such a tax to solve fiscal problems caused by future growth in electronic commerce. See "Australia Concerned Over Tax Revenue Loss " (1997).

4. For a rebuttal, see Federation of the [British] Electronics Industry (1996).

7

Gambling on the Internet

A Case Study in the Politics of Regulation

B ecause cyberspace has lost its special character as a space insulated from the economic and political forces dominating civil society, its normalization has meant that eager entrepreneurs as well as established corporate interests have helped to transform it into prime commercial real estate. As it has become a place for doing business, so government inevitably has been drawn in. In Chapter 6, we saw that politicians have eyed cyberspace as a lucrative source for new tax revenues but have been restrained so far by the fear that they might thwart the future growth of electronic commerce. Business and government have worked together to build a legal structure for doing business online and have attempted to solve the difficult problem of protecting property rights in cyberspace. Business is also interested in establishing consumer trust, which is threatened by fear of loss of privacy on the Net, but, as we have seen, the attempts at self-regulation to protect privacy have so far been ineffective.

Self-regulation is an enduring hope of many of the more libertarian theorists of cyberspace. Self-regulation is a product of what we have called "intra-Net politics"—netizens attempt to control their own affairs. Many believe that intra-Net politics is not only a good way of dealing with regulatory problems, it is the only way. Governments should not attempt to regulate cyberspace, and if they do, they will meet only failure and frustration. We believe that this is unrealistic. The ingenuity of government will enable it to extend its regulatory authority and devise appropriate enforcement mechanisms, though there are problems on the horizon. No doubt there always will be a role for self-regulation in cyberspace, but there is no reason to believe that this role will be any greater there than it is for business in the real world.

Government regulation is part of the process of normalization. As the Internet matures, intra-Net politics will be superseded in importance by politics that affects the Net. Political forces offline, along with online interests, will determine how business can be conducted in cyberspace. To illustrate the complexities of government regulation in cyberspace, this chapter provides an analysis of the attempt to regulate Internet gambling.

Although it is natural to think of regulation as state-imposed restrictions on private conduct,[1] to understand the politics of Internet regulation, we have to expand such understanding to include both public and private forms of regulation. Private regulation has come to be called "self-regulation." There are a variety of self-regulatory mechanisms that have been used as substitutes for government regulation in the real world. These include such things as codes of conduct, voluntary standards, accreditation, third-party certification, and audits. There have been moves to apply such techniques in cyberspace. Furthermore, to understand governmental attempts to regulate cyberspace, we also must be aware of the different levels of government. Public regulation can involve nation-states, subnational units, or international actors and arrangements. One recent scholarly article explored the problem of regulating the Internet:

> Activity on the Internet is as complex and varied as activity in real space and as such its regulatory framework must reflect the complexity. Real space regulation is comprised of a mosaic of self-regulation; local, state, and national regulation; international agreements where international consensus exists; international agreements pledging co-operation where states agree to respect their regulatory differences but provide enforcement assistance; and effects based regulation where jurisdiction is asserted despite tenuous ties to the regulating state. (Geist, 1998)

Cyberspace creates particular problems for regulation. It even has been argued that because physical borders are necessary for the effective operation of a legal system, and cyberspace does not have any borders, we ought to consider it a distinct and separate space with its own jurisdiction; that is, cyberspace should be permitted to generate its own rules free from the attempt of traditional governments to legislate for it (Johnson & Post, 1997).

Regulatory politics is also influenced by values, which change through time and are often in conflict. Disputes about regulation can involve economic as well as social values. They can involve debates about efficiency and freedom of choice and morals. There is no universal consensus on values, and what can seem perfectly appropriate as a target of regulation in one place can be viewed as a purely private matter in another.

Although no one issue area can illustrate all the complexities of Internet regulation, a case study of the attempt to regulate gambling on the Internet illustrates a great number of them. Internet gambling involves the problem of levels of state action, whether regulation should occur at the national or state level or some combination of both, and the role of self-regulation by the Internet gambling industry. Government attempts to regulate gambling also must confront the dilemma of how to regulate a commercial business that may be situated outside its borders but whose product is available to its own citizens. Because Internet gambling occurs in the borderless world of cyberspace, it raises problems of jurisdiction and enforcement that involve international law and politics. Finally, regulating gambling concerns value questions. The United States has a long history of regulating various types of gambling according to its dominant moral values at the time. But a great many other cultures do not share America's ideas about the morality of gambling. This, too, creates problems for Internet regulation.

History of Gambling Regulation

The political debate about Internet gambling is the latest chapter in a long and ongoing controversy about the proper relation between gambling and government. Gambling in the United States traditionally has been controlled by the states and localities, although the federal government under the Constitution has the authority to regulate it when interstate commerce is involved. Americans have experimented with everything from promotion to permission to prohibition. In some jurisdictions, gambling has been a government monopoly; in others, it has become a regulated private business. Today, in many states there is healthy competition—or unhealthy, depending on your values—between government-sponsored gambling, such as state lotteries, and government-regulated private businesses, such as riverboat casino gambling. From the birth of the nation when the Continental Congress authorized a national lottery to help fund the Revolutionary War to the present, various fiscal crises have played a crucial role in turning government from an opponent of gambling into a proponent.

By the early part of the twentieth century, the mood of the country had turned against gambling. Most states outlawed it in any form. Yet, in recent years, inspired by the state of Nevada (which has had legalized gambling since 1931), states gradually relaxed their absolute prohibition. Today, largely as a result of the quest of state governments for new sources of jobs and revenue and changes in federal Indian policy, 48 states and the District of Columbia permit some form of legalized gambling. However, the types of gambling that are legal and the rules under which businesses must operate vary significantly. What has emerged is a complicated system of territorial jurisdiction with great local variance (Raysman & Brown, 1997). Politicians have acquiesced to legalizing gambling in the expectation that it would create local jobs and fill local tax coffers. Those in what is politely known as the "gaming industry" have, for the most part, made their peace with the system of local regulations. Although the industry often has pushed to marginally increase the amount of gambling permitted in various jurisdictions, it has never advocated total legalization, let alone legalization without regulation.

Internet gambling has the prospect of totally destroying this complex symbiosis between government and gambling interests. Many politicians foresee losses of jobs and taxes, as well as the evils of unregulated gambling; some big gambling interests see virtual casinos on the Internet as competition for their multimillion-dollar investments in "bricks and sticks." Tom Bell, the director for telecommunications and technology studies at the libertarian Cato Institute, has lamented the powerful political alliance in the United States between established gambling interests and state politicians who are supporting a proposed ban on Internet gambling. He notes that state and municipal lottery monopolies brought in $43 billion in 1996, and that gives them a direct stake in preventing citizens from shopping around on the Internet for better odds (Bell, 1998).

Given the ambiguous legal status of online gambling, the large gambling corporations are waiting until the legal dust settles before they put their corporate assets at risk by going online. Although at present the serious political advocates in the United States for online gambling are libertarians and

small-time entrepreneurs who have seen the Internet as a way of circumvent-
ing existing U.S. laws, this may change in the future. Bell argues that despite
the opposition of organized interests, most Americans would support
Internet gambling. He points out that at least 56% of Americans gambled in
1996, and legalized gambling represents the fastest growing sector of the entertainment business. For him, it is just another form of business, and going
online would bring all the advantages to the consumer that it would for any
other commercial activity: "Internet gambling can help to satisfy the huge demand for new gambling services and provide competition to ensure that existing services treat consumers well." Bell also makes the argument, so common
to those who have deep faith in the liberating power of cyberspace, that government is really irrelevant to the issue because it cannot control what is going to happen anyway. He contends, "Internet gambling will grow regardless
of what lawmakers and prudes want. . . . Given a chance to vote on an unen-
forceable law that discriminates against Internet users, lawmakers should
walk away from the table" (Bell, 1998). Perhaps they should, but it is not at all
obvious that cyberspace is beyond the long reach of the law.

Enforcement in Cyberspace: Within the United States

Federal and state governments have various laws regulating gambling.
Most legal experts claim that at least some of these laws apply to gambling in
cyberspace, but the legal situation is unclear and untested, and there are significant problems in trying to enforce them. Some of these problems arise
from the special features of cyberspace; others are general problems of enforcing U.S. national law outside its borders. It has been argued that the fact
that cyberspace has no territorial borders challenges the existing legal system
of nation-states. Governments create their own laws and apply them within a
delimited geographical space; thus, the territorial boundaries of nation-states
define the jurisdictional boundaries of different legal systems. The increasing importance of global social, economic, and political activity conducted in
a new medium has the potential to undermine the traditional relation between
physical location and effective legal jurisdiction. Johnson and Post (1997)
claimed that the rise of global computing networks breaks the link between
physical location and the power of governments to control behavior and thus
undermines the legitimacy of their attempts to enforce their rules in
cyberspace.

One example they give of the challenge cyberspace poses to traditional jurisprudence is the case of Minnesota, which has asserted it has criminal jurisdiction over online gambling even if the Web site is located out of state. Although the suit was clearly intended to shut down an online gambling business, what was alleged was false advertising and consumer fraud, not the violation of a state gambling law itself. On July 18, 1995, Hubert Humphrey III, the Attorney General of Minnesota, filed a consumer protection suit against Kerry Rogers, a U.S. citizen, and his company, Granite Gate Resorts, Inc. The suit alleged that an online ad for his proposed sports betting business in Belize, which claimed that such betting would be legal, constitutes false and misleading advertising in violation of the consumer protection laws of Minnesota (Cabot, 1998, chap. 10).

Another state attorney general, Jay Nixon of Missouri, also has been active in asserting the right of his state to restrict online gambling. In June 1997, he brought the first criminal indictment of an online gambling operation. Michael Simone and his Philadelphia-based Interactive Gaming and Communications Corporation were charged with operating an illegal gambling business that accepted bets from Missourians. The casino and sports book was located in Granada, and Interactive Gaming claimed that the players really "arrived" electronically to place their bets (McGuigan, 1997). Nixon has spoken of his fight against Internet gambling:

> [Such gambling is] not really different than our telemarketing fraud cases. . . . It would be illegal to bring a bunch of slot machines and set them up in a back room and invite your neighbors to gamble here in Missouri. The fact that it is done on a computer should not make it legal. We will continue to up the law enforcement ante until those that are profiting from this illegal operation get the message. (Brunker, 1997)

Instead of setting up offshore operations and claiming to be beyond the jurisdiction of the United States, other gambling interests have pushed at jurisdictional limits by going online on Indian tribal land. The Coeur d'Alene Indian tribe believes it has found a loophole in existing federal law that most assume already outlaws online gambling. They established the first online national lottery, called "US Lottery," in January 1998. The tribe operated a bingo operation on its lands in Worley, Idaho, and claimed that a provision of the Federal Indian Gaming Regulatory Act of 1988, which permits them to employ computers and telecommunications to operate noncasino gambling games, gives them the right to operate in cyberspace. The proceeds of the lottery were to go to the reservation for such things as education, health care, and environmental restoration.

The claim to legality is a key to success. Just as we have seen a recent explosion of casino gambling on tribal lands, it is predicted that if the Coeur d'Alene tribe succeeds in stretching the law, it will be followed by others. Despite the cover of federal law, the legality of the US Lottery has been challenged. Missouri Attorney General Jay Nixon filed a lawsuit against the lottery. He said, "It's wrong, it's illegal and we're going to fight it" (Weber, 1998). Howard Goldfrach, Vice President of UniStar Entertainment, which manages the business for the Coeur d'Alene tribe, replied rather sanguinely, "We think we're legal, so we're not particularly worried." Other states also have questioned the legality of the Coeur d'Alene lottery. According to Matt Ross, a spokesperson for the California Attorney General's office, Californians cannot legally participate in the US Lottery unless the Coeur d'Alene make a specific agreement with the state of California such as those that the state has reached with other tribes to permit online parimutuel betting (Swartz, 1998).

After a month of operation, the site had not been a particular success—attracting only about 5,000 players—but David Matheson, a member of the tribe and chief executive of its gambling operations, hoped that marketing efforts such as advertising on the lottery-results page of *USA Today*'s Web site would stimulate business. He assured the public that the tribe will persevere: "Our needs are great, so our innovation has to be great" (Weber, 1998). It remains to be seen whether they will win their legal battles with the courts and how successful they will be in the long run.

The reaction of a few Internet gambling operators to state challenges to their legality, as well as concern over federal law, has been to try to exclude U.S. citizens from using their sites. For example, Virtual Gaming Technologies, based in San Diego, does not permit U.S. residents to get the software necessary to gamble on its site (McGuigan, 1997). Although the threat of prosecution may scare some gambling promoters away from the U.S. market, many observers assert that ultimately the threat will be ineffective. Johnson and Post (1997) claimed that someone who is determined to access such sites can reconfigure his or her connection to make it appear that the communication comes from a different location.

Furthermore, they argued that the claim to have legal jurisdiction over activity in cyberspace because these activities entered a jurisdiction through the Internet, if generalized, can have sweeping unintended effects. If the laws of

Minnesota can apply to gambling on the Internet because gambling sites located outside of the state can be accessed from Minnesota, then potentially the rules of any local jurisdiction can be applied to any activity that that jurisdiction finds offensive. By extension, asserting such a right would seem to provide support for any sovereign nation to regulate the activities of U.S. companies operating according to U.S. law within the borders of the United States. Carried to an extreme, such a claim would support the doctrine that all activity in cyberspace is simultaneously subject to the jurisdiction of all territorial sovereignties (Johnson & Post, 1997).

However the legal and political arguments about applying U.S. law in cyberspace are eventually resolved, some Americans who want to run an online gambling site have tried to avoid the problem by moving offshore, where the action in Internet gambling is, where the laws are accommodating, and where the natives are friendly.

Enforcement in Cyberspace: Offshore

Despite a generally hostile climate among public officials in the United States to the prospect of unlimited gambling in cyberspace, there is no shortage of opportunities to gamble on the Internet. In fact, there has been a rapid growth in Internet gambling sites. As of April 1998, there were at least 140 sites, up from approximately 15 only a few years before. These sites provided a variety of gambling opportunities, including lotteries, bingo, sports betting, poker, and roulette. They use sophisticated multimedia techniques. Some virtual casinos try to make the bettor feel that he or she is part of the action, with a realistic background of electronically generated sounds of clinking glasses, clanking coins, laughter, and roulette wheels in action (Young, 1998).

Most of this increase in gambling activity online has not been conducted by businesses in the United States. Although U.S. citizens are a good percentage of online gambling customers, their activity has not contributed to American tax revenues. The U.S. government claims that operating an online gambling site in the United States is illegal. It is not, of course, that gambling per se is illegal, but, where it is legal, it is highly regulated. Gambling on the Internet is currently not one of the forms of gambling that is permitted.

American entrepreneurs eager to get into online gambling in a legal, or at least quasi-legal, way have tried to get around this problem by going offshore and removing themselves from the jurisdictions of U.S. courts. After a few brushes with U.S. authorities, a number of Internet gambling operators have determined that the United States is simply too hostile a place to carry on their business and have decided to set up elsewhere. A prime location is the Caribbean, where many small island nations have historically been much more accommodating to gambling.

Betting on sports in the United States is big business. Unfortunately, most of this business is illegal. In 1998, it was legal in only two states, Nevada and Oregon. A few technologically inclined American bookies have decided to travel to more hospitable climes. One of their favorite locations has been Antigua, whose prime minister, Lester Bird, is also Minister of Gaming. Antigua has created an economic Free Trade Zone in which bookies can take bets legally and be exempt from corporate taxes. However, the 21 online betting licensees must pay social security and educational taxes and hire local residents. They are also subject to unannounced government inspection ("Internet Gambling Booming in Caribbean," 1997).

Many of these bookies use Web sites to take bets. The customers first transfer money to offshore accounts. The bookies then give them toll-free numbers and personal identification numbers to access accounts and place bets. Customers also can access accounts online by using a password. Sports bookies, as well as other offshore companies, also operate online casinos with real-time interactive games, such as blackjack, poker, and slot machines (Pulley, 1998).

All this gambling activity is perfectly legal, according to the laws of Antigua. Vere Murphy, who is in charge of the Free Trade Zone, explains that gambling not only is permitted but is regulated and carefully supervised. Background checks are done on licensees, and plans are under way to set up testing of casino games of chance to ensure that they are fair ("Will They Fold 'Em?" 1998). In 1998, licenses cost $75,000 for telephone gambling operations and $100,000 for online companies. The reason fees were lower for telephone operations is because they employed more Antiguans. More than 200 local residents were employed by the sports bookies. The government reported that funds from licenses enabled them to open a computer training school that had 180 students. For the Antiguans, gambling has helped to stimulate the economy and reduce unemployment (Pulley, 1998). But, then again, it is a small country.

In late 1998, most gambling sites were located in the Caribbean and Central America, although there were others in Europe, South Africa, Australia, and New Zealand. The United States can do little to shut down gambling operations abroad, assuming, that is, that they are not run by U.S. citizens. If they are and are accepting wagers from the United States, actions by the federal government show a determination to make life very uncomfortable for Americans trying to evade U.S. laws if they reside in the United States.

Let us briefly examine the problem of enforcing U.S. laws in an international context. Lawyers make a distinction between territorial jurisdiction, in which a country may apply its laws to conduct and enforce them, and extraterritorial jurisdiction, in which it may apply its laws to conduct occurring outside its borders but must wait until the individual is within its territory to enforce them. The individual may enter voluntarily or be extradited by another nation.

A number of American gamblers have obtained licenses and set up Internet gambling businesses offshore in jurisdictions where such operations are legal, but they accept bets from U.S. citizens, which the United States claims is in violation of its law. The owners of the operation can set up a number of offshore corporations to make it difficult for law enforcement officials to discover them. Even if evidence of a crime is collected and individuals are identified, if those involved in running the casino or sports book choose to remain outside the territory of the United States, there is little that U.S. officials can do.

The United States could demand that the country sheltering them turn them over to the United States as fugitives from justice. Such requests usually depend on an extradition treaty, but there are two problems with them in this case. The United States does not have such treaties with all countries, and the suspects could be extradited only for crimes specifically covered by the treaty. The government could try to extradite its suspects under the doctrine of comity of nations, in which countries voluntarily surrender fugitives because of their sense of fundamental justice, but the United States rarely uses this method. Without an extradition treaty, it is unlikely that any country would extradite Internet gambling operators, especially in the case of those countries that have welcomed them in to set up shop.

If the federal government were really desperate, it could resort to kidnapping, as in the case of General Manuel Noriega of Panama, abducted and tried in the United States for violating our antiracketeering law. The U.S. government could apply diplomatic pressure to persuade other countries to turn over its Internet gamblers to the United States voluntarily or close down their operations (Cabot, 1998). Realistically, none of these options has much chance of success.

The federal government is waging a campaign against offshore online gambling operations that claim to be legal under the laws of the country where they are located. This crackdown represents a change in federal policy. In January 1998, a Justice Department spokesperson, John Russell, claimed that the federal government had no jurisdiction to prosecute such online gambling operations because "The offense has not been made on U.S. soil" (Freeling & Wiggins, 1998). In March 1998, the federal government filed a case against online gambling operations located offshore. This action was widely reported in the press. Both *The Wall Street Journal* and *The New York Times* covered the story as a case of the feds moving against "online sports betting operations" (the *Times*) and "internet gambling" (the *Journal*). The *Journal* article cited a news conference by Mary Jo White, the U.S. Attorney in New York, which disputed the claim of the industry that the United States lacks jurisdiction over offshore gambling sites: "It's a federal crime to use the Internet to conduct betting operations. You can't hide online and you can't hide offshore" (Quick & Starkman, 1998; Weiser, 1998).

Although the story was reported as a federal crackdown on Internet gambling, it is far from clear that the statute under which gambling operators were charged actually applies to the Internet or cyberspace. They were indicted for conspiracy to violate the Federal Wire Act (1961), which prohibits placing bets over interstate telephone lines. This law was written to prevent sports bookmakers from using the telephone to conduct their business. During a 7-month investigation, FBI undercover agents posed as customers and placed bets on college basketball games, the Super Bowl, and other sporting events. In all cases, bets were placed by telephone. In two cases, bets were placed both by telephone and on the Internet. Not one complaint relied only on online Internet activities to support the charges, though the government did try to equate Internet and telephone use. There is no question that running a bookie operation offshore and taking bets by telephone from the United States is illegal. In *United States v. Blair* (1995), the defendant was convicted for operating an illegal gambling business in the Dominican Republic that accepted bets from Americans using a toll-free number (Freeling & Wiggins, 1998).

If the sports betting operation is not actually taking wagers from bettors in the United States over the Internet but is using its Web site to advertise, post odds, or convey information, it would be difficult for the government to prove that it is violating the Wire Act. In addition, the Wire Act was drafted to close down sports bookmaking businesses; it is far from clear that the law applies to other types of online gambling such as Internet casinos. So far, the federal government must rely on antigambling statutes written before the creation of the Internet, which suffer from a variety of ambiguities and problems when applied to online gambling operations. To remedy these defects, legislation has been proposed to amend the Federal Wire Act.

Proposed Federal Legislation

In 1997, a concerted effort began to pass federal legislation to clear up the ambiguities in federal law and end Internet gambling. The Senate bill, introduced by Senator John Kyl (R-AZ) on March 19, 1997, attracted the most attention. The original bill grew out of recommendations of a working committee of the National Association of Attorneys General. The committee was chaired by Hubert Humphrey III (Minnesota), James Doyle (Wisconsin), and Dan Lungren (California). They concluded that their best strategy was to press for an amendment of the Federal Wire Act to ensure that all forms of Internet gambling would be prohibited, thus permitting prosecutors to obtain jurisdiction.

The attorneys general realized that their problem was whether they had authority, at the state level, over gambling on the Internet that crossed state lines. In pressing for new federal legislation to regulate gambling in cyberspace, they had historical experience on their side. Most of the federal laws regulating gambling were passed as newly developed types of communication media were used for gambling. Federal legislation to prohibit the use of the U.S. mails to advertise or conduct lotteries was passed shortly after the establishment of the federal postal system because the new mail system was quickly used by creative entrepreneurs to conduct national lotteries. Legislation prohibiting the advertising of lotteries on the radio came shortly after radio became a mass medium and was used to promote lotteries; this ban was extended to television after it became widely available (Cabot, 1998).

Existing federal legislation in respect to gambling was written before the most recent innovation in mass communication, the Internet. The federal law most applicable to cyberspace is the Federal Wire Act, which prohibits the use of interstate telephone lines to conduct a betting or wagering business. It was directed against bookies who used telephones to accept bets on sporting events and horse races, but it did not criminalize the placing of bets by individuals. The Kyl bill would expand the Federal Wire Act to cover all communications facilities, including the Internet. It also would extend the law to cover individual gamblers and interactive computer service companies. The bill would allow law enforcement officials to notify an Internet service provider (ISP) about gambling on one of its servers and request that it terminate service. The ISP would be protected from civil liability if it voluntarily terminated service. If it refused to do so, authorities could seek a court injunction. Thus, the ISP, in effect, would become an agent of government law enforcement. The original draft bill had a "Sense of the Senate" section, which asserted that the federal government has extraterritorial jurisdiction over wagering. This section was intended to handle problems of enforcement in the case of Internet gambling businesses that try to avoid U.S. jurisdiction by operating offshore. This provision later was replaced by a section that simply required the Secretary of State to start negotiating with foreign countries to draft treaties that would enforce the antigambling provisions of the law.

The established big-time casino industry supports a ban on Internet gambling—for now—as seen in the words of Frank Fahrenkopf, head of the American Gaming Association and chief spokesperson for the industry:

> We oppose Internet gambling now because the technology does not exist today that would regulate the industry—vetting the operators to be fit to run the business and allowing regulatory control and oversight by law enforcement. But in the long run, appropriate technology will be likely developed. Then the marketplace will take over. (Cabot, 1998)

There is no doubt that casino operators hope that the Internet marketplace of the future will be dominated by those who now dominate the industry, not the small upstart firms operating in legal limbo today.

Those in the horse racing industry feared that the modifications to the Federal Wire Act proposed by the Kyl bill would endanger them. Joe Hickey, president of the American Horse Council, the Washington-based lobbyist group for the industry, said, "There is no more important piece of legislation affecting the horse racing industry than this bill" ("Internet Gambling?" 1997). Hickey also reported that, as a good lobbyist, he attempted to influence the content of the bill:

> We have met with Senator Kyl and he has indicated that he does not wish to impact what the parimutuel industry is doing now. . . . But this is an extremely complicated area, both legally and technically, and we have to watch this legislation carefully. (American Horse Council, 1997)

The horse racing lobby managed to work out a compromise with Senator Kyl for intrastate rather than interstate gambling. In an interview with *The Congressional Quarterly,* Kyl announced a compromise that would allow off-track betting (OTB) or account wagering done by telephone or through an intranet that is not accessible to those on the Internet ("Will They Fold 'Em?" 1998).

The provision inserted as a result of this compromise allowed states to regulate Internet gambling within their own borders. This provision would do more than simply protect existing types of parimutuel betting. It would permit the horse racing industry to go online, albeit in a restricted way. The industry, in general, opposes any federal law that would preclude future efforts to legalize OTB on the Internet. Eight states now allow parimutuel wagering over the telephone, and they see the Internet as a natural extension of this form of betting (Clausing, 1997d).

There are those in the horse racing industry who see the potential for expansion in cyberspace, and with good reason. If OTB migrated from the telephone to the Internet, the betting experience would be enormously enhanced. As of now, someone who wishes to place an off-track bet has to buy a newspaper to see which horses are running and read up on their particular histories. Then he has to go to the OTB facility to receive current information on the race and the odds from a tote board. After analyzing the race, he places a bet at an interactive terminal, and, finally, he settles down to watch a televised broadcast of the race. This transaction involves costs above and beyond the bet itself, as well as a considerable expenditure of time and effort. All this just to place a bet on a horse. Consider the following glowing account of the potential of the Internet for improving the experience of OTB.

> With the Internet, he can simply log on, and go to one site to obtain all the handicapping information that was contained in the newspaper. With the click of a button, he can visit another site to find out which horse the top handicappers like in the race and check the chat room or a bulletin board to swap tips with fellow betters. After making his picks, he can then switch sites again, check the current odds on the tote board and make a bet with the track using his bank debit card. He could then watch the live simulcast of the race on his personal computer. In sum, the

Internet can replace several mediums of communication and make gambling transactions easier, faster, and cheaper. (Cabot, 1998, Introduction)

Not only would this be a good deal for the bettor, it would also be a good
deal for the horse racing industry. The Internet has the potential to entice
many more customers to horse race betting at no significant expense to the industry. The Internet would not create serious competition because the races
would be run anyway. Casino gambling on the Net, on the other hand, has the
potential to provide direct competition with bricks-and-mortar casinos. A
televised Internet version of a real-time casino game in Las Vegas would have
no advantage over one broadcast from Antigua. No one would care whether
an online slot machine video game was located on a server in a casino in At-
lantic City or Timbuktu.

The horse racing interests placed a provision in the Kyl bill that would exempt states that already have legalized gambling by wire, or would do so in
the future, from the general prohibition on wire and telephone gambling.
Senator Dianne Feinstein (D-CA) and other senators believed that this provision was necessary. Without it, the horse racing industry and its OTB system
would be prevented from going online or, perhaps, would be shut down entirely. The only debate about the bill that occurred in the full Senate Judiciary
Committee concerned this clause to protect the horse racing industry. It was
dropped because Senator Joseph Biden (D-DE) and Senator Jeff Sessions
(R-AL) successfully argued that it could be read to allow gambling by telephone (Reiter & Wellen, 1998). They thought the exemption was too broad.
The Judiciary Committee chairman, Senator Orrin Hatch (R-UT), urged the
committee to remove the provision for now, remarking that "those who have
been contacted by horse racing" should seek to find compromise language
before the vote in the full Senate. The provision was struck, and Senator
Feinstein cast the sole negative vote, citing the fact that "I'm obviously concerned about the horse racing industry" (Clausing, 1997d).

The Technology, Terrorism and Government Information Subcommittee
of the Senate Judiciary Committee, chaired by Senator Kyl, held a public
hearing in July 1997 before the bill went to the full Judiciary Committee and
heard from a number of supporters of the ban on Internet gambling. Senator
Kyl himself warned of the dangers of Internet gambling:

Anyone with a computer and a modem has access to a casino. And virtual casinos
make it easier for those with gambling addictions to sink deeper into debt and de-
spair because all they have to do is sit down and log on. (Clausing, 1997a)

Jeff Pash, executive vice president of the National Football League, cited the threat to America's children: "Because no one stands at the door to the virtual casino checking IDs, our children have the means to gamble on the family computer after school" (Clausing, 1997a). The National Association of Attorneys General was represented by its chairman, James Doyle, the Attorney General of Wisconsin. He cited a study that claimed that video gambling was "the crack cocaine of gambling" (Clausing, 1997a). He testified to the fact that it was now possible to gamble on hundreds of Internet sites and spoke of the danger of fraud and abuse: "But we don't know what's behind those cards and cherries, whether they're fair or whether they're being controlled by organized crime." In addition, to no doubt enliven his testimony, he gave a video demonstration of Internet gambling sites that included the Rolling Good Times service, which was taking bets on the chances of Kyl's gambling bill becoming law (Braun, 1997; Clausing, 1997a).

The National Coalition Against Legalized Gambling came out for the Kyl bill because they are opposed to gambling on moral and religious grounds. The American Horse Council was opposed, not, of course, because they are against gambling, but because, despite their efforts, the revised draft had the potential to exclude them from their piece of the action. The National Football League testified in favor of the bill, and the NCAA also lent its support. The reason that the NCAA gave for opposing online gambling is that "it threatens to undermine the integrity of sports contests while jeopardizing the welfare of the student-athlete and the intercollegiate athletic community" (Cabot, 1998, chap. 10). Both amateur and professional sports associations condemn betting on sports events, although one tends to wonder if the Super Bowl would be the Super Bowl or the NCAA basketball tournament would be "March madness" if Americans suddenly lost interest in betting on sporting events. The state attorneys general were in favor because the bill would give them the authority to bring indictments against online gamblers. They could carry out the mandate of their constituents as they see it; safeguard their citizens, including compulsive gamblers and children; and perhaps also protect the revenues of state-sanctioned legalized gambling from untaxed competition.

Senator Kyl was criticized for stacking the subcommittee hearing with supporters of his bill and rejecting all opponents' requests to be heard. Albert J. Angel, of the online gaming information company ICN Ltd. and a board member of the Interactive Services Association (ISA), complained, "It was a grandstand event where the other side never had an opportunity to be heard"

(Clausing, 1997a). Angel said that he and other officials of the ISA's Interactive Gaming Council (IGC) had asked to testify but had been told that there were only a limited number of slots reserved.

Who exactly is on the side that opposes the sweeping ban on Internet gambling? The most vocal group is undoubtedly the ISA. There are two very different reasons why the ISA opposed the Kyl bill. The ISA is a trade association that, for the past 15 years, represented the interactive industry as a whole. Its goal is to "grow the Internet into the consumer mass medium of the 21st century" (ISA Web site, n.d.). The ISA represents businesses such as interactive gaming, interactive marketing, interactive television and entertainment, and the like. It also represents ISPs. The Kyl bill had the potential to affect ISPs because it makes them part of the enforcing process. The bill gave law enforcement officials broad authority to go after individual gamblers, gambling businesses, and ISPs. The federal government may not be able to shut down gambling sites located abroad effectively. However, the Kyl bill would have permitted the authorities to seek injunctions that could force U.S. ISPs to block access to these gambling sites for U.S. citizens. In effect, this would have made ISPs responsible for policing the content of their sites. Kevin Mercuri, manager of counsels for the ISA, voiced his concern:

> This places an undue if not an impossible burden on ISPs to monitor their content to shut down sites. At the very best it is a logistical nightmare for an ISP because the technology is just not there. The fear, which is not that unreasonable, is that any official could shut down any site they don't like on the Web. (Clausing, 1997d)

He also complained that his group was shut out of the hearing. He did note that since the hearing, his group managed to influence the language of the bill a little. The revised version would give only U.S. and state attorneys general the right to take ISPs to court to try to shut down access to gambling sites. The original bill was much broader, because it gave this right to all federal, state, and local authorities (Clausing, 1997d).

In addition to ISPs, the ISA represented the IGC, the trade association created in late 1996 to promote online gambling, or, as they prefer to call it, the "global interactive gaming industry." The IGC opposes the Kyl bill. One might imagine that this group was composed of rugged free marketers who opposed the government messing around in cyberspace. This is not the case. They were not at all hostile to government interference; on the contrary, they welcomed it. Their ultimate intention was to bring the government in as an ally of gambling, not as an enemy. What they opposed is the attitude expressed by Senator Richard Bryan (D-NV), cosponsor of the bill with Senator Kyl. He maintained that because there is no effective way to regulate Internet gambling, the only responsible choice for Congress to make is to prohibit it (Braun, 1997; Lewis, 1997).

The IGC believed that there are actually two ways to regulate, one admittedly more effective than the other. The first is self-regulation, which they optimistically saw as a stepping stone to the second: full-fledged government regulation. The situation of the online gambling business is not typical of many types of businesses that may seek self-regulation. Rather than seeing self-regulation as a way of precluding government from stepping in, they saw it as a model for future international governmental regulation and supervision.

The basic problem for those wishing to set up a casino or other gambling business in cyberspace is the need to build consumer confidence. How are consumers to be sure that an online casino will actually pay the winners what it owes them, and how can they be certain that the odds are fair and the games are not rigged? It is also in their interest to eliminate or control the social evils perceived to be the direct consequences of online gambling, such as access by children and gambling addicts. This is necessary to promote the industry as good, clean fun and stave off moral reformers who would opt for prohibition.

In May 1997, the IGC unveiled a 10-point Industry Code of Conduct for global online gaming. This code covers such issues as regulatory compliance, accountability, consumer privacy, dispute resolution, and truth in advertising. The code requires that steps be taken to limit access to minors and that member firms implement procedures to identify and curtail compulsive gambling. The last canon of the code, titled "corporate citizenship," pledges that those who make money by the PC will also, in fact, be "PC": "IGC members will endeavor to design and implement their services in order that they preserve and protect environmental resources" and make sure "that the services are user friendly and generally accessible to the handicapped" (Interactive Gaming Council, 1997). We guess that it is reassuring to know that those in the gambling business are not simply cold-hearted operators but nice guys with a moral conscience who are sensitive to environmental issues and the handicapped.

The IGC, in collaborating with the ISA, is also developing a process for creating its own Code of Conduct seal that would appear on those sites pledged to adhere to the Code of Conduct. Anyone with a complaint or question about the site could click on the seal and get help from the ISA. They also intend to create their own regulatory authority that would impose the type of strict scrutiny and audits on Internet casinos and betting operations that are now placed on traditional casinos and parimutuel betting businesses.

The IGC has its own Web site, of course. The site outlines its general purposes and provides the visitor with a copy of the Code of Conduct and its press releases and policy statements. It also announced its backing of a grassroots campaign coordinated by another group against the Kyl bill. The IGC site had a link to the Internet Consumers Choice Coalition (ICCC) Web site (http://www.capweb.net/iccc/contact.morph), which included three sample letters to be addressed to a senator or representative. One sample is from an ISP speaking as a small-business person complaining of the high cost they would bear, as well objecting to becoming an agent of the federal government to police the Internet. The second is from a typical net citizen who says that the best way to deal with Internet gambling is to regulate it, not ban it, and objects to the fact that the bill "will create an internet police that can access my private and personal computer files without my permission." The third is from a fan of fantasy sports and "rotisserie" leagues, who fears the bill is so broad as to outlaw their innocent amusements (ICCC, 1997).

The ICCC is an alliance of organizations, including the American Civil Liberties Union, Americans for Tax Reform, Citizens for a Sound Economy, Competitive Enterprise Institute, the First Amendment Coalition for Expression, the U.S. Internet Council, and the ISA. What brings most of these groups together is opposition to government presence on the Internet. The ICCC sent a letter on October 8, 1997, to Senator Hatch, chairman of the Senate Judiciary Committee, requesting that the committee reject the bill. The letter was signed by a number of organizations, including the ISA. It argued that the committee should wait until they get more facts about online gambling, which would be available when the National Gambling Impact Commission reported the next year, and complained of the lack of opportunity for the opposition to voice their views in congressional hearings. They cited two significant areas of concern: (a) the bill entails content restriction and invasion of personal privacy on the Internet, and (b) the bill could negatively affect electronic commerce (ICCC, 1997).

In respect to the first concern, which they claim expressed their general "philosophy," they stated: "We oppose any effort by states to regulate content on the internet, a national and global communications medium that the Supreme Court has found to be especially valuable because of the breadth and diversity of the speech found there." The reference is to the Supreme Court decision that declared the Communications Decency Act unconstitutional. Thus, gambling is analogized to free speech, which is a bit of a stretch. Yet, the IGC and the ISA are not philosophically opposed to governmental regulation of Internet gambling.

As noted previously, the ISA has been developing a voluntary regulatory board that would, among other things, regulate the content of Internet gambling sites. Those opposed to Internet regulation ordinarily make a radical distinction between voluntary self-regulation, which is fine, and governmental regulation, which is an unwarranted intrusion. If there are problems in how netizens conduct themselves on the Internet, the preferred solution is to form associations to set their own rules and standards. The case of online gambling is interesting because the industry would actually prefer government regulation. Stanley Collesano, president of a firm that supplies software to the gambling industry and a cochair of the ISA committee trying to establish voluntary regulations, spoke of this project:

> There is an absolute vacuum right now of regulation. Right from the get go this has been perceived as a temporary fix. . . . This is industry's attempt to fill the vacuum until such time that we get an international or multinational body in place to regulate what is traditionally a regulated industry. (Clausing, 1997b)

The alliance of the online gambling interests with the antigovernment regulation, antitax groups, and the civil libertarians is a matter of convenience rather than conviction. There is no indication that professional gamblers trying to run legalized gambling operations have any philosophical opposition to paying taxes. Given the choice between legalized gambling on the Internet and paying taxes versus existing in quasi-legal limbo and fighting the federal government in court, there is no question they would opt for the former. If anything, paying taxes is one of their strong points in the mind of the public. The lure of new tax money has been one of the major incentives for the recent upsurge in legalized gambling. Nor are they opposed to government regulation of their industry. Those who are currently involved in online gambling are opposed to prohibition, not regulation; they could live with regulation because it would mean legalization.[2]

The coalition letter also argued that the Internet is an international phenomenon and that the Kyl bill would be a bad precedent for the growth of electronic commerce, because it "would attempt to segment the Internet—in effect placing an electronic wall around the United States—to 'protect us from ourselves' much like China and Singapore have tried to do" (ICCC, 1997). They raised the specter of multiple jurisdictions and saw the underlying issue as similar to the problem of Internet taxation, which we discussed in Chapter 6:

> The tendency toward patchwork regulation which S. 474 [the Kyl bill] would legitimize and the low thresholds required for establishing regulatory nexus will also only encourage the nation's 30,000 tax jurisdictions to press for taxes on local Internet access and commerce based on similarly low thresholds of nexus. (ICCC, 1997)

If you could regulate or block a gambling site that was located abroad simply because it was accessible to U.S. citizens, this would encourage all sorts of jurisdictions to claim that they could tax or possibly even regulate all Internet sites that do any business with citizens located within their own boundaries.

Obviously, there would be a problem if national or international commerce were subjected to innumerable small jurisdictions, each with different rules and each trying to get a piece of the action. A solution is to assert national sovereignty to facilitate national commerce. As we saw, this is what happened with the Internet tax moratorium. Because there is no international sovereign authority, on the international level the analogous strategy is to use international treaties. Another alternative is to have gambling regulated on the national level by different countries and simply live with a variety of different rules. Perhaps the gambling sites licensed and supervised by nations with some of the strictest regulations designed to ensure the honesty and integrity of the games will thrive in the marketplace. One never knows. Besides, it is one thing to oppose government regulation of cyberspace for speech and commerce in general, and quite another thing to refuse to make exceptions for activities that, for moral or prudent reasons, are thought to require such regulation.

There was also strong opposition to the original bill by fans of rotisserie fantasy sports leagues, who feared that their hobby would be prohibited. In these games, players draft their own roster of professional athletes in a particular sport and compile points based on their statistics. There are hundreds of Web sites that offer information and support to players and dozens that offer pay-to-play games. It is estimated that half a million people play some kind of fantasy sports game on the Net (Brunker, 1998a). The final version of the bill was modified so that it would not prohibit such games so long as the entry fees are not used to pay off bets. The final bill also included exemptions for state lotteries and OTB on horse or dog racing, as long as they are conducted on "closed-loop, subscriber-based" computer systems that ban out-of-state bettors and the general public.

Senator Larry Craig (R-ID) offered an amendment on the floor that would create an exemption for Indian tribes, but it was defeated by an 82-18 vote. Senator Kyl opposed it because it would create an enormous loophole that could be used by anyone with access to the Net. Kyl remarked, "It goes to any state and into any home and to any child" (Fram, 1998).

On July 23, 1998, the Kyl bill passed the Senate by a vote of 90-10. Although Senator Kyl was able to get his bill through the Senate by an overwhelming vote, similar legislation in the House got bogged down and never got out of committee. The House version of the bill, sponsored by Representative Robert Goodlatte (R-VA), differed in one important way from the Senate's. Although Kyl's bill would impose a ban on gambling on the Net by extending federal regulatory authority into cyberspace, the Goodlatte bill would extend the authority of the states by giving them a right to either permit or prohibit Internet gambling within their borders. Vincent Sollitto, a spokesperson for Kyl, said that the Senator found the direction the House bill was going unacceptable. Despite the general political support for controlling Internet gambling, the difference between the bills could have damaged the chance of either passing.

The House bill, however, got caught up in presidential impeachment politics. It went through the House Subcommittee on Crime and was referred to the House Judiciary Committee just about the time the Starr report was issued. The committee never got around to reviewing the bill. Some blamed the Lewinsky scandal for the death of the bill, but a spokesperson for Representative Goodlatte merely stated, "The clock ran out on us" (Brunker, 1998b). The whole issue finally died when the leadership decided not to add any type of gambling ban to the final massive budget bill, which contained a number of other bills related to the Internet. The fight is not yet over. Both Senator Kyl and Representative Goodlatte promised to reintroduce their respective bills in the 106th Congress, which would convene in February 1999.

The normalization of cyberspace means that many of the regulatory problems that beset government in the real world will also be encountered in cyberspace. The legal and political problems facing citizens and political leaders attempting to decide on the nature and amount of regulation in the offline world also must be faced in cyberspace. Activities like gambling, and commerce in general, have economic and social consequences whether they are conducted online or offline. Their existence generates political controversy, which mobilizes a variety of interests that perceive problems differently. Interests form shifting coalitions, and different coalitions offer different solutions. Many of these solutions entail some governmental presence in cyberspace simply because cyberspace is becoming more and more part of our everyday life.

Perhaps the most vexing problem raised by attempts to regulate cyberspace is jurisdictional. Most business is conducted within a nation's territory, yet once a Web site is put up on the Internet it is available to the entire world. This raises questions about which laws are to apply to Web transactions. Some argue that regulating the Web would be self-defeating because once one country applies its laws to businesses located outside its jurisdiction, what is to prevent other countries from doing the same? This could be a problem, but we must not forget that international commerce offline has coexisted with national sovereignties and conflicting rules and regulations for a long time. The problem of conflict of laws is nothing new. It may be more difficult to adjudicate issues arising from cross-border commercial activity in cyberspace, but we believe that it will be accomplished by the application of familiar legal principles, supplemented, where necessary, by new treaties.

As we have seen, another important aspect of the problem of Internet regulation is how to enforce regulations in cyberspace, and the problem of enforcement is not limited to regulatory issues. Once we accept the idea that the Internet cannot and should not remain immune from the ordinary jurisdiction of government, it becomes evident that government is being drawn into cyberspace to enforce an entire panoply of ordinary law. Establishing law and order and protecting netizens and businesses from online criminal activity is also part of the normalization of cyberspace. Thus, in the next chapter, we turn to the problem of policing cyberspace.

Notes

1. For example, Alan Stone offered the following definition of "regulation": "State-imposed limitation on the discretion that may be exercised by individuals or organizations, which is supported by the threat of sanction" (Stone, 1982, p. 10).

2. In fact, in testimony before the National Gambling Impact Study Commission in February 1999, after the Kyl bill had been defeated, they came out in favor of a comprehensive system of federal, state, and international regulation of online gambling ("Interactive Gaming Council Calls for Regulation," 1999).

8

Criminal Activity in Cyberspace and What to Do About It

Cyberspace has become too complex to exist as a self-contained and self-regulated territory divorced from state jurisdiction. Politicians have argued that governments cannot shirk their duty to examine the regulatory and tax implications of its large commercial sector, and, as seen in Chapters 6 and 7, the commercial sector has not been left to determine its fate through the process of intra-Net politics. Offline politics, both national and international, already affects the Net. Crucial debates about the future shape and direction of the Internet are not occurring primarily on the Net among netizens but in the traditional corridors of power, among bureaucrats and elected officials.

Most businesses in cyberspace would prefer that government leave them alone, but cyberspace needs government. As seen in Chapter 6, there is widespread recognition that government should provide an effective modernized legal infrastructure to facilitate online transactions. We saw that business also needs government to safeguard intellectual property, a form of property peculiarly at risk in cyberspace, and that protecting privacy online is an ongoing problem with which both business and government have wrestled. In Chapter 7, we explored the attempt of government to control Internet gambling, an industry that is highly regulated in real space but exists in legal limbo in cyberspace. In this chapter, we examine another significant role that government has come to play in cyberspace: establishing and enforcing law and order. Just as the intra-Net ideal of self-regulation in practice has proved inadequate to generate the complex rules necessary to serve electronic commerce, so self-regulation alone cannot enforce law and order in cyberspace.

Self-regulation and voluntary enforcement always will be ineffective in preventing sophisticated cybercrime. Flaming, shunning, and kicking people off listservs are no longer adequate sanctions. They cannot compare with the power of government to close down illegal operations and to fine and imprison lawbreakers. A medium of transnational mass communications and commerce cannot be run like a series of informal private clubs very loosely supervised by a shadowy group of self-selected activists and technocrats. The Internet has become the domain of legitimate business professionals, but it also harbors professional criminals, and this, in turn, draws the attention of professional law enforcement agencies. The day of the amateur is over in cyberspace. This, too, is a consequence of the normalization of life in cyberspace.

The analysis of Internet crime that we undertake in this chapter illustrates the perceived need for government intervention, and, in concrete ways, it demonstrates the importance of politics that affects the Net. The police and other government agents seeking to enforce rules and regulations have entered cyberspace, and there is every indication that they are now a permanent feature of life online. Furthermore, it is not enough for government to protect law-abiding netizens from ordinary criminal activity. It is necessary to protect cyberspace itself from terrorists and others with a political agenda. As governments have come to identify cyberspace as a critical component of the economic infrastructure, new justifications are being forged for their further presence in cyberspace.

Crime in Cyberspace

In discussions of criminal activities in cyberspace, commentators employ a variety of terms, such as "cybercrime," "crime on the Internet," and "computer-related crime." All these involve the use of computers to commit illegal acts, but it is useful to distinguish two types of criminal activity that can involve the Internet. We refer to one as *network* crime and to the other as *computer* crime (Ghosh, 1997).[1]

By network crime, we mean a variety of criminal activities that use the Internet but do not entail corrupting or breaking into computers. These crimes either have people, rather than computers, as the victims or entail so-called victimless crimes, such as gambling and pornography. Many types of crimes committed in the real world have their analogues in cyberspace. Crimes such as consumer fraud, stock manipulation, and various types of sexual predation have drawn the attention of law enforcement officials. These crimes are not amenable to technical fixes, but they do reflect the fact that cyberspace has come increasingly to resemble life offline, complete with a host of scammers, crooks, and predators. Not only have such crimes attracted ordinary law enforcement officials, but government agencies that have developed expertise in fighting particular types of crimes have followed the crooks into cyberspace.

Computer crime may or may not employ the Internet in its commission, but, unlike network crime, it has a computer as its object. People are victims of computer crime, but only to the extent that they are involved with the computer that is the object of the criminal activity. Computer crimes involve such things as hacking into computers to steal data, spreading computer viruses, and disabling computer systems. As the Internet comes to play a crucial role in the infrastructure of many nations, the protection of computers from various types of assaults has become a major concern of both industry and government. A technical solution to computer crimes is always superior to traditional law enforcement because, if it works, it becomes impossible to commit the crime again—at least in the same way. Because of the serious threat that such crime poses, government is increasingly interested in working with private industry and academics to devise ways to prevent it. Fighting computer crime, like fighting network crime, also can involve traditional government law enforcement agencies that attempt to track down, identify, and prosecute such criminals.

Network Crime

The Internet has provided a new arena for a variety of traditional crimes, attracting the attention of law enforcement officials as well as organizations dedicated to crime prevention. Many of the types of crimes committed in cyberspace are variations of familiar forms of ordinary criminal activity, but

retooling on the part of law enforcement is often necessary to pursue criminals who employ the Internet in the commission of the crimes.

Using computers and the Internet to break into other computers is a
well-known and well-reported phenomenon, but creative crooks also have
been caught using computers and the Internet to help them break into houses.
One such crime was not particularly high-tech, but it did involve the Internet.
In Ottawa, Canada, two men were arrested by the local police with the aid of
specialized services of the computer crimes section of the Royal Canadian
Mounted Police (RCMP). The men were accused of shopping for used computers either online or in classified ads in newspapers and then contacting the
owners by email and asking when they would be home. When the men received an email reply that no one would be home, they burglarized the houses.
In this case, the Internet was used for one of its fundamental purposes, the exchange of information. It would be hard to imagine a technical software or
hardware fix that would prevent criminals from gathering such information
from consenting adults (Larocque, 1997).

The Canadian thieves used the Internet to commit a crime offline, but the
great majority of network crimes are actually committed online. The Internet
has become home to countless forms of electronic commerce. The tremendous explosion of the online population has attracted its share of predators,
who see cyberspace as an opportunity to make a quick—and illegal—buck. A
variety of government agencies see it as their job to protect consumers
against a host of fraudulent schemes, some fairly new and some simply old
schemes that have migrated to a new place populated by tens of millions of
potential victims. Government agents do not simply respond to complaints
from those who have been caught by an online fraud. In the United States, a
growing network of federal and state organizations, often acting in cooperation with private consumer protection groups, now actively police
cyberspace looking for scams and deceptive ads (Wolf & Shorr, 1997).

From the point of view of law enforcement officials, much of the Internet
is already regulated, and government agents do not require new laws to autho-
rize them to enter the jurisdiction of cyberspace. From the government's
point of view, conduct that violates the law is prohibited whatever the medium, whether it is print, telephone, television, or networked computer.
Sellers online must comply with fraud, truth-in-advertising, and other regulations that apply to sales offline.

The Federal Trade Commission (FTC) has not hesitated to enforce its regulations. The FTC started its investigations of Internet fraud in 1994 and has

been dealing with an ever-growing number of complaints since. It has brought enforcement actions against a number of firms that have made unsubstantiated claims in their Internet advertising (Wolf & Shorr, 1997). It also has gone out looking for violators. On one "surf day" in March 1997, organized by the FTC and the North American Securities Administrators Association, investigators found 215 suspicious Web sites. These sites were issued a warning, and a number of them subsequently were removed ("FTC Cracks Down on Online Scams," 1997). The agency has prosecuted 35 alleged Internet scams. According to Jodie Bernstein, Director of the FTC's Bureau of Consumer Protection, many of the Internet investigations conducted by the FTC have relied on techniques and expertise that were developed in the course of investigating telephone and direct-mail fraud:

> Some people make a little too much of the fancy nature of the Net. A lot are just old-fashioned scams, and [the criminals] have real names, real addresses and telephone numbers and they want their money. . . . Always follow the money. That basic premise still holds. (Bencivenga, 1998)

In 1998, the FTC had more than 300 attorneys and investigators trained in Internet surveillance. There was a special surveillance team composed of about 24 members searching indexing services, Web sites, newsgroups, chat rooms, and email boxes for scams (Bencivenga, 1998).

The FTC has carried out campaigns on the Web to make consumers more aware of the potential for fraud. In an ingenious undertaking to raise public awareness of the dangers of taking Web pages at face value, the FTC set up 11 Web sites that offer get-rich-quick schemes. Each looked authentic and included glowing testimonials. When the visitors worked their way into the site, they encountered an FTC fraud warning. According to Eileen Harrington, associate director of the FTC's Consumer Protection Bureau, most of what they encounter online is not really new, just simply repackaged versions of familiar frauds, such as pyramid schemes. "What is new, and striking, is the size of the potential market and the relative ease, low cost, and speed with which a scam can be perpetrated" (Glave, 1998a).

The FTC also has been instrumental in publicizing the dangers of unsolicited commercial email, better known as "spam." On July 14, 1998, the FTC released its "dirty dozen" list of spam scams. According to the FTC's Jodie Bernstein, this list is "a tip-off to a rip-off." The FTC arrived at its list by soliciting consumers to send them their spam. They received more than 250,000 pieces of spam, which they organized into a searchable database. Not only did they identify targets for law enforcement action, but they also realized that many of the spammers who were making deceptive claims were simply imitating others. The Commission felt that many of them probably did not know that they were violating state and federal laws against deceptive advertising. They sent letters to more than 1,000 spammers identified in their database, warning them that the FTC was watching. Most of these cases concerned chain letters by email. They even received a few responses thanking them for the warning that they were in potential violation of the law. The dirty dozen included business opportunity scams, get-rich-quick schemes, get-something-free scams that require sending in money for memberships, making money by sending bulk email, chain letters, work-at-home schemes, health and diet scams, investment opportunities, cable descrambler kits, guaranteed loans on easy terms, credit repair scams, and vacation prize promotions. The FTC is continuing to monitor fraudulent email and urges the public to send them their junk email because they are probably the only ones who actually want it (Bernstein, 1998).

The Securities and Exchange Commission (SEC) has gone after sellers of unregistered securities on the Internet actively. It also has stopped trading in stocks that have been the object of online "pump and dump" schemes, in which the owners of thinly traded stocks heavily promote them online, thus encouraging unwary investors to buy the stock and drive up the price. They then sell all their shares at the artificially inflated price, leaving the suckers holding the bag. As an aid to enforcement, the SEC also posts investor alerts on its Web site (http://www.sec.gov) and encourages investors to contact them. As the SEC says on its Web site, "If you believe that you have been defrauded by a broker-dealer, an investment adviser or any other person or entity (in which a security is involved), we want to know about it, especially if it relates to the Internet." It also provides an online form for registering complaints. Such reports are crucial for the agency to carry out its enforcement mission because "inquiries and complaints from the general public are the primary sources of leads for detecting law violations in securities transactions" (SEC Web site). The Commodities Futures Trading Commission has a site that similarly informs the public about violations, notes that the general public is an important source of information necessary to develop its cases against violators, and actively solicits such information (http://www.cftc.gov).

The Internet has been a boon to swindlers touting a great variety of fraudulent investment schemes. No longer do they have to resort to making several hundred cold telephone calls a day to potential victims. With the tremendous increase in the number of people online, the opportunity to commit stock fraud also has increased. According to Jupiter Communications, of the 30 million households now online, almost a third use the Internet for doing research and investing in securities. In the old days, the favored method for scamming people was to make cold calls to potential victims. Now, they can simply send out email or set up their own Web page filled with detailed reports on the supposed benefits of getting in on the ground floor of a company with great prospects that no one has ever heard of before. The Internet offers a cheap and simple way to contact millions of investors (Brooker, 1998).

The SEC established an online investor hotline in 1996 and has since received about 100 complaints a day and has been filing new charges on the average of once a month. In August 1998, the SEC created an Office of Internet Enforcement, known as the "Cyberforce," which consists of more than 100 specially trained attorneys who disguise themselves as ordinary investors and surf the Internet looking for fraudulent get-rich schemes. Each member of the team goes online for an hour or two a week looking for "telltale signs, things like 'guaranteed return' and 'safe as a CD,' " said John Stark, the head of the Cyberforce. "Fraud on the Internet can be passed very efficiently. . . . We are continuously scanning message boards, chat rooms, and other postings on the Net to get a break on these people" (Bencivenga, 1998; Mukherjee, 1998b). Stark also spends time working with his counterparts at the state level. State regulators have begun to go onto the Internet looking for securities fraud, although they complain about being underfunded, and they often lack jurisdiction to prosecute cases (Wirth, 1998; Woody, 1998).

Although the SEC claims that the antifraud sections of the Securities Exchange Act of 1934 and current SEC rules are sufficient for them to go after Internet fraud, policing the Internet is no easy task. Despite the best efforts of state and federal regulators, there is no evidence that securities fraud on the Internet has been brought under control, and new variations on old scams are constantly emerging. Some regulators hope that technical solutions will develop to aid in their surveillance of the Internet, envisaging new search engine software using artificial intelligence that will troll the Net looking for scams 24 hours a day. Whatever the future holds in store, more government effort at both the state and federal level will be needed to cope with an expanded volume of Internet securities fraud.

Although government agencies discover online fraud through their own initiative and complaints from the public, they often act on complaints gath-

ered by private watchdog groups. One of the most prominent is the National
Fraud Information Center (NFIC), a division of the National Consumers
League, founded in 1899 as America's first nonprofit consumer protection
group. The NFIC was formed in 1992 to fight telemarketing fraud. The center
saw itself as improving the enforcement capabilities of federal and state
agencies. In 1996, the National Consumers League decided to expand the efforts of the NFIC beyond telemarketing to protect consumers in cyberspace.
It created an NFIC Web site and the Internet Fraud Watch project. The site
provides tips on how to avoid scams, but, importantly, it also collects fraud
reports through its online forms. These reports are entered into the NFIC
database and uploaded daily to the fraud database maintained by the FTC and
the National Association of Attorneys General. The system also automatically faxes these consumer reports to any of more than 160 law enforcement
agencies, according to criteria that match the agency's interest, to alert law
enforcement agencies to possible fraud and to provide them with information
about potential witnesses (Grant, 1998; Thibodeau, 1998; Worth, 1998a).[2]

The National Consumers League list, presented in a Senate hearing, illustrates the types of fraudulent schemes that have been reported on the Internet:

Top Ten Subjects of Reports to Internet Fraud Watch 1997

1. Web Auctions. Items bid for but never delivered by the sellers, value of items inflated, shills suspected of driving up bids, prices hiked after highest bids accepted.
2. Internet Services. Charges for services that were supposedly free, payment for
   online and Internet services that were never provided or falsely represented.
3. General Merchandise. Sales of everything from T-shirts to toys, calendars to col-
   lectibles, goods never delivered or not as advertised.
4. Computer Equipment/Software. Sales of computer products that were never delivered or misrepresented.
5. Pyramids/Multilevel Marketing. Schemes in which any profits were made from
   recruiting others, not from sales of goods or services to the end-users.
6. Business Opportunities/Franchises. Empty promises of big profits with little or
   no work by investing in prepackaged businesses or franchise operations.
7. Work-at-Home Plans. Materials and equipment sold with false promise of payment for piece work preformed at home.
8. Credit Card Issuing. False promises of credit cards to people with bad credit histories on payment of up-front fees.
9. Prizes/Sweepstakes. Requests for up-front fees to claim winnings that were
   never awarded.

10. Book Sales. Genealogies, self-help improvement books, and other publications that were never delivered or misrepresented. (Grant, 1998)

What most of these scams have in common is that sellers who are unknown make false claims about the goods or services that are offered and require payment in advance from unwary consumers. In 1999, the National Consumers League reported that from 1997 to 1999, there was a sixfold increase in consumer complaints about online fraud. Web auction fraud not only remained the most reported type of fraud but accounted for two out of three complaints ("Net Fraud Complaints Jump Sixfold," 1999).

Some of the most serious consumer frauds involve financial services. Although there are thousands of Web sites offering financial services of one sort or another, not all of them are legal. There are a disturbing number that hawk schemes involving tax evasion. Many ordinary folks have received unsolicited email advertising such opportunities, and many others have used the Internet to seek ways to avoid the tax man. Many of these schemes incorporate fraudulent offshore trusts. The most basic of these involves a company that offers to set up an offshore trust for a fee. The consumer transfers assets to the trust, thus supposedly avoiding all taxes on income derived from the use of these assets. Sometimes, these companies do not set up the trust and simply abscond with the funds, or they do set them up but designate themselves as beneficiaries. When the consumer transfers ownership of the assets to the trust, the company becomes the new owner, and the assets are also lost. Even if the trust is set up, and the consumer is able to transfer ownership and retain control, so long as the consumer derives use from the assets, he or she still owes taxes, according to the Internal Revenue Service. In other words, even if the company does what it says it will do (for a fee), the tax evasion scheme still will not work. There are a number of variations on this basic scheme involving more elaborate ploys using offshore trusts to evade taxes (McKee, 1998).

There is an interesting political twist to some of these schemes. Scam artists have discovered that not only can they market their schemes to the average gullible investors, but they also can tailor their appeal to vulnerable citizens who are open to extreme right-wing ideological arguments. Web sites of this sort go way beyond touting the cleverness and profitability of their investment schemes; they start off with several pages of legalistic rhetoric designed to prove that the U.S. government really has no constitutional right to levy taxes on its citizens. They make patriotic appeals to the original Constitution, often dropping references to such *cause célèbre* of the extreme right as Waco and Ruby Ridge. According to Internet Fraud Watch, these scam artists usually do not believe in the ideology, but they know that right-wing extremists can be easy targets for schemes promising to protect their assets from their "criminal" government (McKee, 1998).

Although the FTC has extensive experience in the area of consumer fraud on the Internet, it admits that one case astonished even them. Jodie Bernstein of the FTC remarked: "Just when you think you have seen it all, someone tries to scam consumers by passing themselves off as a champion of consumer protection" (Wolffe, 1998). An advertisement appeared on the Internet that offered, for only $6,000, a chance to open your own local franchise of a fictional body called the U.S. Consumer Protection Agency. For their investment, franchise holders would receive training, licensing, certification, and support services. They would make money by recruiting local businesses and charging them $149 and an annual fee of $250. According to the promotional material, a small agency could generate an annual income of $303,240 based on the "real" track record of an existing franchise. The FTC applied for a permanent injunction against the franchise seller for falsely representing his franchise as a government agency and acting illegally under franchise rules by failing to provide prospective franchisees with full and accurate disclosure documents. Imitation may be the sincerest form of flattery, but in this case, the government was not amused (Wolffe, 1998).

Consumers are not the only victims of fraud in cyberspace; merchants have lost money through false credit card charges. Unlike retail customers, who do not have to pay for unauthorized purchases on their credit cards, businesses are not offered the same degree of protection by banking laws. Sellers of downloadable goods, those who sell bits rather than atoms, have more problems with dishonest customers than do those who sell physical products. Steve Mott, the former senior vice president of electronic commerce for MasterCard International, estimated in 1998 that between 20% and 40% of the charges for downloads were fraudulent. Fraud involving the sale of physical goods via the Internet is less common because criminals are more likely to be caught when goods are delivered through the mails. Merchants are trying to reduce the amount of fraud by adopting fraud-screening techniques similar to those used by catalog sellers, and the credit card associations predict the widespread use of even more sophisticated security systems for online charges in the near future (Crockett, 1998).

Another area of growing concern to law enforcement agencies has been the sale and promotion of various types of drugs, dietary supplements, and medical devices. Health agencies have run across numerous offers for experimental and unproven drugs on the Internet.

To an American, it may come as a surprise to discover the products that can be sold legally on the Net. Businesses dealing in controlled substances exist on the Web, though they are very careful about the destination of their shipments. The firm Amazing Nature of Nijmehen, the Netherlands, sells marijuana seeds and hallucinogenic mushrooms on the Internet, both of which are perfectly legal in the Netherlands if sold in small quantities. The owner, Henk van Velthooven, said, "We try to keep strictly to the rules, because I think if I sold illegal things to the United States, I would soon be out of business" (Crockett, 1998).

The Food and Drug Administration (FDA) has on occasion stepped in to enforce American regulations on the Internet. Contraceptive Technologies Inc. of Bogota, Colombia, was selling do-it-yourself abortion and sterilization kits online. In June 1997, the FDA moved against them on the grounds that the products were dangerous when used by a customer without the direct supervision of a physician. The company's ISP, Rapidsite Inc. of Boca Raton, Florida, decided to remove the advertisements for Contraceptive Technologies on the grounds that they violated U.S. laws and thus breached the company's contract. In this case, it was fairly easy for the FDA to apply pressure to the company's ISP because it was located in the United States. The FDA has little leverage on foreign ISPs. Dwight Rawls of the FDA's Office of Criminal Investigations stated that in the case of ISPs located outside the United States, the FDA notifies the country of origin or attempts to stop shipments of drugs from entering the United States. The FDA also has cracked down on Internet sales of two unapproved drugs, gamma-hydroxybutyric acid, a steroid-like drug, and laetrile, an unproven treatment for cancer (Lu, 1998).

The newest problem relating to drug sales on the Internet concerns the anti-impotence drug Viagra. In California, state health officials investigated an online pharmacy because customers were ordering Viagra and other legal but restricted drugs on the Internet. Medical officials around the country are concerned with Web sites that offer drugs for sale but require that the customer only fill out a short questionnaire and submit a credit card number. This procedure apparently avoids the requirement that such drugs be dispensed only by prescription after consultation with a physician. Mike Takano, a spokesperson for Performance Drugs, one such online business in Colorado, denied that the company was doing anything illegal: "This kind of falls into the frontier. It's in uncharted waters, there are no real statutes for or against it." At the very least, such companies are skirting the law, and if they continue to get away with it, undoubtedly there will be increased enforcement efforts and calls for legislation to deal with the problem ("Illegal Drug Sales Flourish in Cyberspace," 1998).

Because online criminal activity is considered by government agencies to be an extension of ordinary criminal activity, agencies that have had experience with those crimes offline are prone to follow their quarries into cyberspace. Without knowing a bit about the history of law enforcement, it would sometimes be difficult to predict which of the many and often competing government agencies would develop expertise in fighting crime in cyberspace. For example, one of the most active governmental agencies fighting child pornography online is the U.S. Customs Service.

Before the creation of the Web, child pornography consisted primarily of magazines, photographs, and videotapes. Because the overwhelming amount of this form of pornography was, and is, created outside of the United States, the U.S. Customs Service developed expertise in discovering and seizing such material at the borders.

In 1990, the Customs Service executed its first search warrant against a computer bulletin board that they suspected was distributing child pornography. According to Glenn Nick, a senior special agent of the U.S. Customs Service's International Child Pornography Investigation and Coordination Center, "We identified the BBS [bulletin board service] overseas, went in with the Danish authorities, and tracked them back to users in the U.S." Success in that case led to a number of other arrests and convictions in the early 1990s. Because computers are now the most common way child pornography is distributed, this experience established the Customs Service as experts in investigating computer-related child pornography (Littman, 1997).

The Customs Service has invested significant resources in bringing to justice those responsible for online child pornography. In 1997, the agency trained 80 agents in how to conduct Internet investigations and hoped to use this expertise to pursue other forms of online criminality. Despite its track record, the Customs Service shares its jurisdiction over child pornography with other agencies. The FBI also plays a major role in investigating child pornography cases in cyberspace (Littman, 1997).

Ordinarily, a citizen is subject only to the surveillance of the police of his or her own national law enforcement agencies, and crossing a border means subjecting yourself to another set of police officials who are responsible for activity in the new jurisdiction. Though our discussion has focused on American efforts to deal with network crime, one of the consequences of the fact that cyberspace has no frontiers is that going online potentially subjects you to the surveillance of law enforcement officials from any and every land-based jurisdiction.

An article in the *Technological Crime Bulletin,* published by the Communication Unit of the RCMP's Public Affairs and Information Directorate, describes how to use the DejaNews search engine, which covers newsgroups, to investigate and gather evidence for child pornography cases and other types of Internet crime. It suggests that the investigator use the search engine to seek out topics associated with Internet crime. Conducting a search using the terms "child" and "image" will bring up a list of newsgroups where the two subjects are discussed, so the investigator can examine and identify suspicious postings. The article, though, does warn that there are many limitations to this type of cyber-investigation technique. It concludes that, though privacy issues are involved and new privacy laws may make this technique less effective in the future, "For the time being, however, DejaNews provides a simple, quick, desktop tool to help build profiles of suspected newsgroup criminals" (Duncan, 1997).

An investigation of suspicious newsgroup postings will turn up others besides Canadian citizens, though presumably the RCMP would only be interested in following up leads involving Canadians. The fact that cyberspace has no borders means that online surveillance by governments and law enforcement officials is not limited to their national borders. One of the significant differences between doing something online and doing the same thing in real space is that many, many more interested parties may be watching.

Computer Crime

Once upon a time, there was little overt government presence in cyberspace, and there are still many netizens who would prefer to have government stay as far away as possible. Cyberspace seemed to be a territory without the need for a state, especially a state with its own police powers and law enforcement officials. Yet, could cyberspace really get along without cyberpolice? How were people to be protected against those with criminal intent? Did all who passed through the portal of a modem suddenly become virtuous? Computer users always have been aware of the darker side of human nature, but the problem of criminality was, for the most part, perceived as technical and therefore amenable to technical solutions. Designers of operating systems had always been concerned about the security of the data on computers. Since the early days of computing in the 1950s, there have been attacks against computers, but until the 1980s, most of the attacks were perpetrated by those who had an actual account on a computer or access to someone who had one (Denning, 1998). Computer crime consisted mostly of theft or vandalism and entailed some form of trespass. The bad guys got into your machine and messed with your data.

The natural way to deal with attempts to break into computer systems was to build bigger and better locks. The computer community saw the threat of computer crime primarily as a problem of computer security. The rise of the Internet compounded the security problem. Criminals exploited new vulnerabilities, and techies developed new countermeasures. Ideally, if the techies could make computer systems perfectly secure and ensure absolute privacy, and users could be assured that they would have absolute control of their data, then there would be little to worry about. Of course, perfect security is an illusion, but it provided a direction and focus for combating computer crime.

Attacks on computers have become much more sophisticated since the early days. Then, authorized users would access data stored on computers for amusement—or more nefarious purposes—and outsiders would get into systems by guessing at passwords. Attacks now involve much more complex methods of gaining access to individual computers and computer systems. Dorothy Denning (1998), an expert on computer security policy, has created eight general categories of attacks on computers:

1. Eavesdropping and Packet Sniffing. Eavesdropping is the passive interception of network traffic and is performed on the Internet by means of a type of program called a "packet sniffer," which monitors network packets flowing through a computer.
2. Snooping and Downloading. The object of this method of attack is the same as packet sniffing—acquiring information. Rather than intercepting traffic on the Net, the intruder browses through documents and data stored on a computer, downloading what he wants to his own computer. Snooping can be perfectly innocent, but it also can involve everything from stealing credit card numbers, to extortion, to commercial and political espionage.

3. Tampering or Data Diddling. This method entails making modifications to the data or software stored on a computer. It is often used for fraud or embezzlement, though it also can be used for amusement or political protest. Hackers have been known to break into Web sites and alter their content. For example, the Department of Justice home page was once replaced by a page containing a swastika and a nude photograph.

In July 1998, in what may be the largest mass home page attack ever, more than 300 Web sites were victimized. Hackers, part of groups called "Milw0rm" and "Ashtray Lumberjacks," broke into the database of the British ISP EasySpace. They then hijacked the sites in the database and redirected users to their own protest page, which contained an antinuclear message:

> This mass-takeover goes out to all the people out there who want to see peace in this world. Personally, we are fed up of all this nuclear shit and we have started to expose the truth about the countries who are "exploiting" their nuclear power. . . . The world governments and Law Enforcement agencies are trying to find us. . . . WHY? All we are doing is putting forward a message that you people are taking yourselfs [sic] and your countries along the path to SELF-DESTRUCTION. (Shit Must Stop Web site, n.d.)

This was not the first time the hacker group Milw0rm made news. In June 1998, as a protest against the Indian nuclear testing program, they hacked into the computers of the Bhabba Atomic Research Center and downloaded 5 MB of information. They also hacked into a Turkish nuclear facility and stole internal email, memos, and correspondence (Hu, 1998).

4. Spoofing. This occurs when attackers impersonate other users or computers, often as a means of carrying on other types of attacks, such as snooping or tampering. Another significant type of spoofing is forging email. The most common type of forged email is illicit messages to newsgroups, but it also can be used for more serious criminal purposes. Larry Ellison, the CEO of Oracle Systems, was victimized when a former employee used a forged email to assist her in her sexual harassment case against him. She was found guilty of perjury and falsification of evidence (Ferrell, 1997; Pimental, 1997).

5. Jamming or Flooding. This method of attack involves disabling computers by tying up the system resources. Attackers could use up all the available memory or cause a network to shut down by flooding it with so much traffic that no else can use it.

An example of using this technique for political purposes is a new form of radical political action called "electronic civil disobedience." Advocates distinguish it from terrorism, which they see as anonymous and destructive attacks on computer systems. Their intent is to flood a Web site to cause a disruption and make a political point. The intent of their action, as described by proponents of electronic civil disobedience Stefan Wray and Ricardo Dominguez, is to create a form of electronic theater, increase solidarity, and spread their political message. Wray argued that the possibility for new forms of radical political protest now exists because of "a convergence of the computerized activist and the politicized hacker" (Wray, 1998). Unlike older forms of protest in which students engage in a sit-in at the office of a university president or a local consulate, according to Dominguez, the Internet allows for "a virtual sit-in on a mass, global level" (Kaplan, 1998a; Wray, 1998).

Dominguez and two colleagues created a Web site called "Flood Net," which appears on the Internet only at an appointed time to avoid detection. It automatically connects a Web surfer to a selected target site and hits that site's reload button every 7 seconds. If thousands of surfers connect with Flood Net during a particular day, it could disable the site. Wray and Dominguez tested it by posting messages in the Zapatista networks in early April, calling for sympathizers with the cause to link to Flood Net on April 10, 1998. The target was the Web site of Ernesto Zedillo, the President of Mexico. According to Dominguez, 8,141 people around the world connected to Flood Net that day, which disrupted the target site. The Mexican Embassy in Washington acknowledged that there was a protest against government Web sites on April 10, but stated that "there wasn't much negative impact" (Kaplan, 1998a).

Mark D. Rasch, an Internet consultant who formerly led the Justice Department's computer crime force, said in an interview with *The New York Times* that participating in electronic sit-ins is not without risk. Those taking part may be in violation of federal law—18 U.S.C. § 1030(a)(5)(A)—that makes it a crime to distribute a program, software code, or command with the intent to cause damage to a Web site. Rasch said, "These guys are at risk. It may be an electronic sit-in, but people get arrested at sit-ins" (Kaplan, 1998a).

6. Injecting Malicious Code. This usually involves injecting a self-replicating computer virus into a system by means of a floppy disk or through a computer network. Viruses are usually created and introduced into the computer world by those who enjoy doing malicious mischief and demonstrating their programming skills, but, on occasion, viruses have been used for direct criminal purposes. In the United Kingdom, a type of virus known as a "cryptovirus" was intentionally introduced into several business computer systems as part of an extortion scheme. A cryptovirus does not destroy computer data; rather, it encrypts it, making it impossible to use. The perpetrators attempted to extort money from businesses by demanding payment for the decryption key.

7. Exploiting Flaws in Design, Implementation, or Operation. This is a catch-all category for the types of defects in computer system design that can be exploited by attackers to access or sabotage a system and its files. Over the years, thousands of security holes have been found in the software supporting the Internet, and new ones are often discovered when the old ones are plugged.

8. Cracking Passwords, Codes, and Keys. This method involves discovering passwords and keys through systematic attacks, including the use of computer programs specifically designed to discover computer passwords.

Because of the proliferation of techniques for attacking computers, computer crime has attracted the attention of the government. There are three areas of concern, each with its own rationale, that have led government law enforcement agencies to enter cyberspace: (a) attacks on private computers, (b) attacks on government computers, and (c) potential enemy and terrorist attacks on the national infrastructure.

One of the primary functions of government is to protect citizens and private organizations against criminal activities. The results of a 1998 study of computer security conducted by the Computer Security Institute and the FBI's International Crime Squad found a substantial increase in security breaches. Out of more than 500 private organizations, 64% reported such a breach, compared to 48% the year before and 22% the year before that. Although more than half the respondents could not quantify their monetary losses, the 42% who could estimated them at $136 million. One important finding of the study was that about 50% of the companies suspected that the break-ins were the result of industrial espionage by their competitors. The figure rose to 72% among high-tech firms (Richtel, 1998b). Whatever the motivation for computer break-ins, they can cause substantial harm to individuals and businesses and are thus the concern of both federal and state law enforcement officials.

Attacks on government computers involve both civilian and military computer systems. Governments identify with the public interest, so they take breaches of security very seriously. Because of the classified nature of much of the information about break-ins in the Department of Defense (DOD) and other military computer systems, it is difficult to get an accurate account of the number and seriousness of the penetrations. In testimony before a Senate panel in June 1998, an official of the new National Infrastructure Protection Center (NIPC) set up by the FBI said that there had been a half dozen substantial attacks on U.S. government computer systems since February. When asked by Senator Dianne Feinstein if they involved military computers at the DOD, the official chose not to respond directly but noted that the DOD was always a target. In late February 1998, both the Pentagon and the FBI investigated several instances of successful attempts to obtain information from military computers. This was at the same time that U.S. forces were being mobilized for possible military strikes against Iraq (" 'Substantial' Cyber Attacks Reported," 1998).[3] Because national defense is one of the primary reasons for the existence of government in the first place, it is very easy to justify governments taking countermeasures against attacks on military computer systems.

The issue of infrastructure defense requires a broader look at the role the Internet plays within national life. The Internet is one of the critical components of our contemporary infrastructure, and protecting this infrastructure is a matter of national security. Rhetoric about the dangers of computer crime has escalated. Attacking computers is said to pose the danger of massive collapse of crucial sectors of the American infrastructure. This is much more serious than individual economic and personal damage, or even the sabotage of government and military computers. What is at stake is the very survival of our modern industrial society.

In 1996, President Clinton established a President's Commission on Critical Infrastructure Protection (PCCIP). After broad consultation with government and private sector experts on security issues, the PCCIP submitted its report to the White House in October 1997. It portrayed the United States as increasingly vulnerable to disruption by means of assaults on computer networks that play a vital role in the national life:

> The United States is in the midst of a tremendous cultural change—a change that affects every aspect of our lives. The cyber dimension promotes accelerated reliance on our infrastructures and offers access to them from all over the world, blurring traditional boundaries and jurisdictions. National defense is not just about government anymore, and economic security is not just about business. The critical infrastructures are central to our national defense and our economic power, and we must lay the foundations for their future security on a new form of cooperation between the private sector and the federal government. (PCCIP, 1997)

The report also pointed out that there are now millions of people who have the skills to carry out attacks on computer-dependent infrastructures. Modern systems are complex and interdependent, and substantial disruptions to basic services can come from many places. It listed a wide variety of threats: "insiders" who use authorized access for unauthorized purposes; recreational hackers; criminals attacking computers for financial gain; industrial espionage; terrorists who could use disruptive tactics to affect U.S. policy; nations that wish to acquire sensitive information for economic, political, or military purposes; and agents of information warfare carrying out intentional cyber-attacks to disrupt military operations or economic activity (PCCIP, 1997). All types of current and potential computer security breaches are perceived as a potential danger to national security.

Traditionally, lines have been drawn between military and civilian sectors and between foreign and domestic arenas that are at the core of our approach to security issues. These lines have long been seen as part of our constitutional fabric intended to restrain abuses of government power. The PCCIP argued that such distinctions are irrelevant in cyberspace:

> Because our military and private infrastructures are becoming less and less separate, because the threats are harder to differentiate as from local criminals or foreign powers, and because the techniques of protection, mitigation, and restoration are largely the same, we conclude that responsibility for infrastructure protection and assurance can no longer be delegated on the basis of who the attacker is or where the attack originates. Rather, the responsibility should be shared cooperatively among all the players. (PCCIP, 1997)

The PCCIP recommended a broad array of programs for education, research, and cooperation between the public and private sectors ("Commission Calls for a Defensive Posture," 1997; Staten, 1997).[4]

Although its current recommendations are fairly benign, this report provides one of the broadest rationales for bringing government into cyberspace. Government agencies already have moved ahead on implementation. The report also has received attacks from critics who question the reality of the danger and the motives of the government, and who fear that it potentially threatens freedom in cyberspace.

The FBI has created the NIPC in response to the PCCIP's findings. In an interview, Michael Vatis, the new deputy assistant director of NIPC, explained that the center will have an Analysis and Warning section that will gather information from private industry and foreign intelligence; a Watch and Warning unit to receive and respond to reports of unauthorized intrusions; and a Training, Administration, and Outreach unit for education. He noted that they have an interagency mandate and looked forward to a significant role for the government in cooperation with the private sector:

> We expect contributions from the Department of Defense, the intelligence community, and state and local law enforcement. But the private sector is on the forefront of these intrusions. They're in the best position to implement the security measures that will prevent these crimes. (Reiter, 1998)

In her speech in February 1998 at the Lawrence Livermore National Laboratory announcing the creation of the new NIPC, Attorney General Janet Reno assured the American public that they have nothing to worry about: "We must not and we will not sacrifice any constitutional protections" (Kesten, 1998).

One of the strongest arguments for government presence in cyberspace is the threat of cyber-terrorists attacking the United States. The PCCIP report alluded to the terrorist bombings of U.S. forces in Saudi Arabia, the World Trade Center in New York City, and the federal building in Oklahoma City and explained that the President was inspired to create the commission "in recognition of comparable threats to our national infrastructures." Yet, critics have questioned the claim that there is a significant threat of cyber-terrorism. Despite all the press reports about break-ins in sensitive DOD computers, there seems very little evidence of it. On May 4, 1998, U.S. intelligence officials reported what they asserted was the first known attack by a terrorist group on a country's computer system. This incident happened in 1997 and involved an attempt by ethnic Tamil guerrillas to swamp Sri Lankan embassies with email.[5] An official said that the incident "did cause us to sit up and take notice" because it was the first computer assault conducted by a known terrorist organization and a possible "portent of worse things to come" ("First Cyberterrorist Attack Reported by U.S.," 1998). Although this was not a terribly sophisticated or dangerous act of terrorism, more dangerous terrorist activities may lay ahead.

Not all experts agree with the official American position on the severity of the cyber-terrorism threat. Peter Sommer, a senior research fellow at the London School of Economics, said that the dangers from computer terrorism and cyber-warfare are mainly theoretical and that penetrating and manipulating computer networks pose awesome problems for the would-be attacker:

> To hit a major network you need to know how it works, what back-up there is, you need a great deal of information. You would need to infiltrate someone into the organization. They would need to know how to write code and introduce it onto the system. I'm not saying it cannot be done, but for quick effect it may be better just to place a bomb. ("Fear of Cyber-Terrorism," 1998)

In response to a question about hackers getting into Pentagon computers, Sommer pointed out that the U.S. military has more than 2 million computers, most of which are insignificant, and most secure systems are isolated.

> These big hacker cases—sixteen year olds could get in, not because they were clever but persistent and basic standards of security were very poor indeed. Lots of money will be spent on curing this problem and nearly all of it will be wasted on

sexy sounding projects. What you really need is auditors to check systems. ("Fear of Cyber-Terrorism," 1998)

President Clinton's call for safeguarding American computer systems because of our increasing vulnerability to cyber-attacks was also treated with skepticism by Dr. Ross Anderson of Cambridge University's computer laboratory: "Information warfare seems to be a marketing exercise rather than anything else. It's the computer security community trying to increase sales to the [U.S.] Federal government" ("Fear of Cyber-Terrorism," 1998).[6]

Other experts come to very different conclusions. An essay by Clark Staten, the Senior Analyst of the Emergency Response and Research Institute, states that their own analysts as well as many other experts, both in and out of government, all agree on three things:

> 1) Americans, from all sectors of society, can expect to be dramatically affected by both the promise and potential disasters associated with the rapidly progressing computerization of our society. 2) Protection of our essential infrastructure should be among the highest of our future priorities. . . . 3) Were we to collectively lose a number of these critical services [such as information and communications, banking and finance, energy, and transportation] in a short period of time, our current society could be expected to sink into something resembling "chaos" in a very short period of time. . . . It would appear incumbent on us all, in both the public and private sectors, to begin to work together to plan, prevent, and protect our critical infrastructure. We must develop a system of "electronic civil defense," before it is too late. If we don't do so, the quality of our lives and America's prosperity are at stake. (Staten, 1997)

It remains to be seen how this debate will be resolved, but the concerns raised by computer crime and cyber-terrorism will be a source of increasing political debate in the years to come. They raise profound issues of national security and of the proper role of government in cyberspace.

Conclusion

The normalization of cyberspace has meant that some of the more unpleasant aspects of ordinary reality have become entrenched on the Internet. It should come as no surprise that not all of the millions of new netizens in cyberspace are law-abiding citizens. Criminal activity is part of life in the real world and, as cyberspace grows to resemble the real world, crime has become a part of it. There is a great variety of crime online, but so far, at least, it is not possible to commit violent bodily assaults on the Internet. But cyberspace does carry its own risks. Although it is possible to protect business, netizens, and the Internet itself from certain types of crime through improved security techniques, much of it can be dealt with only by law enforcement agencies, and different types of crime must be fought by different enforcement agencies, as in the real world. Consequently, cyberspace crime has attracted the attention of a wide variety of governmental agencies, and policing the Internet has become a routine activity.

The Internet also has become a vital part of the infrastructure of modern industrial society. It is argued that cyberspace itself, not just those who choose to enter it, needs to be safeguarded against terrorist attacks. This could prove to be a new subject for political controversy because of its potential for providing a new and powerful rationale for government action that could greatly affect life in cyberspace.

We believe that our normalization thesis has enabled us to deflate the more revolutionary expectations that have surrounded the development of the Internet. Indeed, money and politics have domesticated the Web. Market forces largely will shape the fate of cyberspace, and politics, especially politics conducted offline in the real world, will play an important role in molding its future. We are more skeptical about claims that political uses of the Net will have a comparable effect on the real world. In the next and concluding chapter, we consider further implications of our normalization thesis and evaluate the political implications of the Internet for democracy and of democracy for the Internet.

Notes

1. This terminology is adapted from Interpol terminology. Interpol divides digital crime into three areas: (a) computer crime, which includes piracy, data theft, and computer break-ins; (b) computer-related crime, which is mainly bank fraud and pornography; and (c) network crime, the use of the Internet for transactions that are already illegal, such as child pornography or to aid illegal activity, such as the drug trade, customs evasion, and money laundering (Ghosh, 1997).

2. The Better Business Bureau (BBB) also collects information about consumer fraud online, but it forwards the complaint to a local BBB bureau based on the zip code of the company or to its national office. Because the BBB basically tries to resolve disputes, only in the most extreme cases does it refer its file on a company to a law enforcement agency (http://www.bbb.org).

3. An extensive literature on computers and national security issues, updated monthly and online, is available at ttp://www.infowar.com/.

4. To have a chance of succeeding, such cooperative efforts must overcome industry suspicion caused by years of disputes about security issues and the use of encryption. See also Staten (1997).

5. As we noted in Chapter 1, in 1977 the Sri Lankan government set up its own Web site to counter what it considered distorted propaganda by the Tamils on their Web site.

6. For a scholarly account that takes seriously the dangers of information warfare and cyber-terrorism, see Arquilla and Ronfeldt (1998).

9

Democracy and Cyberspace

A Peek Into the Future

This book has scrutinized many claims for the transformative power of the Internet. This chapter sorts out the reasonable predictions from the unreasonable. The Internet provides a fascinating new field for political scientists to study, but judgment must be applied in evaluating the claims that have been made for it. The Net will affect our daily lives, but we cannot endorse claims about the future that amount to little more than wishful thinking. Our scholarly conscience and experience forbid us from accepting all the hype about the great potential for the Internet to change our very being. Although both of us read science fiction on occasion, neither of us writes it.

When we began our forays into the politics of cyberspace in 1994, the territory really was unsettled. Although technical standards had been established for email and for the various Nets that connected to the Internet backbone, the power of the World Wide Web had barely been recognized, and Netscape Navigator, the commercially developed browser that would unleash that power, had yet to be released. Even though the U.S. government had subsidized development and use of the Internet, public access was disproportionately limited to those connected with institutions of higher learning, research organizations, governmental units, and those who worked for or with private organizations that underwrote access for their employees and associates. Proprietary networks such as America Online and CompuServe also offered some Internet access to subscribers, notably email, but they emphasized their own user-friendly sources and services, not the abstruse features of the Internet.

Many aspects of the early Internet made it an elitist medium. Those with access tended to be better off financially and better educated than their fellow citizens. Even though enthusiasts like Rheingold (1993) foresaw opportunities for a wide variety of virtual communities to establish themselves in cyberspace, the Internet was not friendly toward new users. Instructions for invocation of the required commands were scattered among fugitive documents, and not all commands were standardized. Although each virtual community could develop its own rules for governing its network, those who connected to the Internet also were expected to follow a set of norms called "netiquette." Aside from the rule that precluded conducting commercial transactions via the government-sponsored backbone, rules of netiquette were loosely defined. Self-selected groups made up of technologically sophisticated "old hands" enforced the rules, strictly or indifferently, and sometimes capriciously (Seabrook, 1994; Wiener, 1994).[1]

That technological elite may still hold sway over Usenet and some other network domains. But their rule has shrunk to virtual insignificance for most of today's Web users. Interactions among commercial domains far exceed other transactions over the Internet. Users now need only a modicum of technological skills to access the Net, and millions of novices have entered cyberspace with hardly a concern for netiquette. Politics within the Net no longer has primacy. Users are far more affected by and concerned about politics that affects the Net. Real-world governments, as opposed to virtual ones, increasingly impose the rules. Their attention has turned to cyberspace because the major interests of the real world, most of them commercial, have joined the WWW. As the Web facilitates the routine conduct of business and the exchange of information over the Internet on a worldwide basis, demands for rules and regulations arise, and governments respond. Politics that affects the Net comes to the fore.

Because those who use the Internet are by no means passive or indifferent to government policy, they, too, respond to demands for rules and regulations. Although most of the interests that conduct substantial amounts of business over the Internet have contact with governments in the real world, they also can make political uses of the Internet to extend or enhance their efforts to influence government policy. These uses can include electoral activity, petition drives, email letter-writing campaigns, fund-raising, information-sharing, and organizational activities to enhance the effectiveness of political activities in the real world. The effectiveness of such political uses of the Net remains to be demonstrated, but they are growing in number, and they appear of more salience to most users than politics within the Net.

How the Net Will Not
Contribute to Democracy

We expect that the Internet will foster democracy in the long run but not in the way utopians have trumpeted. It will influence politics and democratic government, but before we can focus on which changes are likely, we must be clear about which are not. It is unlikely that there will be a massive increase in political participation because of the Internet. There has been a tremendous increase in the number of people now on the Net, but there is no indication that their presence will inaugurate a new era in mass politics. The Internet has become a mass medium, but the numbers tallied by those who estimate the growth of the Internet have not been translated into comparable growth in political participation.

The Net is a new means of participating in politics because it provides new conduits for the expression of public opinion. The future undoubtedly will bring some form of voting online. It may provide instant public feedback about the events of the day, but it is unlikely to lead to the triumph of popular sovereignty and direct democracy.

The old Rousseauian dream of direct democracy in which all the citizens assemble at one time to participate directly in the great process of democratic decision making now seems a possibility. It seems that modern technology can overcome the limits of physical space. Why could the great assembly of the people not be held in cyberspace, the General Will be articulated, and the government become a true servant of the people? The idea that the modern nation-state could be transformed into the functional equivalent of a small ancient city-state or be reborn as a New England town meeting with its citizens imbued with civic virtue through the miracle of modern technology is truly utopian.

However, even if direct democracy were a good idea—and there are many reasons to believe that it is not better than representative democracy—it simply will not happen. Direct democracy is not appropriate for a complex industrial or postindustrial society. The unity, equality, and devotion to the public good, which are the prerequisites for a successful participatory democracy, according to traditional democratic theory, are not present. Public policy issues are too complicated and citizens too distracted to devote the time and effort to public affairs that such a society would require. To be sure, if public affairs were becoming less complex, then the Internet would be a potent force for direct democracy. Although it could be argued that history does show the growth of democracy as a long-term secular trend, this simply means that more societies are adopting the Western model of representative government with competitive political parties, the rule of law, and the like. The world is indeed becoming more democratic, but there is no evidence that existing democracies are metamorphosing into a new form of direct democracy based on significant increases in the quantity and quality of political participation. The changes that the Internet will bring to modern democracies will be important, but hardly revolutionary.

Another radical democratic vision sees the Internet as empowering the powerless by providing them with a new voice and leverage that will shift power away from entrenched economic interests. In the past, democratic power, the power of numbers, has been used to redistribute resources and opportunities formerly monopolized by elites. Many have seen the Internet as a way to combat elite domination. Even if the Net will not initiate a new golden age of direct democratic participation, at least it could be used to magnify the power of the powerless. More concretely, some believe that the democratic process in advanced societies could be invigorated if the minor parties of today used the Internet to get their message of hope and change across to the broad mass of the citizenry. Unfortunately, there is little evidence to support that belief. The access of marginal movements to a new and powerful medium of mass communication has not led them to make significant headway in the real world. The problem seems to lie more in the message than in the medium. In any case, the evidence shows that those who have been powerful in the past—the established organizations, the wealthy, and the privileged—are moving into cyberspace and taking their advantages with them.[2]

Whatever new exposure minor parties and movements have gotten by entering cyberspace has yet to be translated into real-world shifts of power and resources (Margolis, Resnick, & Lu, 1997; Margolis, Resnick, & Wolfe, 1999; Roper, 1998). Most Net surfers today pay little attention to the radical fringe in cyberspace. If one or more new radical parties emerge into prominence in the twenty-first century, no doubt they, or their ancestors, will have been on the Web. However, it is doubtful that the Internet will have been directly responsible for their rise to prominence. Almost certainly, no significant shift in power from the haves to the have-nots will occur simply because the have-nots are able to exploit the democratic potential of the Internet. Indeed, the evidence reviewed in Chapters 3, 4, and 5 indicates that the parties, interests, news media, bureaucracies, and public officials who dominate politics in the real world have become more adept at exploiting the Web for political purposes than have their real-world rivals who lie outside the mainstream.

The Internet also will not create the global village, at least in any meaningful political sense. True, cyberspace is a realm without borders. People using a computer equipped with a modem, a browser, and Internet access can contact Web sites without regard to their location around the globe. Indeed, while users click and follow hotlinks, unless they carefully observe the URL, they often find it hard to tell where in the world they have landed. Marvelous though this is, people and computers are located in real space, and real space is divided into national sovereignties. The Internet undoubtedly creates new difficulties for nation-states asserting their sovereign authority, but the aspects of the Internet that now evade national jurisdictions are unlikely to be the foundations for a worldwide erosion of the power of the nation-state. There are many processes connected with international economic trends that lead some observers to claim that the days of the nation-state are doomed, but we doubt that it will cease to be the dominant form of organized political life in our lifetimes or those of our children.

The Internet will further those trends that have made it more difficult for nations to control what flows across their borders. Certainly, they can no longer so easily police what their citizens see and think. If nations wish to participate in the modern world, they must accept the inevitable invasion of their space by ideas, attitudes, and lifestyles that they might otherwise prefer to keep at bay. It will be more difficult to run a closed society and still benefit from the fruits of modern technology, but that is a long way from having a world without borders. As we have pointed out in Chapters 6, 7, and 8, the Internet poses new difficulties for the fight against international crime and for regulating international trade, but none of these difficulties is insurmountable. Nation-states have been around for a long time, and they possess deep reservoirs of power and legitimacy. The Internet presents challenges to them, but in our judgment, nation-states will meet the challenges and incorporate solutions within the existing structures of governance.

How the Net Will
Contribute to Democracy

Some pundits look to a newly energized wired citizenry to spread democracy. Although it is true that the Internet can be used as a tool for democratic participation, it also has great potential to stimulate economic development and create wealth. A modern telecommunication infrastructure is a great aid to economic development, and the Internet is becoming a crucial component of that infrastructure. Economic development, in turn, promotes and stabilizes democratic regimes. Ironically, it may be the commercial aspect of cyberspace, its ability to connect individuals and businesses to each other for commercial purposes, that will have a more profound effect on the increase and stabilization of democratic regimes than its ability to nurture online political life.

We believe that a more mundane but ultimately more powerful effect of the Internet holds out a greater chance of fostering democracy. The Internet will help to spread democracy, but not because more people will conduct more of their politics online. Rather, as we enter an age in which information will be at the center of new forms of economic wealth, the Net will facilitate the spread of that wealth. Areas of the world lacking old-fashioned sources of wealth rooted in natural resources, such as vast tracts of arable land or scarce minerals, can now compete with nations more abundantly endowed. As the world as a whole becomes increasingly information-rich, this richness will have profound effects on many nations that are now both poor and governed despotically. Because the information spread via the Internet will contribute to general world economic wealth, and because economic wealth facilitates the rise of democratic government, the Internet will contribute to the spread of democracy.

The Internet also will help dissident groups in authoritarian societies. The Net adds to the technological arsenal of the communications revolution, whose weapons, such as the fax and the cell phone, already have breached national barriers to the flow of information. During the days of the Cold War, Western governments invested millions in short-wave radio to beam information behind the so-called Iron Curtain, and Communist governments spent millions jamming the signals. With these new types of decentralized technological innovations—the Net being but the latest and most powerful—it is difficult for an authoritarian regime to monopolize the sources of public information.

In the industrialized democracies of the developed world, which already have the rule of law and a tradition of free speech, the extra freedom provided by the Internet will do little to change democracy and spread democratic values. Its real radical political potential lies in the less-developed areas of the world. The liberating aspect of criticism directed at repressive regimes will help spread democracy, but only in countries where the ordinary means of public dissent are stifled.

Governments in the developed world now have a very visible presence in cyberspace. Elected officials have their own Web sites and email addresses, and so do agencies at all levels of government. We can clearly document this change, but its exact significance for the future of democratic politics is not clear. The greatly increased presence of government agencies online is an achievement. Although it represents a genuine effort on the part of government officials to provide better service and to bring government closer to the people, it represents no significant increase in citizen participation in public policy development (see Chapter 5).

Democratic government should be responsive to the will of the people, but there are two levels of responsiveness. The first is responsiveness to policy initiatives. Citizens in a democracy expect their government to pass laws, adopt new regulations, and create new instruments to solve pressing problems. Sometimes they demand that government stop doing what they perceive to be harmful. They might want government to lower taxes and to balance the budget, to intervene abroad or to bring the troops home. The second type is responsiveness to how government implements its existing policies. Citizens who claim benefits from government want the process made simpler. Citizens want easy access to government information. They also want the government to make it easy to fill out forms, file reports, and do what the government requires of them in their everyday lives. In short, they want to reduce the transaction costs of interacting with government.

For many, the Internet promises increased responsiveness to citizens' policy initiatives. Email and Web pages enable citizens to wage campaigns for change in new ways. The Internet makes it easier to organize, to bring pressure on legislators and government officials, and to make them aware of what citizens want. Yet, despite the advantages, so far there is little evidence that initiatives organized through the Internet to have government adopt significant new policies or alter existing ones have been successful (Gurak, 1997). No doubt in the future, efforts to lobby government via the Internet will become more sophisticated and more successful, but this process is essentially an extension of ordinary democratic politics. Some public policies will change because some always change. There will probably be online activity crucial to these changes in particular cases, but a systematic increase in governmental responsiveness to policy initiatives due to political activity on the Internet seems unlikely.

The argument for the Internet bringing about an increase in responsiveness in the second sense, implementing government policies, is much stronger. Most of the increased presence of government in cyberspace is an attempt to be responsive to citizens as clients and customers. The Internet provides new ways for government to interface with citizens. Many of the advantages that advocates of electronic commerce cite for doing business online also apply to government. Government Web sites are up 24 hours a day. Citizens do not have to waste time visiting government offices or trying to contact employees by phone. They can access the information they need whenever they want. The day is fast approaching when many of the routine interactions between government and citizen—such as applying for permits, requesting forms, paying taxes, and even voting—will be conducted online. Thanks to the Internet, government in the future will be more responsive, more efficient, and less bureaucratic.

Paradoxically, one of the hardest things to predict is whether the Internet will improve the quality of democracy by creating a more informed citizenry. We say paradoxically, because it seems obvious that because the Internet provides instant and almost cost-free information, it should enable the ordinary citizen to be fully informed about all relevant policy areas. Citizens also can follow government activity in ways that never were possible in the past. Will the dream of an enlightened citizenry finally be realized? We remain skeptical—not about the Internet as a source of information, but about the predilection of ordinary citizens to use it to better inform themselves about public issues. To be sure, the Net is now and will continue to be a boon to those who already have an active and sustained interest in public affairs, but there is little evidence that the Internet by itself will increase the attentive public.

Inequalities in Cyberspace

Unequal access to the Internet is a topic of concern to those who see it as a necessary tool for participating in social and economic life in the coming century, as well as those who conceive of it as vital to a more meaningful democracy. Many policymakers believe that universal access is a goal we should vigorously pursue. Vice President Al Gore requested a recent U.S. government study of who has access to modern telecommunications facilities to further the administration's goal of connecting all Americans to the information infrastructure. The National Telecommunications and Information Administration (1998) issued the report *Falling Through the Net II* and based it on Census Bureau data compiled in October 1997. It is the second such report; the first was based on data collected in 1994. These reports give a picture of how Americans of different types are connected to the telecommunication infrastructure by cross-tabulating information gathered according to variables such as income, race, age, education, and geographic categories. The report documents a digital divide between the haves and have-nots of American society. It is clear from the data that the overall growth of computer ownership and use have been distributed unevenly.

Income and race appear to make a difference. The disparity between higher and lower income groups in ownership of computers has increased since 1994. The gap between households earning $10,000 to $14,000 and those earning $50,000 to $74,999 grew from 38.2 percentage points in 1994 to 47.7 percentage points in 1997. In 1997, the difference in PC ownership between white and black households was 21.5%, nearly a 5-point increase from the 16.8% difference reported in 1994. Similarly, there has been an increase in the gap between white and Hispanic households from 14.8 percentage points in 1994 to 21.4 points in 1997. Among the least connected are the traditional have-nots of American society: the rural poor, rural and central city minorities, and female-headed households (National Telecommunications and Information Administration, 1998).[3]

How significant is this digital gap? The report argues that policies should focus on segments of the population that are not wired; these are the people who could most use the Internet for finding jobs, housing, or other services. Because it will take time for those people to get connected at home, policymakers should ensure that schools, libraries, and other community centers provide access to computers and the Internet. In their "Net Equity" study of levels of access among different segments of the population, Moss and Mitra (1998) reached similar conclusions. They argued that the current subscription-driven model of Internet access may never be able to provide access for all. They believe that, for the impoverished, libraries, schools, and community centers "may be the *primary* Internet access channels" (Moss & Mitra, 1998).

Despite these arguments, the picture of a future in which the affluent and privileged in America will have access to the Internet at home at their leisure and the poor have to trudge to a public library or a community center seems a bit overdrawn. The need for public provision of Internet access may be only temporary. Just as time and the market erased, for all practical purposes, the gap that once existed between those with access to television and those without it, so there will come a day in the not too distant future when basic Net access also will be affordable to practically anyone who wants it, at least in advanced industrial countries.

It would be naive to assume that current trends can be projected into the future—that the gap between the digital haves and have-nots will necessarily widen or remain the same. The price of computers is dropping rapidly. At this time, a well-equipped computer and modem for connecting to the Internet costs roughly the same as a large-screen television set. For even less money, you can buy a box that attaches to a TV set to provide Internet access. As computer prices drop and a variety of new ways to connect to the Internet become commonplace, we can project a narrowing of the digital gap, at least to the extent that it is caused by lack of household financial resources. It is not implausible to think that in the fairly near future, Internet appliances at home will be almost as ubiquitous as telephones and television sets are today. The achievement of universal Internet access will come not because it fills the need that government experts and academic pundits have identified—its practical use being to provide information for those needing jobs, housing, and services—but because it will become a cheap source of entertainment and communication.

The digital gap between the haves and have-nots in the United States pales when access rates in the United States are compared to those in underdeveloped countries. In 1998, the United States had 27.8% of the population online, compared to 0.49% for India, 0.08% for China, and even smaller percentages for much of Africa. Only 3.6% of the entire world was online (NUA Internet Surveys). Although the economics of Internet access looks favorable for the have-nots of advanced industrial societies, even a relatively inexpensive Internet appliance would be an unaffordable luxury for much of the world's population. And even if they could afford the hardware, the telecommunications infrastructure would still be a barrier. Many countries and telecommunications suffer from slow speed and high price. For example, in Egypt, the highest speed connections are 256 kilobits per second; in Senegal the highest are 64 kilobits. A phone line can cost more than $1,000 to install, and the wait may be 2 years or more (Spangler, 1998). New modes of connecting to the Internet that do not depend on old-fashioned copper wires are emerging, but they are spreading slowly in the Third World.

The United States is pledged to take some action to reduce the international digital gap. On November 11, 1998, Ira Magaziner, who was then the Clinton administration's Internet czar, announced at a U.N. trade and investment conference in France that the United States was adopting an initiative to help poor countries get online. He said that developing countries "in our view have a responsibility to participate and to make it a major priority to try to bring this new information age throughout the globe" ("U.S. Plans Program to Help Poor Countries Onto Internet," 1998). According to an official administration memorandum, the initiative is going to be rather modest. The Secretary of State is directed to cooperate with relevant U.S. agencies and multilateral organizations to initiate a program to accelerate the spread of the Internet and electronic commerce to developing countries:

> This shall include a demonstration of successful models for development in a small number of interested countries and should highlight and create incentives for public/private sector partnerships to serve as a catalyst for successful private action. (Clinton, 1998)

Despite rhetoric about the responsibility of the developed world to spread the digital revolution around the globe, the current political climate in the United States is not favorable to expensive new programs, let alone those involving foreign aid. Given the size of the problem, the administration proposal will, at best, have only a limited impact on developing countries. We also do not foresee any major initiative by other industrialized countries to assist the developing world to improve its telecommunications infrastructure. Poor countries will have to rely on the international economic market and whatever modest public investments they can generate for themselves.

The percentage of the population online in many parts of the world is minute, but this does not mean that their being online is insignificant. Those who are now online will form the core of the new information society in their respective countries, and we expect this online elite will press for radical improvement in their telecommunication infrastructure. The economic benefits that will accrue from this upgrading should be more than enough to pay for itself. With increasing wealth, education, and technical improvements will come an increase in the number of citizens with access to the Internet.[4]

The Internet and Hopes for World Peace

One utopian dream that has been used to hype the importance of the Internet is that it can bring world peace and understanding. Schoolchildren in a class in one country get online with a class halfway around the world and exchange stories about their everyday lives. It is now relatively easy to contact a stranger from a different culture online and start up a chat or exchange email. The Internet has undoubtedly increased the number of such cross-cultural contacts by ordinary people enormously. Yet, although getting to know other cultures is a good thing, it is doubtful that it will initiate a more peaceful world. In many cases, citizens of rival nations get to know each other better only after their countries have settled their political differences, not before. How many international conflicts really stem from the sorts of misunderstandings that can be overcome if only people knew each other better? We sincerely hope that events in the next century will show our informed skepticism to have been mere baseless cynicism. For now, we remain skeptical.

Although the Internet can facilitate understanding and fraternity, as a relatively unregulated international medium of communication it also can spread hate and bigotry. Marginal hate groups have taken advantage of the free speech available to them in cyberspace and set up Web pages to spread their messages. These sites have made the views of hate groups available to people who might never have encountered them otherwise. It is impossible to guarantee that these groups will remain marginal and that the Internet will foster a more tolerant world. It would be wonderful if debate, openness, and intellectual freedom turned out to be sufficient to counter such dark forces without the need for censorship (Legister, 1998). Many countries outside the United States, having had different experiences with hate groups, have adopted more repressive policies. It remains to be seen whether the American liberal faith in unfettered political speech will triumph in future encounters with the forces of censorship around the world. We doubt that it will, but we are convinced that the struggle for free speech in cyberspace will continue to be a source of political controversy.

The Internet will not bring about a perfectly harmonious world, but we do expect that it will have a significant impact on international trade. Although retail electronic international commerce will grow, the more important economic impact will be on business-to-business trade. The Internet will foster international competitiveness and create new opportunities for import and export by making it easier for suppliers and potential customers to connect with each other. The transaction costs of doing business internationally definitely will be reduced, assuming that national governments do not create new barriers to international trade. Business, however, is only business: It is not likely that increased international contacts and exchanges will so intertwine nations as to significantly reduce the possibility of war. History simply affords too many counterexamples. In the past, nations that traded with each other also went to war with each other. There is no reason to expect the future will be different (Grieco, 1988).

Setting Internet Policy in the Years Ahead

Will the impact of politics on the Internet be good or bad? Certainly, the growth of the Internet has caught the attention of politicians. In the United States in the 105th Congress, more than 300 bills with the word "Internet" were filed. There were just 75 in the previous Congress. We have discovered in the course of our research that politicians and governmental officials have acquired an increasingly sophisticated awareness of cyberspace and its importance for public policy. Speaking for the Internet Alliance, a trade association based in Washington, DC, Brian O'Shaughnessy echoed this judgment. He described the quality of debate over Internet policy during the last session of Congress:

> The level of sophistication on both sides was clearly raised this year, not only among the technology sector but also among legislators and policy makers. Everyone on both sides, I think, has reached a certain understanding about the importance of each other. (Clausing, 1998a)

Although members of Congress have become more advanced at the political game of drafting new policy for cyberspace, this does not necessarily mean that the results will reflect the concerns of the have-nots. It may only portend a better accommodation of established interests.

Nevertheless, the ability of the political process in the United States to confront new policy issues in increasingly sophisticated ways is truly impressive. The executive branch of government has been able to hire people who are highly knowledgeable about developments in cyberspace. Many members of Congress may not know much about computers and the Internet, but the organization of Congress—with its network of specialized committees, subcommittees, and staff and the input of industry and public interest lobby-ists—ensures that the system will develop its own expertise.[5]

Many early Internet enthusiasts were extremely hostile to government and felt that it had no role to play in the development of cyberspace. They feared that government would try to control what it could not understand. It was certainly seen as unnecessary and unwelcome in cyberspace. This can be seen in "A Declaration of Independence of Cyberspace," a widely circulated piece on the Internet written in 1996, in which John Perry Barlow wrote:

> Governments derive their just powers from the consent of the governed. You have neither solicited nor received ours. We did not invite you. You do not know us, nor do you know our world. Cyberspace does not lie within your borders. Do not think you can build it, as though it were a construction project. You cannot. It is an act of nature and it grows itself through our collective actions. (Barlow, 1996)

Cyberspace, of course, is not an act of nature. In fact, it was underwritten by government and created by its agents, mostly to facilitate computer-based military and scientific research. As the Internet grew beyond its original purposes and became a mass medium for information, commerce, and entertainment, governmental officials could hardly remain ignorant of the universe whose creation had largely resulted from their sponsorship. Barlow's manifesto assumed those in cyberspace were a breed apart, and government would forever be dominated by clueless old fogies: "Our world is different. . . . You are terrified of your own children, since they are natives in a world where you will always be immigrants" (Barlow, 1996). Such attitudes reflected the assumption that those left behind did not understand what was happening in cyberspace and never could. It was as if the borders of cyberspace let in only those who were technically sophisticated and pure of heart and those who shared an anarcho-libertarian view of the world.

Ironically, it was technological progress itself that betrayed the fundamental flaws in this view. New technology, new users, and new functions have made such a declaration irrelevant. Cyberspace has evolved. Until the 1980s, a person needed a fair degree of technological sophistication to use computers. This is no longer the case. Moreover, technology is created by real human beings who are paid to create it, and those who pay ultimately will decide how the technology is used. Those entrusted with governing in the real world become cognizant of new technology when it begins to make a substantial impact on social and economic life. Cyberspace is not a brave new world, and government will not go away. The Internet has become an important component of modern society.

This naïveté about the ability of others to understand cyberspace was reinforced by a naive technological determinism and an underestimation of the ingenuity of governments. James Boyle, Professor of Law at American University, has identified three assumptions that early Internet advocates held that led them to conclude that the Internet would remain immune from state regulation. In Boyle's (1997) view, these assumptions are so widely circulated on the Net that they have become cliches. The first is that the technology itself prevents any interference. This cliche is expressed in the statement of John Gilmore, one of the founders of the Electronic Frontier Foundation: "The Net interprets censorship as damage and routes around it" (Boyle, 1997). It harks back to the (false) idea that the Internet was designed to survive nuclear war, and that if a message finds one path blocked, it simply discovers another one. The second assumption is that the international scope of cyberspace means information can escape the jurisdiction of any single sovereign entity and be retrieved from servers located anywhere in the world. The third is that the nature of the content makes it immune from state regulation. In cyberspace, "Information wants to be free," and therefore information cannot be the exclusive property of any one person. Information is nearly costless to copy and should be spread as widely as possible. For those who accept such a claim, "The Net is the ultimate natural environment for information and trying to regulate the Net is like trying to prohibit evolution" (Boyle, 1997).

In our view, these assumptions should be seen as yesterday's cliches; they are hardly truisms. To begin with, the Internet was built not actually to survive nuclear attack but to facilitate communication among expensive mainframe computers (see Chapter 2). Although it is certainly more difficult to regulate and enforce law and order in this new medium, difficulties are not impossibilities. Indeed, how can anyone seriously believe that cyberspace cannot be regulated when in fact it is now being regulated? As electronic commerce is growing exponentially on the Internet, governments around the world are adapting existing commercial regulations to cover such transactions (see Chapter 7). Governmental agents are now roaming cyberspace to uncover fraud and other crime (see Chapter 8). It is also obvious that no biological or technical imperative requires that information must be free in cyberspace. The United States, in cooperation with the international community, has developed new laws to protect intellectual property in cyberspace (see Chapter 6). In short, to maintain that the nature of cyberspace precludes meaningful state intervention and regulation is a fantasy.

Politicians and government officials have been rather cautious, however, in their attempts to bring this new phenomenon under control. Despite the dramatic increase in the number of bills dealing with the Internet introduced in Congress each year, the U.S. government has not adopted a simple top-down regulatory approach. As we have pointed out in our discussion of regulation, the Clinton administration has seen regulation by government as a fallback position. Industry is to take the leading role in creating workable solutions to Internet problems. Government has recognized that the process of drafting rules and regulations is relatively slow, and technology changes rapidly. Policymakers realize that the private sector has the advantage of flexibility, and they remain wary of codifying policy solutions into laws that could hamper the growth and development of the Internet.

Legal codes, rules backed by the threat of force, cannot always yield preferred policy solutions. Some solutions entail adopting voluntary industry codes; others require creating new software. It has been said that in cyberspace technical architecture is also policy. How software operates determines, in a very strong sense, the limits of what can be done online. The 1998-99 antitrust action against Microsoft reflected the fear that a private monopoly of access software—like a prescribed legal code—could stifle innovative development of the Internet. As discussed in Chapter 8, cyberspace is difficult to police by traditional methods. Many of the strategies to reduce crime on the Internet involve new technical means of security. The cooperation of the private sector with government law enforcement officials is absolutely necessary to develop and implement these strategies successfully.

Some public policy problems regarding the Internet seem beyond the ability of the United States or any single nation to resolve because of jurisdictional and enforcement limits. Negotiating international agreements and treaties is an even slower and more cumbersome process than rule making in individual countries. Not only do interests conflict in the international sphere as they do in domestic politics, but arriving at an international consensus entails overcoming deep cultural differences. The Internet will affect nations differently, and these differences will have to be worked out.

It has been argued by David Johnson, founder of the Cyberspace Law Institute and the Aspen Institute Internet Policy Project and former chairman of the Electronic Frontier Foundation, that the age of the Internet has ushered in a new form of public policy making because it has overturned many of the premises on which the old system was based. The traditional relationship between lobbyists and government officials has been reversed. In American politics, lobbyists typically pressured government to recognize problems facing their backers. Lobbyists pushed their groups' solutions and opposed the solutions of others that they believed harmful. Ultimately, it was up to government to create an authoritative compromise among contending interests. According to Johnson (1998), the government has a new role to play:

> Government, often unable to use its legitimate monopoly over the use of physical force to police the global Net, and unable to write sensible top-down rules for an ever-changing global electronic environment, finds another role: speaking as an advocate on behalf of harmed constituencies. And the private-sector players, who might once have been content to advocate narrow interests, are being asked to come up with workable solutions, effective compromises, and new forms of private sector "self-regulation."

Although government is not the preferred final locus of policy making, it still has an important role to play when it comes to the formation of Internet policy. It has the power to educate, persuade, and speak on behalf of broad constituencies. It has the financial resources to fund research and development. Johnson (1998) argued that by using these tools, government will coax the private sector to create policy in the public interest. Whereas government once would have created rules and regulations, now it will, in effect, lobby business to come up with solutions. Government will endorse private sector solutions, fund new prototypes, convene industrywide meetings to lend legitimacy to the private sector initiatives, and provide antitrust exemptions for standard setting. In short, according to Johnson, government will provide incentives for creative private sector policy making rather than making policy itself and imposing it by means of old-fashioned rules and sanctions (Johnson, 1998).

This claim that the Internet is introducing a new way of making public policy, however, should be evaluated with some care. Many of Johnson's concrete observations about the role of lobbyists and the government are correct and pertinent to understanding Internet policy making. Certainly, the pattern of relations between government and private industry that Johnson identified is already emerging, but the conclusion that private sector policy making in response to government lobbying represents something new in American politics is debatable. There is at least one good old-fashioned American slang term for such governmental activity—"jawboning." Government repeatedly has attempted to achieve voluntary compliance with policy guidelines by applying public pressure. Use of the bully pulpit as well as the threat of new governmental initiatives often has been enough to influence recalcitrant actors in the private sector. There are also precedents for government cooperation with private industry to develop solutions to ongoing problems. It is much too simple to conceive of the intricate process of public policy formation and implementation only in terms of legal codes and rule making. Trade associations and private standard setting are nothing new either. Government attempts to rely on them to solve public policy problems go back at least as far as the 1920s, when Herbert Hoover was Secretary of Commerce.

The argument that the special technology of the Internet requires a radically new approach to public policy also should be met with skepticism. The phrase "architecture is policy" is catchy, but thinking about the phrase suggests that architecture is also policy in the real world. Structural engineering is a profession much older than computer engineering. In general, how things are built determines how things can be used, and myriad decisions incorporating solutions to problems are made every day by those who build things in the real world. These decisions reflect a complex mix of technical considerations, market forces, and legal requirements. Why should we expect cyberspace to be different?

The decision to avoid a top-down regulator regime for the Internet also reflects a general retreat from the "era of big government." There is currently a worldwide appreciation for the importance of free markets, as numerous governments have become disillusioned with the regulatory state. Though governments vary in terms of their willingness to rely on the private sector, all advanced industrial countries are now much more willing to consider private sector solutions to public policy problems than they have been for many years. Given this worldwide trend, it would not have been hard to predict that governments' first response to cyberspace as a new public policy arena would be cautious. We cannot predict with certainty whether this cautious approach will continue in the twenty-first century. What we can predict is that the shroud of technical mystery that has enveloped cyberspace will dissipate fairly rapidly. The Internet will become part of everyday life, and although it will create new public policy problems, it is doubtful that either the solutions or the process of arriving at them will strike an observer as radically new.

Notes

1. For examples, see Fisher et al. (1996a, 1996b) and Negroponte (1995).

2. See Chapters 3, 4, and 5.

3. See Moss and Mitra (1998) for a study of the correlation between income and other demographic variables with subscription to an ISP. This study also documents the gap in access between the haves and have-nots.

4. See Roche and Blaine (1996) for a general discussion of economic development and access to the Internet. Heeks (1996) assessed the impact of India's software industry on the development of communications infrastructure.

5. See Casey (1999) for a summary of developments regarding Congress and the Internet.

References

Alger, D. E. (1996). *The media and politics* (2nd ed.). Belmont, CA: Wadsworth.

American Horse Council. (1997). *Internet gambling bill introduced by Kyl.* Retrieved July 30, 1999, from the World Wide Web: http://www.horsenews.com/break/mayjune97/ahc1.htm

Anderson, R. H., Bikson, T. K., Law, S. A., Mitchell, B. M.; with Kelzier, C., Kettner, B., Paris, C., Pliskin, J., & Srinagesh, P. (1995). *Universal access to e-mail: Feasibility and societal implications.* Santa Monica, CA: RAND.

Angwin, J. (1996, November 6). Internet users overwhelm many election Web sites. *San Francisco Chronicle.* Retrieved August 26, 1999, from the World Wide Web: http://www.sfgate.com/cgi-bin/article.cgi?file=/chronicle/archive /1996/11/06/MN70331.DTL

Armstrong, D. (1996, November 4). Digital democracy: The Internet is crawling with ideas at election time. *San Francisco Examiner,* p. B1.

Arquilla, J., & Ronfeldt, D. (Eds.). (1998). *In Athena's camp: Preparing for conflict in the information age.* Santa Monica: RAND.

Arterton, F. C. (1987). *Teledemocracy: Can technology protect democracy?* Newbury Park, CA: Sage.

Associated Press. (1999, December 6). "WTO Talks Collapsed Amid Protests." Retrived from the World Wide Web: wysiwyg://5/http://www.nytimes.com/aponline/f/AP-World-Trade-Future.html

Australia concerned over tax revenue loss via the Internet. (1997, February 1). *The Age* [Australia]. Retrieved from the World Wide Web but no longer available.

Bagdikian, B. (1989, June 12). The lords of the global village. *The Nation, 248*(23), 805-820.

Band, J., & Kennedy, J. (1998). Battle lines form over WIPO copyright bills. *National Law Journal.* Retrieved July 30, 1999, from the World Wide Web: http://www.ljx.com/copyright/0126wipo.html

Barber, B. (1984). *Strong democracy: Participatory politics for a new age.* Berkeley: University of California Press.

Barlow, J. P. (1996). *A declaration of independence of cyberspace.* Retrieved July 30, 1999, from the World Wide Web: http://www.dawn21.com/Journal21/DeclIndp.shtml

Bell, T. W. (1998, January 6). *Internet Gambling Ban Faces Losing Odds.* Retrieved July 30, 1999, from the World Wide Web: http://members.aol.com/tomwbell/papers/Gamble.html

Bencivenga, D. (1998, September 3). Internet cyberforce: SEC and FTC crack down on on-line fraud. *New York Law Journal.*

Bennett, W. L. (1996). *The governing crisis: Media, money and marketing in American elections* (2nd ed.). New York: St. Martin's Press.

Bernstein, J. (1998, July 14). *Statement of Jodie Bernstein, Director Bureau of Consumer Protection, Press Conference on 'Spam.'* Retrieved July 30, 1999, from the World Wide Web: http://www.ftc.gov/opa/1998/9807/jbspam.713.htm

Birdsall, D. S., Muzzio, D., Taylor, H., & Krane, D. (1996, June/July). A new political marketplace: The Web snares voters. *The Public Perspective, 7*(4), 33-35.

Bonchek, M. S. (1995). Grassroots in cyberspace: Using computer networks to facilitate political participation. *Political Participation Project.* Retrieved July 30, 1999, from the World Wide Web: http://www.uni-koeln.de/themen/cmc/text/bonch95a.htm

Bonchek, M. S. (1996). Message to candidates: It's about community, stupid. *iGuide.* Retrieved July 30, 1999, from the World Wide Web: http://institute.strategosnet.com/msb/ppp/stupid.html

Borland, J. (1998). Net companies promise to protect privacy. *TechWeb.* Retrieved July 30, 1999, from the World Wide Web: http://www.techweb.com/wire/story/TWB19980622S0018

Boyle, A. (1996a, November 11). Governments take on the Net. *MSNBC.* Retrieved from the World Wide Web but no longer available.

Boyle, A. (1996b, November 11). Internet issues on the international stage. *MSNBC.* Retrieved from the World Wide Web but no longer available.

Boyle, J. (1997). *Foucault in cyberspace: Surveillance, sovereignty, and hard-wired censors.* Retrieved July 30, 1999, from the World Wide Web: http://www.wcl.American.edu/pub/faculty/Boyle/Foucault.htm

Braun, D. (1997, July 28). Online gambling not in Congress's card. *TechWeb News.* Retrieved July 30, 1999, from the World Wide Web: http://www.techweb.com/se/directlink.cgi?WIR1997072814

Brinkley, J. (1998, September 21). F.T.C. "losing patience" with business on Web privacy. *The New York Times.* Retrieved August 18, 1999, from the World Wide Web: http://search.nytimes.com/search/daily/bin/fastweb?getdoc+site+site+77087+0+wAAA+Joel%7EBrinkley%7EAND%7EF.T.C.

Brooker, K. (1998, October 26). The scary rise of Internet stock scams. *Fortune Investor, 138*(8).

Brunker, M. (1997, October 24). *Strike two! Internet gambling disputes the call.* Retrieved July 30, 1999, from the World Wide Web: http://www.gamemasteronline.com/InfoBigBrother Content1.html

Brunker, M. (1998a, March 26.). Fantasy sports ban included in Net gambling bill. *MSNBC.* Retrieved from the World Wide Web but no longer available.

Brunker, M. (1998b, October 21). Net gambling ban dead 'til next year. *MSNBC.* Retrieved from the World Wide Web but no longer available.

Bryan, R. F. (1995). *Remembering the significant contributions of Dr. Glen J. Culler.* Retrieved July 30, 1999, from the World Wide Web: http://kk.ucsb.edu./culler/stories/bryan.html

Cable Communications Policy Act of 1984. 47 U.S.C. § 521 (1984).

Cable Television Consumer Protection and Competition Act of 1992. 47 U.S.C. § 222 (1992).

Cabot, A. (Ed.). (1998). *Internet gambling report II.* Retrieved April 4, 1998, from the World Wide Web: http://www.hotelcasinomedia.com/trace/index.html, but not available as of August 20, 1999.

Caruso, D. (1996, May/June). The Net nobody knows. *Utne Reader,* 41-49.

Casey, C. (1996). *The hill on the Net: Congress enters the information age.* San Diego, CA: Academic Press.

Casey, C. (1999). *The hill on the Net—Electronic update No. 20* (Mailing list). Retrieved July 30, 1999, from the World Wide Web: http://www.casey.com/index.html

Chaddock, G. R. (1997, January 10). English Web sites in France flamed by language police. *Christian Science Monitor.* Retrieved from Lexus/Nexus as Section, International, p. 1.

Clausing, J. (1997a, July 29). Online businesses critical of hearing on Net gambling. *CyberTimes.* Retrieved August 20, 1999, from the World Wide Web: http://search.nytimes.com/search/daily/bin/fastweb?getdoc+site+si te+17662+2+wAAA+Clausing%7Eand%7Egambling

Clausing, J. (1997b, December 23). Online gambling industry seeks regulation to save itself. *CyberTimes.* Retrieved August 20, 1999, from the World Wide Web: http://search.nytimes.com/search/daily/bin/fastweb?getdoc+site+site+18490+10+wAAA+Clausing%7Eand%7Egambling

Clausing, J. (1997c, September 4). Scrambling to tax the golden goose. *CyberTimes.* Retrieved August 20, 1999, from the World Wide Web: http://search.nytimes.com/search/daily/bin/fastweb?getdoc+site+si te+17860+0+wAAA+Clausing%7Eand%7Egoose

Clausing, J. (1997d, October 24). Senate panel votes to block access to gambling sites. *CyberTimes.* Retrieved August 20, 1999, from the World Wide Web: http:// search.nytimes.com/search/daily/bin/fastweb?getdoc+site+site+18153+11+wAAA+Clausing%7E and%7Egambling

Clausing, J. (1998a, December 28). Government and the Internet got acquainted in 1998. *CyberTimes.* Retrieved August 20, 1999, from the World Wide Web: http://search.nytimes.com/search/daily/bin/fastweb?getdoc+site+site+78132+0+wAAA+Clausing%7E and%7EInternet%7Eand%7EGovernment%7Ean d%7Eacquainted

Clausing, J. (1998b, July 18). House reaches compromise on digital copyright law. *CyberTimes.* Retrieved August 20, 1999, from the World Wide Web: http://search.nytimes.com/search/daily/bin/fastweb?getdoc+site+si te+76463+3+wAAA+Clausing%7Eand%7EDigital%7Eand%7ECopyright%7Eand% 7Elaw

Clinton, W. (1997, February 5). State of the union address. *The New York Times.*

Clinton, W. (1998, November 30). *Memorandum for the Heads of Executive Departments and Agencies. SUBJECT: Successes and Further Work on Electronic Commerce..* Retrieved August 19, 1999, from the World Wide Web: http://www.pub.whitehouse.gov/uri-res/ I2R? urn:pdi://oma.eop.gov.u s/1998/11/30/6.text.1

Commission calls for a defensive posture. (1997, October 20). *USA Today.*

Communications Decency Act, (1996). http://www.epic.org/cda/cda.html

Conway, M. M. (1991). *Political participation in the United States* (2nd ed.). Washington, DC: CQ Press.

Copyright bill clears Congress. (1998, October 12). *Wired News.* Retrieved August 4, 1999, from the World Wide Web: http://www.wired.com/news/print_version/politics/story/15571.html

Cordell, A. J. (1996). New taxes for a new economy. *Government Information in Canada,* 2(4). Retrieved from the World Wide Web: http://www.usask.ca/library/gic/v2n4/cordell/cordell.html

Crockett, B. (1998). Virtual sales; real crimes. *MSNBC.* Retrieved August 18, 1999, from the World Wide Web: http://www.msnbc.com:80/news/173432.asp#BODY

Cyberspace Law for Non-Lawyers Web site. (1999). Retrieved July 30, 1999, from the World Wide Web: http://www.ssrn.com/update/lsn/cyberspace/csl_lessons.html

Dart, B. (1997). Internet copyright treaty: The stakes are high. *Cox News Service.* Retrieved July 30, 1999, from the World Wide Web: http://www.computernewsdaily.com/237_082597_094213_1037.html

Davis, R. (1999). *The Web of politics: The Internet's impact on the American political system.* New York: Oxford University Press.

December, J., & Randall, N. (1994). *The World Wide Web unleashed.* Indianapolis, IN: Sams Publishing.

Demchak, C., & Colón, V. (1998, September). *Evaluating openness in agencies on the Web: Empirical black holes and potential solutions.* Paper presented at the annual meeting of the American Political Science Association, Boston.

Denning, D. E. (1998). Cyberspace attacks and countermeasures. In D. Denning & P. Denning (Eds.), *Internet Besieged* (pp. 32-40). New York: ACM.

Diamond, E., & Silverman, R. A. (1995). *White House to your house: Media and politics in virtual America.* Cambridge: MIT Press.

Duncan, R. (1997). Using DejaNews to profile suspected Internet newsgroup criminals. *Technological Crime Bulletin.* Retrieved from the World Wide Web: ttp://www.rcmp-grc.gc.ca/html/te-crime.htm but not available August 20, 1999.

Duty-free Net? (1998, October 26). *Industry Standard.* Retrieved August 25, 1999, from the World Wide Web: http://www.thestandard.com/articles/display/0,1449,2178,00.html

Dyson, E. (1997). *Release 2.0: A design for living in the digital age.* New York: Broadway Books.

Dyson, E. (1998). Privacy protection: Time to think and act locally and globally. *First Monday.* Retrieved July 30, 1999, from the World Wide Web: http://131.193.153.231/issues/issue3_6/dyson/index.html

Englehart, D. C. (1962). *Augmenting human intellect: A conceptual framework.* Retrieved August 25, 1999, from the World Wide Web: http://www.histech.rwth-aachen.de/www/quellen/engelbart/ahi62index.html

E-ratecentral.com. (1998, December 11). *Information on Waves 1 and 2 released by the SLC.* Retrieved July 30, 1999, from the World Wide Web: http://www.e-ratecentral.com/

Europe said to embrace Internet. (1998, September 16). *Ch7Europe.* Retrieved August 23, 1999, from the World Wide Web: http://www.ch7Europe.com/archive/news/1998/199809/19980916.htm

European commission vetoes bit tax for data networks. (1997, April 4). *Ethos.* Retrieved July 30, 1999, from the World Wide Web: http://www.tagish.co.uk/ethosub/lit9/7aae.htm

European Union. (1997). *A European initiative in electronic commerce.* Retrieved July 30, 1999, from the World Wide Web: http://www.cordis.lu/esprit/src/ecomcomx.htm

EU Seeks to Tax E-Commerce. (1998, June 17). *CNET.* Retrieved July 30, 1999, from the World Wide Web: http://www.news.com/News/Item/0,4,23292,00.html?st.ne.1.head

E.U.-U.S. (1997, December 5). *Joint E.U.-U.S. Statement on Electronic Commerce.* Retrieved July 30, 1999, from the World Wide Web: ttp://www.qlinks.net/comdocs/eu-us.htm

Fear of cyber-terrorism more hype than reality. (1998, June 8). *Reuters.* Retrieved from the World Wide Web but no longer available.

Federal Trade Commission. (1998). *Privacy online: A report to Congress.* Retrieved July 30, 1999, from the World Wide Web: http://www.ftc.gov/reports/privacy3/toc.htm

Federal Wire Act. 18 U.S.C. § 1084(a) (1961).

Federation of [British] Electronics Industry. (1996, November 11). *FEI position paper on the "bit tax proposal."* Retrieved July 30, 1999, from the World Wide Web: http://www.fei.org.uk/fei/public/position/bittax.htm

Fenno, R. (1978). *Home style: House members in their districts.* Boston: Little, Brown.

Ferrell, K. (1997). Net crimes: Don't be a victim. *CNET.* Retrieved July 30, 1999, from the World Wide Web: http://www.cnet.com/Content/Features/Dlife/Crime/index.html

Finifter, A. W. (Ed.). (1993). *Political science: The state of the discipline II.* Washington, DC: American Political Science Association.

First cyberterrorist attack reported by U.S. (1998). Reuters. Retrieved from the World Wide Web but no longer available.

Fisher, B., Margolis, M., & Resnick, D. (1996a, Spring). Breaking ground on the virtual frontier: Surveying civic life on the Internet. *American Sociologist, 27,* 11-29.

Fisher, B., Margolis, M., & Resnick, D. (1996b, September). Surveying the Internet: Democratic theory and civic life in cyberspace. *Southeastern Political Review, 24,* 399-429.

Fisher, B., Margolis, M., Resnick, D., & Bishop, G. (1995). Survey research in cyberspace: Breaking ground on the virtual frontier. In *Proceedings of the International Conference on Survey Measurement and Process Quality* (pp. 178-183). Alexandria, VA: American Statistical Association.

Flynn, L. J. (1998, March 18). With Goto.com's search engine, the highest bidder shall be ranked first. *The New York Times,* p. D-5.

Fram, A. (1998). Senate bans Net gambling. *ABCNEW.com.* Retrieved July 26, 1999, from the World Wide Web: http://abcnews.go.com/sections/tech/DailyNews/gambling980723.html

Freeling, K., & Wiggins, R. (1998, March 30). Internet law. *National Law Journal,* p. B7. Retrieved July 30, 1999, from the World Wide Web: http://test01.ljextra.com/na.archive.html/98/03/1998_0323_81.html

Freeman, J. (1997). Feds hate the Web. *Forbes ASAP.* Retrieved July 30, 1999, from the World Wide Web: http://www.forbes.com/asap/97/0825/078.htm

Frendreis, J. (1994). Voters, government officials, and party organizations: Connections and distinctions. In D. M. Shea & J. C. Green (Eds.), *The state of the parties: The changing role of contemporary parties* (pp. 339-348). Lanham, MD: Rowman & Littlefield.

Froomkin, A. M. (1995). *An introduction to the "governance" of the Internet: I. The Internet: An orderly anarchy.* Retrieved July 30, 1999, from the World Wide Web: http://www.law.miami.edu/~7Efroomkin/seminar/ilsx.htm

FTC cracks down on online scams. (1997). *ZDNet AnchorDesk.* Retrieved August 4, 1999, from the World Wide Web: http://www5.zdnet.com/anchordesk/story/story_866.html

Fulbright, J. W. (1971). The Pentagon propaganda machine. New York: Vintage Books.

Gaffin, A. (1996). *The Electronic Freedom Foundation guide to the Internet.* Retrieved July 30, 1999, from the World Wide Web: http://www.eff.org/

Gay, L. (1997). Revenuers raise a ruckus over Internet booze business. *Scripps Howard.* Retrieved December 23, 1998, from the World Wide Web but no longer available.

Geist, M. (1998, July). The reality of bytes: Regulating economic activity in the age of the Internet. *73 Washington Law Review, 73.* Retrieved August 2, 1999, from the World Wide Web: http://www.law.washington.edu/wlr/geist.htm

Georgia Tech: Graphics, Visualization & Usability Center (GVU). *Semi-annual WWW user surveys 1994-1998.* Retrieved August 2, 1999, from the World Wide Web: http://www.cc.gatech.edu/gvu/user_surveys

Ghosh, R. A. (1997, October 31). Exclusive: Interpol's top Internet crimefighter speaks out. *American Reporter* (Reproduced as an addendum to Roger Clarke's *Technological aspects of Internet crime prevention*). Retrieved June 26, 1998, from the World Wide Web, http://www.anu.edu.au/people/Roger.Clark/II/ICrimePrev.html, but not available as of August 2, 1999

Gibson, R. K., & Ward, S. J. (1998, September). *The Internet and intra-party democracy: Discourse and dissent.* Paper presented at the annual meeting of the American Political Science Association, Boston.

Gidari, A., & Aglion, M. (1998, August/September). EU directive on privacy may hinder e-commerce. *IP Magazine.* Retrieved August 2, 1999, from the World Wide Web: http://www.ipmag.com/dailies/980629.html

Gilster, P. (1994). *The Internet navigator* (2nd ed.). New York: John Wiley.

Gilster, P. (1997). *The Web navigator.* New York: John Wiley.

Ginsberg, B., & Shefter, M. (1999). *Politics by other means: Politicians, prosecutors, and the press from Watergate to Whitewater.* New York: Norton.

Glave, J. (1998a, June 25). FTC cracking down on Net fraud. *Wired News.* Retrieved August 2, 1999, from the World Wide Web: http://www.wired.com/news/news/politics/story/13268.html

Glave, J. (1998b, August 25). Keeper of the flame. *Wired News.* Retrieved August 2, 1999, from the World Wide Web: http://www.wired.com/news/news/story/14631.html

Glave, J. (1998c, June 22). New try at privacy "self regulation." *Wired News.* Retrieved August 2, 1999, from the World Wide Web: http://www.wired.com/news/news/story/13158.html

Global co-operation needed to avoid multiple taxation on the Internet. (1996, October 12). *Internet IT Informer.* Retrieved from the World Wide Web but no longer available.

Global Information Infrastructure Commission. (1998). *A global action plan for business with governments toward electronic commerce.* Retrieved August 2, 1999, from the World Wide Web: http://www.gii.org/pubs/e_biac.pdf

Graber, D. (1996, March). The "new" media and politics: What does the future hold? *PS: Political Science & Politics, 29,* 33-36.

Graber, D. (1997). *Mass media and American politics* (5th ed.). Washington, DC: CQ Press.

Grant, S. (1998). *Fraudulent schemes on the Internet: Remarks to the Senate Permanent Committee on Investigations.* Retrieved August 2, 1999, from the World Wide Web: http://www.fraud.org/news/1998/feb98/021098.htm

Gray, M. (n.d.). "Internet statistics." Retrieved August 2, 1999, from the World Wide Web: http://www.mit.edu/people/mkgray/net/printable

Green, G. (1997, January 14). Who owns facts within databases? *CyberTimes.* Retrieved August 2, 1999, from the World Wide Web: http://search.nytimes.com/search/daily/bin/fastweb?getdoc+site+site+15384+0+wAAA+%22Geoffrey%7EGreen%22%7Eand%7Edatabases

Green, H., Yang, C., & Judge, P. C. (1998, March 5). A little Net privacy please. *BusinessWeek.*

Greenberg, E. S., & Page, B. I. (1995). *The struggle for democracy* (2nd ed.). New York: HarperCollins.

Greenhouse, L. (1997, June 27). High court voids curb on "indecent" Internet material. *The New York Times.* Retrieved August 19, 1999, from the World Wide Web: http://search.nytimes.com/search/daily/bin/fastweb?getdoc+site+site+17400+1+wAAA+%22Linda%7EGreenhouse%22%7Eand%7EIndecent%7Eand%7E Einternet

Grieco, J. (1988). Anarchy and the limits of cooperation. *International Organization, 42*(3), 167-186.

Grun, B. (Ed.). (1982). *The timetables of history.* New York: Simon & Schuster.

Guissani, B. (1997a, June 10). French court dismisses suit on Georgia Tech site. *The New York Times.* Retrieved August 2, 1999, from the World Wide Web: http://www.nytimes.com/library/cyber/week/061097georgia.html

Guissani, B. (1997b, February 18). A plan to tax cyberspace, bit by bit. *CyberTimes.* Retrieved August 2, 1999, from the World Wide Web: http://www.nytimes.com/library/cyber/euro/021897euro.html

Gurak, L. J. (1997). *Persuasion and privacy in cyberspace: The online protests over Lotus Market-place and the clipper chip.* New Haven, Ct: Yale University Press.

Hacker, A. (1967). Power to do what? In W. Connolly (Ed.), *The bias of pluralism* (pp. 67-80). New York: Atherton.

Hafner, K., & Lyon, M. (1996). *Where wizards stay up late: The origins of the Internet.* New York: Simon & Schuster.

Hansell, S. (1998, December 13). Mouse attack in cyberspace: With Go Network, Disney steps into portal wars. *The New York Times,* pp. 1, 10 (Section 3).

Hardesty, D. (1998a). *European commission says electronically delivered products are services.* Retrieved August 2, 1999, from the World Wide Web: http://www.mshb.com/ec/062398.htm

Hardesty, D. (1998b). *House passes Internet Tax Freedom Act—Senate next.* Retrieved August 2, 1999, from the World Wide Web: http://www.mshb.com/ec/062798.htm

Hardy, H. E. (1993). *USENET: The history of the Net.* Unpublished master's thesis, Grand Valley State University, Allendale, MI. Retrieved August 2, 1999, from the World Wide Web: http://www.ocean.ic.net/ftp/doc/nethist.html

Harmon, A. (1998, April 3). In cyberspace, is there law where there is no land? *The New York Times.* Retrieved August 2, 1999, from the World Wide Web: http://search.nytimes.com/search/daily/bin/fastweb?getdoc+site+site+75886+0+wAAA+Harmon%7Eand%7EPam%7Eand%7Esamuelson

Harris, W. H., & Levey, J. (Eds.). (1975). *The new Columbia encyclopedia* (4th ed.). New York: Columbia University Press.

Hauben, M. (n.d.). History of ARPANET: Behind the Net—The untold history of ARPANET." Retrieved August 2, 1999, from the World Wide Web: http://www.dei.isep.ipp.pt/docs/arpa.html

Hauben, M., & Hauben, R. (1997). *Netizens: On the history and impact of Usenet and the Internet.* Los Alamitos, CA: IEEE Computer Society Press.

Hayward, D. (1997, September 9). Internet tax plan is needed, Net creator says. *TechWeb News.* Retrieved August 2, 1999, from the World Wide Web: http://www.techweb.com/wire/news/1997/09/0909tax.html

Heeks, R. (1996). *India's software industry.* Thousand Oaks, CA: Sage.

Heilemann, J. (1996, December 2). Netizen columnist bids farewell to the year of the Net. *Wired.* http://www.wired.com/news/news/story/729.html

Helling, B. (1998). Web-site sensitivity to privacy concerns: Collecting personally identifiable information and passing persistent cookies. *First Monday.* Retrieved August 2, 1999, from the World Wide Web: http://www.firstmonday.dk/issues/issue3_2

Hill, K. A., & Hughes, J. E. (1998). *Cyberpolitics: Citizen activism in the age of the Internet.* Lanham, MD: Rowman & Littlefield.

Hiskes, R. P. (1996, June/July). Acts of democracy: Reconceptualizing politics, participation, and competence. *Public Perspective, 7*(4), 40-44.

Hu, J. (1998). Political hackers hit 300 sites. *CNET.* Retrieved August 2, 1999, from the World Wide Web: http://www.news.com/News/Item/0,4,23881,00.html?st.ne.fd.mdh

Huber, P. (1996, December 2). The end of law, and the beginning. The digital revolution: Where do we go from here? *Forbes ASAP,* pp. 63, 68.

Human Rights Watch. (1998). *World Report 1998.* Retrieved August 2, 1999, from the World Wide Web: http://www.hrw.org/worldreport/Table.htm

Human Rights Watch. (1999). *World Report 1999.* Retrieved August 2, 1999, from the World Wide Web: http://www.hrw.org/worldreport99/

ICCC Web site: http://www.capweb.net/iccc/contact.morph

Illegal drug sales flourish in cyberspace. (1998, July 3). *Reuters*. Retrieved from the World Wide Web but no longer available.

Intel unveils controversial chip. (1999, February 18). *The New York Times*. Retrieved August 2, 1999, from the World Wide Web: http://search.nytimes.com/search/daily/bin/fastweb?getdoc+site+site+79395+0+wAAA+Intel%7Eand%7EUnveils%7Eand%7EControversial%7Eand %7Echip

Interactive Gaming Council. (1997). *IGC code of conduct*. Retrieved August 2, 1999, from the World Wide Web: http://www.igcouncil.org/code.html

Interactive Gaming Council calls for comprehensive regulation of online gaming. (1999, February 10) [IGC press release]. Retrieved August 2, 1999, from the World Wide Web: http://www.igcouncil.org/news/regulation990210.html

Interactive Services Association Web site. (n.d.). *About ISA*. Retrieved April 17, 1998, from the World Wide Web, ttp://www.isa.net/aboutisa/index.html, but not available on August 2, 1999.

Intermedia. (1998). *Legal and privacy notification* [Brochure]. Covington, KY: Author.

Internet Consumers Choice Coalition. (1997). *Letter to Senator Orrin Hatch*. Retrieved August 2, 1999, from the World Wide Web: http://www.aclu.org/congress/lg100897a.html

Internet gambling booming in Caribbean. (1997, December 17). *CyberTimes*. Retrieved August 2, 1999, from the World Wide Web: http://search.nytimes.com/search/daily/bin/fastweb?getdoc+site+site+18458+0+wAAA+INternet%7Eand%7EGambling%7Eand%7EBooming%7Eand%7Ecaribbean

Internet gambling? Not so fast! (1997, July 20). *Daily Racing Form*. Retrieved from the World Wide Web, ttp://sportstalk.total.net/howie/messages/1573.html, but not available on July 30, 1999.

Internet Tax Fairness Coalition Web site. (n.d.). Retrieved August 2, 1999, from the World Wide Web: http://truth.apk.net/stopnettax/joinus.asp

Inter-University Consortium for Political and Social Research. (1994). *Guide to resources and services, 1994-1995*. Ann Arbor, MI: Author. Retrieved August 2, 1999, from the World Wide Web: http://www.icpsr.umich.edu

Jaszi, P. (1998, September 10). *Oral testimony of Peter Jaszi on behalf of the Digital Future Coalition before the Senate Foreign Relations Committee*. Retrieved August 2, 1999, from the World Wide Web: http://www.dfc.org/issues/wipo/pjorltst/pjorltst.html

John Marshall Law School Cyberlaw Web site. (1999). Retrieved August 2, 1999, from the World Wide Web: http://www.jmls.edu/cyber/index.html

Johnson, D. R. (1998, December). Who's lobbying whom? *IP Magazine*. Retrieved August 2, 1999, from the World Wide Web: http://www.ipmag.com/98-dec/johnson.html

Johnson, D. R., & Post, D. G. (1997). The rise of law on the global network. In B. Kahin & C. Nesson (Eds.), *Borders in cyberspace* (pp. 3-47). Cambridge: MIT Press.

Johnston, D. C. (1997, November 10). Online sales collide with off-line tax question. *CyberTimes*. Retrieved August 20, 1999, from the World Wide Web: http://search.nytimes.com/search/daily/bin/fastweb?getdoc+site+site+18223+0+wAAA+online%7Eand%7Esales%7Eand%7Ecollide

Jones, D. (1999, December 3). "Will WTO hurt e-commerce?" *USA Today*.

Jupiter Communications. (1998). *Portals emerge as dominant source for online news: Jupiter warns mainstream news providers that brevity, not depth, wins*. Retrieved August 2, 1999, from the World Wide Web: http://www.jup.com/jupiter/press/releases/1998/1208a.html

Kamark, E. C. (1999, February). *Campaigning on the Internet in the off-year elections of 1998*. Retrieved August 2, 1999, from the World Wide Web: http://ksgwww.harvard.edu/visions/kamarck.htm

Kaplan, C. S. (1998a, May 1). For their civil disobedience, the "sit-in" is virtual. *CyberTimes*. Retrieved August 20, 1999, from the World Wide Web: http://search.nytimes.com/search/daily/bin/fastweb?getdoc+site+site+75925+0+wAAA+Civil%7Eand%7EDisobedience%7Eand%7Evirtual

Kaplan, C. S. (1998b, October 9). Strict European privacy law puts pressure on U.S. *CyberTimes*. Retrieved August 20, 1999, from the World Wide Web: http://search.nytimes.com/search/daily/bin/fastweb?getdoc+site+site+77466+0+wAAA+Strict%7Eand%7EEuropean%7Eand%7EPrivacy%7Eand%7EL aw%7E

Kazmierczak, M. (n.d.). *Internet history: Birth of ARPANet*. Retrieved August 23, 1999, from the World Wide Web: http://www.mkaz.com/ebeab/history/part3.html

Kemeny, J. (1972). *Man and the computer*. New York: Scribner.

Kernell, S. (1997). *Going public: New strategies of presidential leadership* (3rd ed.). Washington, DC: CQ Press.

Kerstetter, J. (1998, August 31). Web merchants battle for space in high-rent and high risk online districts." *PCWeek, 15*, pp. 1, 14-15.

Kesten, G. (1998, February). Attorney general announces crime center to tackle cyberattacks. *TechWeb*. Retrieved August 2, 1999, from the World Wide Web: http://www.techweb.com/wire/story/TWB19980228S0004

King, M. (1997, June 16). Quebec's language cops slammed over Net policy. *Calgary Herald Online.*. Retrieved from the World Wide Web but no longer available.

Klass, G., & Cooley, S. (1994, Summer). Internet lists for political scientists. *Social Science Computer Review, 12,*(2), 261-265.

Kyl reading to go with Bill. (1998, March 13). *Rolling Good Times Online*. Retrieved from the World Wide Web, http://www.rgtonline.com/, but no longer available.

Larocque, C. (1997). It's hard to catch criminals on the Net, police say. *Online Reporter*. Retrieved August 3, 1999, from the World Wide Web: http://www.uwo.ca/journ/reporter/Mar3197/internet.htm

Lassman, K., & O'Donnell, R. (1997, December 8). Internet poses taxing puzzle. *Denver Business Journal*.

Lavin, P. (1998, June 25). The cyber VAT man cometh in Europe. *CNNFN*. Retrieved August 2, 1999, from the World Wide Web: http://www.cnnfn.com/digitaljam/newsbytes/113774.html

Legister, F. S. J. (1998, April). *Global village idiots: The racist right on the Internet*. Paper presented at the annual meeting of the Midwest Political Science Association Chicago.

Leiner, B., Cerf, V. G., Clark, D. D., Kahn, R. E., Kleinrock, L., Lynch, D. C., Postel, J., Roberts, L. G., & Wolff, S. (1998). *A brief history of the Internet*. Retrieved August 3, 1999, from the World Wide Web: http://www.isoc.org/internet-history/brief.html#clark

Levin, D. (1995, September 14). Internet's coming, but what'll it do? *Detroit News*, p. C1.

Lewis, P. (1997, September 22). Can lawmakers control online gambling? *CyberTimes*. Retrieved August 25, 1999, from the World Wide Web: http://search.nytimes.com/search/daily/bin/fastweb?getdoc+site+site+19254+0+wAAA+Lawmakers%7Eand%7EControl%7Eand%7EOnline%7Eand%7E gambling

Lindblom, C. (1977). *Politics and markets: The world's political economic systems*. New York: Basic Books.

Littman, J. (1997). The Net's finest: Law enforcement goes online. *CNET*. Retrieved August 3, 1999, from the World Wide Web: http://www.news.com/News/Item/0,4,16790,00.html?st.ne.fd.mdh

Locke, J. (1988). *Two treatises of government* (P. Laslett, Ed.). Cambridge, UK: Cambridge University Press. (Original work published 1689)

Lohr, S. (1997, December 15). Cyberspace staying duty-free. *CyberTimes*. Retrieved August 20, 1999, from the World Wide Web: http://search.nytimes.com/search/daily/bin/fastweb? getdoc+site+site+18446+0+wAAA+Cyberspace%7Eand%7Estaying%7Eand%7Eduty

Lowi, T. J. (1994). Toward a responsible three-party system. In D. M. Shea & J. C. Green (Eds.), *The state of the parties: The changing role of contemporary parties* (pp. 45-60). Lanham, MD: Rowman & Littlefield.

Lu, S. (1998, March 23). Concerns raised by unregulated drug sales on Web. *The New York Times*. Retrieved August 26, 1999, from the World Wide Web: http://search.nytimes.com/ search/daily/bin/fastweb?getdoc+site+site+76004+0+wAAA+Concerns%7Eand%7ERaised %7Eand%7EUnregulated%7Eand %7EDrug%7Eand%7ESales%7Eand%7Eweb

Macavinta, C. (1996, December 24). Law schools note Net law boom. *CNET*. Retrieved from the World Wide Web but no longer available.

Macavinta, C. (1998a, July 30). E-rate boosted by digital divide concerns. *CNET*. Retrieved from the World Wide Web but no longer available.

Macavinta, C. (1998b, June 30). Gingrich talks crypto in Valley. *CNET*. Retrieved from the World Wide Web but no longer available.

Macavinta, C. (1998c, October 30). Rockefeller: E-rate will survive. *CNET*. Retrieved from the World Wide Web but no longer available.

Mann, B. (1995). *Politics on the Net*. Indianapolis, IN: Que Corp.

Mansbridge, J. (1980). *Beyond adversary democracy*. New York: Basic Books.

Margolis, M. (1970, March). "OSIRIS" and "SPSS": New computer packages for the analysis of social science data. *Historical Methods Newsletter, 3,* 15-18.

Margolis, M. (1979). *Viable democracy*. New York: St. Martin's Press.

Margolis, M. (1996, September). *Electioneering in cyberspace: Parties, interest groups, and the 1996 presidential race on the Internet.* Paper presented at the annual meeting of the American Political Science Association, San Francisco.

Margolis, M., Resnick, D., & Tu, C.-C. (1997, Winter). Campaigning on the Internet: Parties and candidates on the World Wide Web in the 1996 primary season. *Harvard International Journal of Press/Politics, 2*(1), 59-78.

Margolis, M., Resnick, D., & Wolfe, J. (1999, Fall). Party competition on the Internet: Minor versus major parties in the UK and USA. *Harvard International Journal of Press/Politics, 4*(3), 24-47.

Markoff, J. (1998, July 1). U.S. and Europe clash over Internet consumer privacy. *The New York Times*. Retrieved August 26, 1999, from the World Wide Web: http://search. nytimes. com/search/daily/bin/fastweb?getdoc+site+site+76898+0+wAAA+U.S.%7Eand%7EEurope %7Eand%7EClash%7Eand%7EInternet%7Eand%7EConsumer%7Eand%7Eprivacy

Marx, K. (1978). On the Jewish question. In R. C. Tucker (Ed.), *The Marx-Engels reader* (pp. 24-51). New York: Norton. (Original work published 1843)

Maryland Business School. (n.d.). *Howard Frank named Dean.* Retrieved August 20, 1999, from the World Wide Web: http://www.rhsmith.umd.edu/pr/news-new-dean.html

Mayhew, D. (1974). *Congress: The electoral connection.* New Haven, CT: Yale University Press.

McChesney, R. (1997). *Corporate media and the threat to democracy.* New York: Seven Stories Press.

McDonald, S. (1997, October 31). The laws of cyberspace: What colleges need to know. *Chronicle of Higher Education, 44,* p. A68.

McGinniss, J. (1969). *The selling of the President, 1968.* New York: Trident.

McGookin, S. (1995, December 27). Internet "may give stimulus to democracy." *Financial Times*.

McGuigan, P. P. (1997, November 3). Stakes are high in battle to bar Internet gambling. *National Law Journal.* Retrieved August 3, 1999, from the World Wide Web: http://www.ljx.com/internet/1103gambling.html

McGuire, E. (1997, December 31). E-commerce faces Euro fire. *ZDNet.* Retrieved August 3, 1999, from the World Wide Web: http://www.zdnet.com/zdnn/content/zdnn/1231/267866.html

McKee, P. C. (1998, January 14). Internet special alert: Remarks to the National Trust Conference Public Awareness Day (sponsored by the IRS). Retrieved August 3, 1999, from the World Wide Web: http://www.fraud.org/internet/irsremarks.htm

McMurray, S. (1996, June 26). Surf the Net—But first a word from our sponsor. *Toronto Sun,* p. 48 ("Connect" section).

Mendels, P. (1998, July 30). Education Secretary defends technology in schools. *CyberTimes.* Retrieved August 20, 1999, from the World Wide Web: http://search.nytimes. com/search/daily/bin/fastweb?getdoc+site+site+76486+0+wAAA+Education%7Eand%7E Secretary%7Eand%7EDefends%7Eand %7Etechnology

Mendler, C. (1996, June 24). Electronic levy could mean a taxing time for Belgians. *Communications Week International.* Retrieved August 25, 1999, from the World Wide Web: http://www.totaltele.com/cwi/167news6.html

Meredith, R. (1998, February 2). Building Internet 2. *The New York Times,* p. C3.

Miley, M. (1996, April 1). Good interactive sites take time, hard work. *MacWeek,* pp. 32-34.

Mill, J. S. (1991). *Considerations on representative government.* Buffalo, NY: Prometheus Books. (Original work published 1861)

Mill, J. S. (1998). *Utilitarianism.* New York: Oxford University Press. (Original work published 1863)

Miller, M. C. (1996, June 3). Free the media. *The Nation, 262*(22), 9-14.

Miller, M. C., & Biden, J. B. (1996, June 3). The national entertainment state. *The Nation, 262*(22), 23-27.

Miller, W., & Shanks, J. M. (1996). *The new American voter.* Cambridge, MA: Harvard University Press.

Mitchell, A. (1998, April 14). 1998 candidates advertise early and expensively: Record spending likely. *The New York Times,* pp. A-1, A-16.

Mockapetris, P. (1983). *Domain names—Concepts and facilities* (RFC 882). Retrieved August 3, 1999, from the World Wide Web: http://www.cis.ohio-state.edu/htbin/rfc/rfc882.html

Mockapetris, P. (1987). *Domain names—Concepts and facilities* (RFC 1034). Retrieved August 3, 1999, from the World Wide Web: http://www.cis.ohio-state.edu/htbin/rfc/rfc1034.html

Montgomery, K. C. (1998, June). Viewpoint: Government must take lead in protecting children. *Advertising Age.* Retrieved from the World Wide Web, ttp://www.adage.com/interactive/articles/19980622/articles3.htm l, but not available on August 3, 1999.

Moss, M., & Mitra, S. (1998). *Net equity* (Taub Urban Research Center, New York University). Retrieved August 25, 1999, from the World Wide Web: http://urban.nyu.edu/research/ net-equity/

Mukherjee, S. (1998a, November 16). E-mail is becoming a popular lobbying tool. *San Antonio Business Journal.* Retrieved August 25, 1999, from the World Wide Web: http://www.amcity.com/sanantonio/stories/1998/11/16/smallb2.html? h=mukherjee

Mukherjee, S. (1998b, September 14). SEC "cybercops" crack down on Internet scams. *Puget Sound Business Journal.* Retrieved August 25, 1999, from the World Wide Web: http://www.amcity.com/seattle/stories/1998/09/14/smallb6.html

Munro, N. (1998, April 11). A tough sell on Internet taxes. *The National Journal.* Retrieved August 25, 1999, from the World Wide Web: http://Cox.house.gov/nettax/natjour.html

National Education Association E-rate. (n.d.). Retrieved August 3, 1999, from the World Wide Web: http://www.nea.org/lac/

National League of Cities. (n.d.). *State and local leaders support Internet commerce.* Retrieved August 3, 1999, from the World Wide Web: http://www.nlc.org/pres-icm.htm

National Telecommunications and Information Administration. (1998). *Falling through the Net II.* Retrieved August 3, 1999, from the World Wide Web: http://www.ntia.doc.gov/ntiahome/net2/

Negroponte, N. (1995). *Being digital.* New York: Knopf.

Net fraud complaints jump sixfold. (1999, February 23). *USA Today Tech Report.* Retrieved August 26, 1999, from the World Wide Web: ttp://www.usatoday.com/life/cyber/tech/cte465.htm

Net subsidies frozen, not iced. (1998, June 12). *Wired News.* Retrieved August 4, 1999, from the World Wide Web: http://www.wired.com/news/news/politics/story/12968.html

Net tax bill nears final hurdle. (1998, October 9). *USA Today Tech Report.* Retrieved August 26, 1999, from the World Wide Web: http://www.usatoday.com/life/cyber/tech/ctd610.htm

Net tax moratorium passed. (1998, June 23). *Wired News.* Retrieved August 4, 1999, from the World Wide Web: http://www.wired.com/news/news/politics/story/13222.html

Neuman, W. R. (1998). The global impact of new technologies. In D. Graber, D. McQuail, & P. Norris (Eds.), *The politics of news: The news of politics* (pp. 238-250). Washington, DC: CQ Press.

NUA Internet Surveys. (n.d.). *How many Online?* Retrieved August 3, 1999, from the World Wide Web: http://www.nua.net/surveys/how_many_online/

O'Harrow, R., Jr. (1998, July 13). Protecting privacy online. *The Washington Post,* p. F17.

Oppose the Euro Bit Tax Web site. (n.d.). Retrieved August 3, 1999, from the World Wide Web: http://www.personal.u-net.com/~7Eamiga/EuroBitTax.html

Organization for Economic Cooperation and Development. (1998). *Economic and social impacts of electronic commerce.* Retrieved August 3, 1999, from the World Wide Web: http://www.oecd.org//subject/e_commerce/summary.htm

Parenti, M. (1993). *Inventing reality: The politics of news media* (2nd ed.). New York: St. Martin's Press.

Pearlstein, S. (1999, December 5). "WTO faces hard lessons" *The Washington Post,* p. A47.

Pew Research Center for the People and the Press. Web site. (1998). *Event-driven news audiences: Internet news takes off.* Retrieved August 3, 1999, from the World Wide Web: http://www.people- press.org/med98rpt.htm

Phillips, K. (1995). Virtual Washington. *Time, 145,*(12), 65-68.

Pimental, B. (1997, January 29). Woman who accused Oracle chief guilty of perjury. *San Francisco Chronicle,* p. A11.

Pitkow, J., & Kehoe, C. (1995). *GVU's 3rd WWW user survey.* Retrieved August 3, 1999, from the World Wide Web: http://www.gvu.gatech.edu/user_surveys/survey-04-1995/

Polsby, N., & Wildavsky, A. (1996). *Presidential elections: Strategies and structures of American politics* (9th ed.). Chatham, NJ: Chatham House.

Postel, J. B. (1982). *Simple mail transfer protocol* (RFC 821). Retrieved August 3, 1999, from the World Wide Web: http://www.cis.ohio-state.edu/htbin/rfc/rfc821.html

President's Commission on Critical Infrastructure Protection. (1997). *Critical foundations.* Retrieved August 3, 1999, from the World Wide Web: http://www.info-sec.com/pccip/web/report_index.html

Project Vote Smart. (1997a). *The reporter's source book.* Corvallis, OR: Author. Retrieved August 3, 1999, from the World Wide Web: http://www.vote-smart.org/about/services/publications.html

Project Vote Smart. (1997b). *Vote Smart Web yellow pages.* Corvallis, OR: Author. Retrieved August 3, 1999, from the World Wide Web: http://www.vote-smart.org/about/services/publications.html

Project Vote Smart. (1998). *Vote Smart Web yellow pages, 1998-99 edition.* Corvallis, OR: Author. Retrieved August 3, 1999, from the World Wide Web: http://www.vote- smart.org/about/services/publications.html

Proxicom. (1996). *Majority of Americans favor voting by Internet* [Press release]. Retrieved August 3, 1999, from the World Wide Web: http://www.pollingcompany.com/pollingcompany/press/120996.html

Public Broadcasting Act of 1967. 47 U.S.C. 396 (1967).

Pulley, B. (1998, January 31). On Antigua, it's sun, sand and 1-800 betting. *CyberTimes.* Retrieved August 3, 1999, from the World Wide Web: http://search.nytimes.com/search/daily/bin/fastweb?getdoc+site+site+18749+0+wAAA+Pulley%7Eand%7EAntigua%7Eand%7E Betting

Quick, R., & Starkman, D. (1998, March 6). U.S. may face enforcement hurdles in crackdown on Internet gambling. *The Wall Street Journal,* p. B2.

Quill Corp. v. North Dakota, 504 U.S. 298 (1992).

Randolph, E. (1996, December 16). Heard on the beat. *Los Angeles Times.* Retrieved August 25, 1999, from the World Wide Web: http://www.latimes.com/cgi-bin/archsearch-cgi ?DBQUERY=Eleanor+and+Randolph+and+December+and+16&DATE=1996&SECT=&SORT=d%3Ah&NITEMS=2 5

Raney, R. F. (1999, February 27). Even on the Web, major political parties have the edge. *The New York Times.* Retrieved August 23, 1999, from the World Wide Web: http://search.nytimes.com/search/daily/bin/fastweb?getdoc+site+site+79105+0+wAAA+Raney%7Eand%7E Major%7Eand%7EPolitical%7Eand%7EParties% 7Eand%7Eedge

Raysman, R., & Brown, P. (1997). Cyber-casinos: Gambling meets the Internet. *New York Law Journal.* Retrieved August 3, 1999, from the World Wide Web: http://www.ljx.com/internet/0812cycasinos.html

Reid, R. H. (1997). *Architects of the Web: 1,000 days that built the future of business.* New York: John Wiley.

Reiter, L. (1998, March 6). CyberCrime interviews new anti-hacker agency chiefs. *ZDTV.* Retrieved August 3, 1999, from the World Wide Web: http://www.zdnet.com/zdnn/content/zdtv/0306/292020.html

Reiter, L., & Wellen, A. (1998, March 25). CyberCrime special: What's the deal with gambling on the Net? *ZDNET.* Retrieved August 3, 1999, from the World Wide Web: http://www.zdnet.com/zdnn/content/zdtv/0325/298019.html

Reno v. American Civil Liberties Union. 117 S. Ct. 2329, 138 L. Ed.2d 874 (1997).

Rheingold, H. (1993). *The virtual community: Homesteading on the electronic frontier.* Reading, MA: Addison-Wesley.

Richtel, M. (1998a, April 22). ISPs and content producers reach copyright agreement. *CyberTimes.* Retrieved August 3, 1999, from the World Wide Web: http://search.nytimes.com/search/daily/bin/fastweb?getdoc+site+site+75824+0+wAAA+Content%7Eand%7EProducers%7Eand%7ECopyright%7Eand%7Eagreement

Richtel, M. (1998b, March 5). Study finds rise in computer crime. *CyberTimes.* Retrieved August 3, 1999, from the World Wide Web: http://search.nytimes.com/search/daily/bin/fastweb?getdoc+site+site+75496+0+wAAA+Richtel%7Eand%7EStudy%7Eand%7Efinds%7Eand%7ECompu ter%7Eand%7Ecrime

Roche, E. M., & Blaine, M. J. (Eds.). (1996). *Information technology, development and policy: Theoretical perspectives and practical challenges.* Brookfield, VT: Avebury.

Roper, J. (1998). New Zealand political parties online: The World Wide Web as a tool for democratization or for political marketing? In C. Toulouse & T. W. Luke (Eds.), *The politics of cyberspace* (pp. 69-83). New York: Routledge.

Saunders, M. (1996, September 6). Internet hums with political inquiries. *Boston Globe.* Retrieved from the World Wide Web but no longer available.

Save the E-Rate Now Web site. (n.d.). Retrieved August 3, 1999, from the World Wide Web: http://congress.nw.dc.us/e-rateplus/e-rate4.html

Schiesel, S. (1998, June 6). FCC preparing to scale back school Internet programs. *CyberTimes.* Retrieved August 3, 1999, from the World Wide Web: http://search.nytimes.com/search/daily/bin/fastweb?getdoc+site+site+76668+0+wAAA+FCC%7Eand%7EPreparing%7Eand%7EScale%7Eand%7EBack%7Eand%7ESchool%7Eand%7EInternet%7Eand%7E programs

Schiffrin, A. (1996, June 3). The corporatization of publishing. *The Nation, 262*(22), 29-32.

School-wiring subsidy in peril. (1998, June 5). *Wired News.* Retrieved August 3, 1999, from the World Wide Web: http://www.wired.com/news/news/politics/story/12771.html

Schwartz, E. (1996). *Net activism: How citizens use the Internet.* Sebastopol, CA: Songline Studios.

Scobilionkov, D., & Glave, J. (1998, July 22). Magaziner: Back off, big brother. *Wired News.* Retrieved August 3, 1999, from the World Wide Web: http://www.wired.com/news/news/story/13910.html

Seabrook, J. (1994, June 6). My first flame. *New Yorker,* pp. 70-79.

Shit Must Stop Web site. (n.d.). Retrieved August 23, 1999, from the World Wide Web: http://www.flashback.se/hack/1998/07/02/1/

Sidlow, E., & Henson, B. (1998). Politics in cyberspace. In E. Sidlow & B. Henson (Eds.), *America at odds: An introduction to American government* (pp. 307-331). Belmont, CA: Wadsworth.

Soete, L., & Kamp, K. (1996). *The "bit tax": The case for further research.* Retrieved August 3, 1999, from the World Wide Web: http://www.ispo.cec.be/hleg/bittax.html

Spangler, T. (1998, December 2). Africa's Net challenge: Overcoming regulation, poor telecom infrastructure. *Interactive Week.* Retrieved August 26, 1999, from the World Wide Web: http://www.zdnet.com/intweek/stories/news/0,4164,375096,00.html

Sri Lanka takes war against rebels to cyberspace. (1997, December 7). *Reuters.* Retrieved from the World Wide Web but no longer available.

Staten, C. (1997, October 23). *Reflections on the 1997 Commission on Critical Infrastructure Protection (PCCIP) Report.* Retrieved August 3, 1999, from the World Wide Web: http://www.emergency.com/pcciprpt.htm

Stone, A. (1982). *Regulation and its alternatives.* Washington, DC: CQ Press.

"Substantial" cyber attacks reported. (1998, June 10). *San Jose Mercury News* (Reuters).

Sussman, G. (1997). *Communication, technology and politics in the information age.* Thousand Oaks, CA: Sage.

Sutin, A. N. (1998, July 13). Roadblocks stall electronic commerce. *New York Law Journal.* Retrieved August 3, 1999, from the World Wide Web: http://www.ljx.com/internet/0713roadcomm.html

Swardson, A. (1996, December 24). French groups sue to bar English-only Internet sites. *Washington Post Foreign Service.* Retrieved from the World Wide Web, ttp://wp1.washingtonpost.com/wp-srv/inatl/europe/dec/24/georgia.htm, but not available on August 3, 1999.

Swartz, J. (1998, January 16). Tribe to start national online lottery but Californians can't legally play. *San Francisco Chronicle.* Retrieved August 3, 1999, from the World Wide Web:

http://www.sfgate.com/cgi-bin/article.cgi?file=/chronicle/archive/1998/01/16/MN67248. DTL

Swett, C. (1995, July 17). *Straight assessment: The Internet* (Office of the Assistant Secretary of Defense for Special Operations and Low-Intensity Conflict). Retrieved August 3, 1999, from the World Wide Web: http://www.copi.com/articles/IntelRpt/swett.html

Talking Internet commerce: IC interview with Ira Magaziner. (1997, July 24). *Intellectual Capital.com.* Retrieved August 2, 1999, from the World Wide Web: http://www. intellectual capital.com/issues/issue98/item2489.asp

Tanouye, E. (1997). Governors say Internet taxes are essential. *Hearst Newspapers.* Retrieved from the World Wide Web, ttp://meritbbs.rulimbury.nl/cybertax/tanouye.html, but not available on August 3, 1999.

Thibodeau, P. (1998). FTC database aims to aid consumers. *Computerworld.* Retrieved August 3, 1999, from the World Wide Web: http://www.idg.net/crd_ftc_9-64094.html

Tumulty, K., & Dickerson, J. F. (1998, May 25). Gore's costly high-wire act. *Time.* Retrieved August 26, 1999, from the World Wide Web: http://www.pathfinder.com/time/magazine/1998/dom/980525/nation.go res_costly_high1.html

Ubois, J. (1996, April 1). Ten essential steps for maintaining a Web site. *MacWeek,* 28-30.

UCLA Online Institute for Cyberspace Law and Policy. (1999). Retrieved August 3, 1999, from the World Wide Web: http://www.gseis.ucla.edu/iclp/hp.html

United States v. Blair, 54 F.3d 639 (10th Cir. 1995).

U.S. House of Representatives. (1998). *The Internet Tax Freedom Act H.R. 4105, Long Summary.* Retrieved August 2, 1999, from the World Wide Web: http://cox.house.gov/nettax/suml.html

U.S. Internet Council. (1998). *Logging on: State lawmakers discuss the Net.* Retrieved August 3, 1999, from the World Wide Web: http://www.usic.org/survey.htm

U.S., Japan agree on Net rules. (1998, May 15). *Wired News.* Retrieved August 4, 1999, from the World Wide Web: http://www.news.com/News/Item/0,4,22164,00.html?st.ne.fd.mdh

U.S. Mission to the European Union. (1997, July 9). *Ira Magaziner Press Conference on Electronic Commerce.* Retrieved August 23, 1999, from the World Wide Web: ttp://www. useu.be/archive/ira.html

U.S. plans program to help poor countries onto Internet. (1998, November 11). *Nando Media.* Retrieved August 25, 1999, from the World Wide Web: http://www.techserver.com/newsroom/ntn/info/111198/info8_25296_no frames.html

U.S. seeks accord on Internet free trade. (1998, February 10). *Nando.net.* Retrieved August 25, 1999, from the World Wide Web: http://www.techserver.com/newsroom/ntn/info/021098/info1_12649.html

van de Donk, W. B. H. J., & Tops, P. W. (1995). Orwell or Athens? Informatization and the future of democracy: A review of the literature. In W. B. H. J. van de Donk, I. T. M. Snellen, & P. W. Tops (Eds.), *Orwell in Athens: A perspective on informatization and democracy* (pp. 13-32). Amsterdam: IOS Press.

Verba, S., Schlozman, K. L., & Brady, H. E. (1995). *Voice and equality: Civic voluntarism in American politics.* Cambridge, MA: Harvard University Press.

Vesely, R. (1997, July 17). Cities, states decry Net tax ban. *Wired News.* Retrieved August 3, 1999, from the World Wide Web: http://www.wired.com/news/news/story/5275.html

Virtual country "nuked" in cyberwar. (1999, January 28). *MSNBC.* 1999. *MSNBC.* Retrieved August 4, 1999, from the World Wide Web: http://www.zdnet.com/zdnn/stories/news/0,4586,2195840,00.html

Wade, B. (1998, May 24). States embrace the Web. *The New York Times.* Retrieved August 26, 1999, from the World Wide Web: http://search.nytimes.com/search/daily/bin/fastweb?getdoc+site+site+1724+0+wAAA+States%7Eand%7EEmbrace%7Eand%7Eweb

Wasserman, E. (1998, July 29). Privacy policy differences holding back e-commerce says top official. *Industry Standard.* Retrieved August 26, 1999, from the World Wide Web: http://www.thestandard.net/articles/display/0,1449,1249,00.html

Weber, T. E. (1998, February 4). Idaho tribe uses loophole to put gaming on Web. *The Wall Street Journal,* p. B1.

Weiser, B. (1998, March 5). U.S. charges 14 with online sports betting operations. *The New York Times.* Retrieved August 26, 1999, from the World Wide Web: http://search.nytimes.com/search/daily/bin/fastweb?getdoc+site+site+28468+0+wAAA+Online%7Eand%7ESports%7Eand%7EBetting%7Eand%7Eoperations

Wells, B. (1997, February 27). Internet leaders see threat to local taxes. *CyberTimes.* Retrieved August 23, 1999, from the World Wide Web: http://search.nytimes.com/search/daily/bin/fastweb?getdoc+site+site+15463+3+wAAA+INternet%7Eand%7ELeaders%7Eand%7ESee%7Eand%7Ethreat

White House. (1997). *A framework for global electronic commerce.* Retrieved August 3, 1999, from the World Wide Web: http://www.ecommerce.gov/framework.htm

Who's on the playing field: Where's the real journalism on the Net? Where's the challenger to CNN? (1996). *American Journalism Review.* Retrieved July 30, 1999, from the World Wide Web: http://ajr.newslink.org/menu.html

Wiener, J. (1994, June 13). Free speech on the Internet. *The Nation,* 825-828.

Will they fold 'em??? (1998, March 22). *Rolling Good Times Online.* Retrieved from the World Wide Web but no longer available.

Wirth, G. (1998, November 16). Policing the universe. *Industry Standard.* Retrieved August 3, 1999, from the World Wide Web: http://www.thestandard.net/articles/display/0,1449,2488,00.html

Wolf, C., & Shorr, S. (1997, January 13). Cybercops are cracking down on Internet fraud. *National Law Journal,* p. B12. Retrieved August 4, 1999, from the World Wide Web: http://www.ljx.com/internet/0113cops.html

Wolffe, R. (1998, July 4). FTC discovers consumer protection scam on the Internet. *Financial Times.* Retrieved August 26, 1999, from the World Wide Web: http://www.techserver.com/newsroom/ntn/info/070498/info11_29868_noframes.html

Woody, T. (1998, November 16). The SEC's Internet ranger. *Industry Standard.* Retrieved August 3, 1999, from the World Wide Web: http://www.thestandard.net/articles/display/0,1449,2490,00.html

Worth, M. (1998a). Fighting against scamming, slamming and cramming. *Microsoft Internet Magazine.* Retrieved August 4, 1999, from the World Wide Web: http://home.microsoft.com/reading/home3.asp

Worth, M. (1998b, June 9). *The U.S. government online: Federal agencies at your fingertips.* Retrieved August 3, 1999, from the World Wide Web: http://home.microsoft.com/reading/archives/business-5-25-98.asp

Wray, S. (1998, April 7). *Transforming Luddite resistance into virtual Luddite resist: Weaving a World Wide Web of electronic civil disobedience.* Retrieved August 4, 1999, from the World Wide Web: http://www.nyu.edu/projects/wray/luddite.html

WTO: No Net taxes for a year. (1998, May 20). *Wired News.* Retrieved August 4, 1999, from the World Wide Web: http://www.news.com/News/Item/0,4,22354,00.html?owv

Young, E. (1998, April 20). Betting on the Web. *The Sacramento Bee,* p. B1.

Zakon, R. H. (n.d.). *Hobbes' Internet timeline v3.1.* Retrieved August 4, 1999, from the World Wide Web: http://info.isoc.org/guest/zakon/Internet/History/HIT.html

Ziegler, B. (1996, January 18). Web trap? Internet's popularity threatens to swamp the on-line services. *The Wall Street Journal,* p. A1.

Index

About the Authors

Michael Margolis is Professor of Political Science at the University of Cincinnati. He received his A.B. from Oberlin College and his M.A. and Ph.D. from the University of Michigan. He has served on the faculties of the University of Pittsburgh and the Universities of Strathclyde and Glasgow in Scotland, and as Fulbright Lecturer at Hankuk University of Foreign Studies in Seoul, Korea. His publications include *Political Stratification and Democracy* (1972), *Viable Democracy* (1979), *Manipulating Public Opinion* (1989), *Machine Politics, Sound Bites and Nostalgia* (1993), *Free Expression, Public Support, and Censorship* (1994), and numerous articles in professional and popular journals.

David Resnick is Associate Professor of Political Science at the University of Cincinnati and Director of the Center for the Study of Democratic Citizenship. He received his A.B. from Columbia College (Columbia University) and his Ph.D. from Harvard University. Before coming to the University of Cincinnati, he taught in the Department of Government at Cornell University. He has published numerous articles about the history of political theory in addition to his recent scholarly work on cyberspace.